THE
NARROW
BRIDGE

THE
NARROW
BRIDGE

Jewish Views on Multiculturalism

EDITED BY

Marla Brettschneider

RUTGERS UNIVERSITY PRESS
New Brunswick, New Jersey

Manufactured in the United States of America
Published by Rutgers University Press, New Brunswick, NJ

Library of Congress Cataloging-in-Publication Data

The narrow bridge : Jewish views on multiculturalism / edited by
   Marla Brettschneider.
     p.   cm.
   Includes bibliographical references.
   ISBN 0-8135-2289-7 (cloth : alk. paper). — ISBN 0-8135-2290-0
(pbk. : alk. paper).
    1. Jews—United States—Politics and government.   2. Jews—United
States—Identity.   3. Multiculturalism—United States.   4. United
States—Ethnic relations.   I. Brettschneider, Marla.
E184.J5N27   1996
323.1'1924073—dc20   95-43322
                                              CIP

British Cataloging-in-Publication information available

This book is in honor of
my grandmother, Evelyn Reinstein,
who emigrated to the United States
in 1921 from Russia

and dedicated to the Legacies of
New Jewish Agenda
North American Jewish Students Appeal

Contents

Foreword

CORNEL WEST

If all the black, brown, red, and yellow people in America were to disappear tomorrow, leaving behind no trace of their histories, the country would still be multicultural. But there would not be a heated debate about multiculturalism. This is so primarily because of the tremendous weight of white supremacy—with its influential constructs of positively charged whiteness and negatively debased Blackness—in the American past and present. The sheer gravity of race overshadows the rich multicultural diversity among white Americans. And the relatively mild Gentile supremacy—as measured against white supremacy—has rendered Jewish identity problematic. (It is important to note that a small yet significant number of Jews in America are of Middle Eastern and African origin. This complicates Jewish identity in America even more.) Yet since anti-Semitism is as Christian as the New Testament and as American as cherry pie, Jews in America have been forced to forge identities between the Scylla of religion and the Charybdis of race.

Since the early American Jewish settlements—especially in New York, Charleston, Newport, and Philadelphia—Jewish identity has oscillated between an inescapable suspicion of Christian America and an incredible recognition that they were not *the* despised and degraded underdog in White supremacist America. Although they were barred from residing in Massachusetts, Connecticut, and New Hampshire, forbidden to build a synagogue in New York in the late seventeenth century, and not entitled to hold public office during much of the eighteenth century, the major targets of white Anglo-American hostility were Catholics, Indians, and Blacks. By the early nineteenth century, significant assimilation had set in—a governor of Georgia, a mayor in Richmond, a mayor in Charleston, cadets in the first classes at West Point and Annapolis, U.S. senators in Florida and Louisiana, the chief justice of the California Supreme Court, four generals in the Union Army, and the commander of the Mediterranean fleet were

Jews. To put it bluntly, the fact that Jews were defined as on the white side of the fundamental racial divide meant that Jewish identity—despite anti-Semitic perceptions and practices—was superseded by white-skin privilege in racist America.

Needless to say, the urban Jewish experience in anti-Semitic Europe—with the cultivation of skills in business and finance, the coping with marginal status, and the distinctly religion-based zeal for learning—produced noteworthy material prosperity for some Jews and a concentration of most Jews in certain occupations. For example, in New York in 1880 roughly 80 percent of all retail and 90 percent of all wholesale clothing firms were Jewish-owned. In Columbus, Ohio, in 1872 every retail clothing store in town was owned by Jews. And of the twenty thousand itinerant traders in America on the eve of the Civil War, the majority were Jews. So before the arrival of over a million and a half East European Jews between 1881 and 1910, significant inroads into middle-range economic success in America had been made by some Jews.

East European Jewish immigration complicated Jewish identity in America. The immigrants arrived with no money, craft backgrounds, a hunger to succeed, and left-wing sensibilities. The conflicted consciousness at the center of twentieth-century Jewish identity set in—many Jews assimilated into conservative subcultures of American education and business and at the same time opposed the xenophobic practices of American government and economy. This tension-ridden stance resulted in an incredible educational and professional success alongside courageous political and ideological critiques of American society. In 1919 Jews comprised just over 2 percent of the U.S. population; nonetheless, Jewish students made up 40 percent of the undergraduates at Columbia, 20 percent at Harvard and Yale, and 25 percent at the University of Pennsylvania. Quotas would drastically cut back these numbers. In 1930 in New York (when Jews comprised 25 percent of the population), Jews made up 55 percent of that city's physicians, 65 percent of its lawyers, and 64 percent of its dentists. And the ranks of American liberalism and radicalism—from Louis Brandeis to Arthur Miller—were disproportionately Jewish. In addition, American popular culture—with George Gershwin, Irving Berlin, Jerome Kern, and Richard Rogers in music and innumerable notables backstage and onstage in show business and Hollywood—was deeply shaped by Jews.

These facts entail neither a Jewish conspiracy nor typical American ethnic success. Instead, they signify a unique Jewish cultural amalgam that has yielded both relative material prosperity and existential anxiety. This amalgam consists roughly of a distinctive history of autonomous institution building, an obsession with the life of the mind in the form of a deep love affair with texts, an incurable fear of being targeted and attacked as powerless underdog or omnipotent masterdog, and an indescribable anguish in the face of a perennial homelessness, hence restlessness. Is it a mere accident that the Hare Krishna group and Reverend Sun Yung Moon's church are disproportionately Jewish?

With the founding of Israel in 1948 (after one out of three Jews in the world were murdered by the Nazis in Europe), the entree of a majority of Jews into the American middle class and the vast human and financial Jewish support of the civil rights movement in the 1950s and 1960s, Jewish identity becomes even more complicated and conflicted. After the European Holocaust are not Jews undeniable underdogs in this blood-drenched century? What are the tensions between this understandable underdog mentality in light of the class status of the many middledogs and a few topdogs in American society (7 percent of the senior executives in corporate America and 23 percent of Forbes' top four hundred richest Americans are Jewish)? How do we account for the socioeconomic status and liberal voting behavior of Jews (78 percent voted Democratic in 1994?) But yet in spite of prevailing stereotypes of Jewish prosperity, we often overlook the fact that significant numbers of Jews are working-class and poor. Will the complex, ambivalent special relationship of Jews with Blacks—the visible underdog and pariah people of America—persist in the coming years? Are the state of Israel and palpable anti-Semitism the only solid pillars for Jewish identity and continuity in light of a Jewish exogenous marriage rate of over 50 percent in America?

These urgent questions form the backdrop of the ever-expanding debate about Jews and multiculturalism, especially in the academy. With 87 percent of college-aged Jews enrolled in higher education (compared with 40 percent for the general population) and a disproportionate number of Jewish faculty and administrators in elite universities and colleges, this debate has immense implications.

First, at the intellectual level, we are just beginning to revise our understanding of the premodern and modern West in light of the rich traditions of Jews within the ghettoes and behind the walls in Jerusalem, Alexandria, Madrid, Amsterdam, Rome, Vienna, Berlin, and New York. This means we must no longer settle for those visible, usually assimilated Jewish thinkers like Josephus, Maimonides, Spinoza, Marx, Durkheim, Wittgenstein, Weil, Trilling, and Einstein. We should also relate them to what they were often running away from—those indigenous yet usually cosmopolitan Jewish thinkers we have silenced or marginalized. Furthermore, we must reexamine the non-Jewish classic figures by keeping track of how anti-Semitic "Otherness" shapes or influences their profound formulations and blind prejudices. How would St. Jerome, Erasmus, Luther, Hegel, Ezra Pound or T. S. Eliot—exemplary canonical anti-Semitic figures—fare in such an analysis?

Second, on the historical front, we have yet to fully embark on understandings of how Jewish doings and sufferings are related to the rise and decline of major empires like Rome, Spain, Portugal, Britain, Habsburg, Russia, and America. How have the Jewish historical cycles of stigmatization, segregation, expulsion, pogroms, incorporation, assimilation, and annihilation shaped these empires? How has gender and sexual orientation figured in such configurations?

Finally, on the political front, we need to pursue lines of inquiry in regard to how the plights and predicaments of Jews have fanned and fueled as well as impeded and obstructed exemplary efforts to transform the energy of kinship into democratic citizenship. How has this worldly focus on transformation in prophetic Judaism or the otherworldly orientation of mystical Judaism contributed to democratic sensibility and civil sentiments? In what ways have Jewish intellectual traditions constructed and expanded notions of tolerance, pluralism, tragicomic visions, and democratic vistas?

In short, we have much work to do in infusing and inserting the rich history and culture of Jews into the multicultural debate—not because it is fashionable or faddish, but because it is part of the ageless human quest for knowledge and truth, goodness and beauty. And such a quest embraces the torment, freedom, and hope so central to Jewish identity in the twentieth century.

Acknowledgments

In 1992, as I was making some final adjustments to my Ph.D. dissertation, I had a strange experience. I had long been a Jewishly identified activist in multicultural politics and my writing thus far had been mostly in Jewish-based multicultural theory. In rereading the paragraph in the introduction to my dissertation, where I termed the work *Jewish* and *multicultural,* I thought I ought to include a citation to works previously written on the topic of Jews and multiculturalism. And this is what happened: I went to my bookshelves to find the book, and it wasn't there. I thought, "That's weird," and dutifully went off to the library for the reference. But I couldn't find the book in the library either. In fact, after some research, what I *did* find was that the book on Jews and multiculturalism did not exist.

Subsequently, at various conferences, meetings, and speeches, I often felt myself wanting to hold up this nonexistent book. In the midst of the tensions, stereotyping, and misconceptions by and about Jews that invariably arose in progressive, multicultural settings, I wanted to say, "Please, read this book." That book would give a different picture of the role of Jews in multicultural work and the promise of multiculturalism in Jewish life; it would clarify confusions, challenge stereotypes, complicate the issues and ideas that had somehow gotten misleadingly simplified through mass politics; and it would offer new interpretations, bringing the debate ever forward. It took some time before I realized that I, long-time activist and soon-to-be Ph.D., could make that book come to be.

At that point I was faced with a choice: I could write this much-needed book myself, or get others to write it. Now, in 1996, as I work over the final drafts of the contributions to this anthology, I cannot express how glad I am that I chose to edit, rather than write, this book. Sending out a call far and wide to find new voices, and soliciting pieces from some of the very best the Jewish community has to offer, has resulted in a book that is diverse and rich, with analysis so much deeper than I could have written on my own. My first word of thanks, therefore, goes to the contributors and to all of those who submitted their work for review.

When it suddenly occurred to me that if such a book needed to be out there, I was in a position to make it happen, I almost knocked myself out. The concept was incredibly exciting—so exciting that I got so nervous I couldn't even bring myself to tell anyone. After what felt like ages, I finally approached Bertell Ollman (who would probably even call himself a most unlikely choice). His crazy sort of enthusiasm for the project gave me the courage to start talking and exploring. I owe him much thanks.

In large part this anthology was made possible by the earlier collections of Jewish feminists that set in motion the contemporary Jewish exploration of our multiple identities. Works such as Koltun's *The Jewish Woman,* Heschel's *On Being a Jewish Feminist,* Klepfisz and Kaye/Kantrowitz's *The Tribe of Dina,* Torton Beck's *Nice Jewish Girls,* and Plaskow and Christ's *Woman Spirit Rising* have changed Jewish life forever. I am honored that many women who were involved in these projects have contributed their writing and visions to this volume, especially Melanie Kaye/Kantrowitz. I am also delighted to introduce a new generation of writers.

Patricia Moynagh, H. Mark Roelofs, and Nancy Gentile-Ford were sources of great encouragement, and their comments on the introduction were invaluable. Rebecca Alpert's feedback was essential and Navah Levine has been a important friend and editor. I thank Hilary Levey for her friendship and for explaining to me (when we were in college) that she wasn't saying "peacey," but "p.c."

The aid of the Bloomsburg University Political Science Department, including Christie Shuman and the work-study students, has been greatly appreciated. Gloria Cohen and Mark Stern shared their knowledge of the American Jewish Congress and Michelle Seligman of the North American Conference on Ethiopian Jewry her contacts in the Ethiopian Jewish community. Jonathan Springer has been a great help with the Jewish gay and lesbian community.

It is unfortunate that additional perspectives could not be included in this volume. I was able to proceed on this project, making difficult choices as to which contributions to include, only by assuming that this would be the first of many books on the topic. In addition, a number of writers with whom I worked, especially some of the younger ones, eventually decided that their subjects remained too difficult to put into writing at this point. I wish them the best of luck and want to remind them that we need to hear from them.

Numerous journals and organizational newsletters published the original call for papers and many individuals distributed flyers at conferences, mailed announcements to colleagues, posted notices in organizational offices, and listed the call on electronic bulletin boards, helping make the solicitation process tremendously democratic. As testimony to the community's need for such a volume, many of these acts were performed anonymously: I learned of many such publications quite accidentally.

I would like to thank Deborah Waxman, particularly for her early involvement in the project. Her sensitivity, intellect, and editorial skills were, as always, of great service; but the lessons of friendship she has taught me along the way have been extraordinary. I would also like to thank the participants in the workshop that Deborah and I led on Jews and multiculturalism at the 1993 National Havurah Institute; the shifting community at the NHIs has provided much stimulating and warm support. At a later point, the participants in the workshop at the International Conference on Gay and Lesbian Jews (summer 1995) were also helpful.

Much love goes to Tamar Frolichstein and Joanne Jacobson for their friendship and support. The cover painting is Ellen Wertheim's *Crash of the Heavens* ink on paper from the collection of Sariel Beckenstein. (Thank you again, Ellen.) Again, Martha Heller and the people at Rutgers University Press have been wonderful at each step along the way. The folks at Bretmar, also, have been helpful and fun. Thanks, of course, to my family. Finally, I want to remember Agnes Hochberg and Barbara Hinckley. May their memories be for a blessing.

THE
NARROW
BRIDGE

כל העולם כלו גשר צר מאד
והעקר לא לפחד כלל.

All the world is a very narrow bridge
and the main thing is not to fear at all.

Rabbi Nachman
of Bratslav

Introduction
Multiculturalism, Jews, and Democracy: Situating the Discussion

MARLA BRETTSCHNEIDER

A s the most recent development in the struggle with difference in the pursuit of justice, multiculturalism fundamentally affects Jews. Jews have long been situated as "Other": in different times and in relation to different dominant cultures since the destruction of the Second Temple and the resulting dispersion two thousand years ago, Jewish identity has been continually re-created in marginal spaces so rich on the inside, so often despised from the outside. Knowing "Otherness" and prepared by history, many Jews are deeply involved on all levels of the current debate. There exists, however, a need for careful, reflective analysis of the role, importance, and even the dangers of multiculturalism to the Jewish community; in addition, there exists a need for newly honed Jewish visions as we reweave the tapestry of American life. This anthology was developed in an attempt to determine what multiculturalism is and what it can be to the Jewish community as well as what Jewish experience has added and can add to broader multiculturalism.

Multiculturalism in the United States, as we have known it and practiced it thus far, has been both good and bad for Jews. It has given us a language comprehensible to others in which we can do Jewish politics in larger public spheres. For example, our identity has long informed our politics, we have long known "Otherness," and we have long experienced ourselves as a community. As multiculturalist politics has evolved, spaces have opened within the Left to be Jewish politically and to address Jewish concerns from a progressive perspective.[1] In today's multicultural environment, Jewish-based politics is increasingly welcomed as a contribution to progressive movement generally.

However, multiculturalist politics is also often tricky for Jews. As identities become fair game in politics, Jewishness takes a beating from

1

the Left in ways Jews more usually are accustomed to being attacked from the Right. Even in a politics that courageously seeks to understand, name, and overcome oppression as well as to rethink and to rewrite history, historic anti-Semitic fantasies have resurfaced at times—now from marginalized, rather than powerful, groups—about how Jews run the world and are to blame for all the world's problems. Recent media attention to particular anti-Semitic Black Muslim speakers or the "Holocaust hoax" problem only amplifies what Jews and multiculturally oriented student activists have faced every day around the country. The campus has felt like a battleground and Jews too often have found complications with progressive efforts to diversify canonically based curricula. Despite our community's apparent success, we remain marginalized from the majority Christian culture; adding insult to injury, despite our minority status and experience, often we are marginalized in multicultural circles.

The Roots of Multiculturalism in the United States

I am often asked to explain what multiculturalism is. As an activist and political philosopher, I answer that multiculturalism is a recent attempt to approach the complications of democracy and difference. Given the problems we have had with diversity since the founding of the Republic, multiculturalism stands as the third major response to diversity attempted in this century, with interesting effects on the unstable situation of Jews.

Difference in the Early Republic

Americans have long grappled with the difficulty of creating a union with such heterogeneous raw material for its citizenry. Early Republicans maintained that "natural diversity" has a disastrous effect on society and the body politic. James Madison thought that the diverse faculties "sown in the nature of man" lead us always to "vex and oppress each other."[2] Expression of group solidarity was understood as the "violence of faction" that is "adverse to the rights of other citizens, or to the permanent and aggregate interests of the community." If well constructed, our union would effectively "break and control . . . this dangerous vice."

Madison and others developed a framework for politics, as laid out in the Constitution, which seeks to subsume our differences. For example, Benjamin Rush, signer of the Declaration of Independence, prominent scientist, and commentator on social issues of his day, wrote that the problem with African slaves rested in their leprosy-like disease that made them different from whites.[3] There was a common assumption among the Founders that politics is possible only when we are cured of the differences that cause dis-ease in the body politic.

The battle over our differences raged on through the nineteenth century. The Civil War realized the battle most literally, and abolitionist ideas gave rise to the suffragist movement. During the nineteenth century Americans were also busy dismantling some class-based barriers to participation as well as passing new laws concerning the native peoples. Thinking about multiculturalism from a Jewish perspective, however, it is particularly important to note that by the turn of the twentieth century this country was faced with a new challenge of difference. The flood of millions of new immigrants from a vast array of foreign cultures necessitated a new response within American politics.

The Melting Pot Response

Still assuming politics to necessitate sameness, "nativists" launched a campaign to "Americanize" the immigrants.[4] From settlement houses to civics classes, the United States was presented as a great melting pot where all the "different" ingredients are thrown together into a single kettle to create a tasty soup.[5] Although there were different understandings of what the melting pot metaphor actually symbolized, the basic conception reflected a perceived need to melt away differences in order to "naturalize" the new immigrants. European Balkanization was seen as the result of Old World prejudice between groups stubbornly clinging to their ancient, outworn distinctions. In America, the New World, it was felt that "in the crucible of love, or even co-citizenship, the most violent antithesis of the past may be fused into a higher unity."[6]

The melting pot vision was grandly optimistic. Speaking of the immigrants as "the great American problem" (though his poetic rendering is also expressive of the plight of African Americans who did not choose to come here and, in certain ways, that of Native

Americans to whom the United States itself was an uninvited entity), Frederick J. Haskin wrote,

> When I pour out my blood on your altar of labour, and lay down my life as a sacrifice to your god of toil, men make no more comment than at the fall of a sparrow.
> But my brawn is woven into the warp and woof of the fabric of your national being.
> My children shall be your children and your land shall be my land because my sweat and my blood will cement the foundations of the America of To-Morrow.
> If I can be fused into the body politic, the Melting-Pot will have stood the supreme test.[7]

The problem, it seems, concerned what was meant by "fusion." It was felt that "though the peoples now in process of formation in the New World are being recruited by mainly economic forces, it may be predicted they will ultimately harden into a homogeneity of race, if not even of belief."[8] Over time, however, people felt the problems involved with an expectation that our differences of culture and heritage should melt away so that we can become "homogeneous." Some felt that this would be impossible; others believed homogenization was actually undesirable.[9] In short, people began to question whether the expectation of assimilation to some generalized American standard would indeed free us from the oppression many of us experience based on our "differences."

The Development of Pluralism

By midcentury, melting pot theories gave way to a pluralist view of American political life.[10] The emergence of pluralism marked a move toward the incorporation of difference into democratic theory in that it did not demand a complete homogenization of our given diversity. This was accomplished by distinguishing between private and—according to this theory, the more politically relevant—public aspects of diverse group life. Pluralism allows for the retention of distinctive characteristics in the private cultural lives of groups, but still relies on an assumption of the need for sameness in what it considers to be politics.

For example, pluralism allows some to attend Mass and others synagogue, some to eat spaghetti and others curry or kubeh. However, despite being an adaptation of Marx's group vision, pluralism remained Liberal-Capitalist to the core: in the public realm all groups are understood to be similarly selfish, competing to maximize their interests. Each group is assumed to be politically homogeneous within itself fighting it out with other, similarly understood, groups in an Hobbesian war of each against all, a Darwinian struggle for existence. Pluralism's promise of equality and freedom stems from the assumption that no one group will lose—or win—this war all the time. Within this model, the call of justice is a distributive one restricted "to the morally proper distribution of benefits and burdens among society's members."[11]

Critics of pluralism charged that the problem of this "heavenly chorus" was that it "sang with an upper class accent."[12] Not long after the pluralist Robert Dahl captured the American political imagination with a vision of his typical city, smoothly functioning according to the pluralist paradigm, was that same city (New Haven) set ablaze by groups who had been consistently "losing the war."[13] This was, after all, the 1960s and groups such as Puerto Ricans and African Americans did not see politics running as equitably as Dahl had supposed.[14]

Multiculturalism

Out of the burst of activism in this country during the 1960s, later aided by developments in French postmodernist thinking, multiculturalism emerged as the third major effort in this century to focus directly on questions of difference.[15] This 1960s activism in the United States marked a shift from "old" style politics to a "newer" politics: the "Old Left" ideology, based on the orthodox Marxist idea of the primacy of economic class, gave way to a more complicated group-based analysis of oppression.[16] The multiculturalism of the 1960s social movements expanded the purview of "relevant" political groups to include an array of those based on identity beyond class, such as race, gender, ethnicity, religion, sexual orientation, ability, size, and age.

In contrast to pluralism, however, multiculturalism claims that these identity-based groupings do not belong in some apolitical cultural sphere, but are politically relevant in and of themselves. The multiculturalist view clarifies that pluralism has, in its pretense to be "difference-blind," left many nondominant groups stifled and disenfranchised. Furthermore, pluralism's response to difference virtually precludes overcoming this situation by depoliticizing the sphere—the privatized culture or identity—from which these groups experience one of the most profound aspects of politics: oppression. Multiculturalism does away with the pretense of a separate private sphere to which difference can be relegated by asserting that privatizing difference means privatizing real oppression and thus barring it from public scrutiny. The feminist movement first asserted that "the personal is political," and multiculturalism suggests "celebrating difference" as a mode of politics itself.

Multiculturalism is developing democratic praxis which, rather than squelching diversity, seeks to welcome difference in the creation of a vibrant and inclusive public sphere (or spheres).[17] Multiculturalism is founded on a notion of justice that focuses on transcending oppression in the various ways in which different individuals and groups experience it, rather than on an abstract universalism or an attempt at some slight redistribution of material resources. It is this alternative vision of justice that has directed the multiculturalist attention to hearing our "voices."[18] This mode acknowledges the importance of individuals and groups figuring out (not necessarily fighting out) their own needs and aspirations and defining the nature of their oppressions for themselves (in conjunction with and with the aid of others when appropriate).[19] It calls on the citizenry to encourage and welcome others into the public sphere to raise their distinct voices in common dialogue.[20]

In developing this alternative vision of the point and process of politics, multiculturalism has also unmasked the pluralist assumption that its political sphere is a neutral, objective space.[21] By relegating cultural difference to an apolitical sphere, pluralism implicitly assumes politics to be acultural, unbiased by group particularities.[22] Multiculturalist critique shows the fallacy of this claim to neutrality, for example, in its analysis of the relationship of pluralist self-interest with the common good. If, as in the pluralist view, groups engage in politics for their selfish interests, then particular group claims can be refused "legitimately" in the interest of the common good. Certainly, not all particular claims belong on the public agenda at all times. A critical reading, however, reveals that nondominant groups have been viewed excessively as having the dangerous "differences" that threaten the so-called common good. This "common good" was thus exposed as a means to protect certain particular privileges and inequalities.

In short, a multicultural analysis demonstrates that the political sphere is not as culturally neutral as pluralists would have us believe. A theory of politics that understands public involvement as a way to attend to our differing needs, perspectives, and aspirations acknowledges the ways in which culture and identity are themselves often politically relevant aspects of life. A multiculturalist may acknowledge that some groups do, in fact, act selfishly. However, one also notes that groups that assert their needs in the public sphere are not all solely selfishly competitive actors. Such a perspective makes it incumbent on the public to take groups' claims seriously, rather than dismiss them.[23] In doing so, multiculturalism gives us a vision of justice based on our responsibility to listen to—and to engage honestly with—each other as we communicate in our distinct voices while we work toward goals of overcoming oppression and meeting our ever-changing and constantly reinterpreted needs as individuals, groups, and as a whole.

When we recognize the potentially liberating aspects of difference, rather than perceive only threat, we allow for critical awareness of our cultural identities and the historical-social forces that have helped shape them. In facing our fears of difference, of the "Other," and of the painful realities of our identity-based oppressions and exclusion from the public sphere, we open spaces for deeper identity exploration. Through such inward-focused exploration we come to see the multiplicity of identities each of us experiences: outward connections and intersubjective understandings begin to develop. Delving into the complicated world of multiple identities (which is what I would call "multiculturalism at its best") thrusts us into a dialectic of particularism and generalism that encourages us to renavigate the problematics of sameness and difference.

For instance, when I take seriously my position in the world as a Jew, I must also acknowledge that I am a woman, an Ashkenazi (Eastern European Jew and lighter-skinned "Semite") in a country obsessed with racial bifurcation. The process continues with other aspects of my identity, which I come to realize are politically relevant in this time and place in which I live and for which I suffer degradation, marginalization, and discrimination as well as enjoy access, privilege, and choice. Now I gather with Jews to celebrate our history, to examine anti-Semitism, to uncover Jewishly meaningful ways of

living in and repairing the world; now I gather with women to uncover our untaught history, to examine sexism, and to recover the va-
rieties of women's ways of knowing that seem essential to creative and
caring solutions necessitated by our rationalistic and formalistic dead-
ness. And I know I must keep gathering, finding home in now so many
houses. The particular, we learn in the process, is no longer singular:
from the one particular gathering of a Shabbat service there are many
particulars. I meet in time with both men and women, Jew and Gentile, white and colored, queer and straight, working class and differently abled as the common public space is brought to life by a full and
developing diverse citizenry who share so many of those different and
radically particular identities—even as those identities are themselves
constantly in flux.

As we remember Martin Buber's "in each Thou we address the
eternal Thou," we come to see that identities are particular, though
identity takes on the hue of a universal.[24] Attention to difference,
therefore, stimulates a reconceptualization of the sameness of our
shared identities, of our common humanity, of the enfranchised and
participating citizen. Given the history of identity-based oppression,
to envision and create a just and democratic public sphere in our time
is to be immersed in the intricacies of the multiculturalist dialectic.
Struggling within this multiculturalist dialectic, activists and philoso-
phers are reconstituting the public space (even at times decentralizing
it into politically relevant public spaces) and reminding us that we will
ever be reconstituting it. We are refocusing currently on meeting our
needs and overcoming oppression, all the while remembering that we
may want to redefine the point of politics in other ways in the future.
Politics thus understood—complicated, extended, and open-ended—
can be treacherous, there is no doubt, many of the essays in this
anthology demonstrate just how so. Thus understood, however, politics can also be a matter of exciting, meaningful, and joy-filled explorations and experiments, and the tales of some of these are told in the
following pages as well.

So, Where Do Jews Fit In?

In my explorations of the complicated relationship of Jews and
multiculturalism, I was fascinated to discover that political visions

from within the American Jewish community (stimulated by attempts to cope with its own minority position and overcome its own identity-based oppression) have paralleled the development of those in the United States generally. As the American public at large moved from melting pot theory to pluralism and more recently to multiculturalism, so, too, did the American Jewish community. Such a connection suggests the import of the Jewish experience to American democratic development as well as the significance of democratic grappling with difference to a strong and vibrant Jewish community.

Jews and the Melting Pot

The greatest influx of Jews into the United States occurred during the period of mass immigration to this country generally. The years 1880 to 1920 saw nearly two million Jews, predominantly of Eastern European descent, immigrating to these shores. As the Eastern European Jews came to outnumber even the German Jews, the Jewish community in the United States was transformed from a largely Sephardi (Spanish) to an Ashkenazi (European) community. Such a move has resulted in Ashkenazi cultural dominance to this day.[25]

However, it was the title and character of *The Melting Pot: A Drama in Four Acts*, written in 1908 by the European Jewish playwright Israel Zangwill, which crystallized the turn-of-the-century assimilationist approach to difference. The play's high-pitched, heartrending story explores the trials of assimilation faced by a family of Russian Jewish immigrants to the United States. The play was "designed to bring home to America both its comparative rawness and emptiness and its true significance and potentiality for history and civilisation."[26] In 1914 Zangwill wrote of his play, "it has had the happy fortune to contribute its title to current thought, and, in the testimony of Jane Addams, to 'perform a great service to America by reminding us of the high hopes of the founders of the Republic.'"[27]

In the context of this anthology, however, we must remember that Jane Addams, founder of Hull House, also wrote that the settlement house "insists upon similarities rather than differences."[28] Thus, as late as the 1950s we can see working-class Jewish girls, children of immigrants—as Felice Yeskel describes herself in these pages—taking violin and dancing lessons at the settlement house in an effort to become "American" by acquiring middle-class cultural skills. Additionally, in the civics classes of our public schools we sought to, as we were sought out to, assimilate.[29] In this volume, Leora Saposnik and Ellen Osterhaus's essay on Jews and cultural diversity in the public schools makes a significant contribution by critically addressing this phenomenon from within the more recent context of multiculturalism.

In addition to lending the theory its very name, Jews (for the most part as a community) not only accepted the melting pot call to assimilation, but quite consciously helped promote it. For example, contemporary philosopher of education Maxine Greene writes that Julia Richman

> made it brashly clear where she thought the public schools should stand when it came to fitting children into the system. Their parents, [Richman] once said, "must be made to realize that in forsaking the land of their birth, they were also forsaking the customs and traditions of that land; and they must be made to realize an obligation, in adopting a new country, to adopt the language and customs of that country."[30]

This "opportunity" to assimilate distinguished Ashkenazi Jews and other European immigrants from more racially distinct minority groups, causing tensions among them that continue to surface in the new multicultural politics. In contrast, Rebecca Posner's contribution to this volume complicates Jewish-race issues by looking at how racial and cultural differences among Ashkenazi, Sephardi, and Mizrachi Jews in Canada's formalized multicultural politics affects this racial/ethnic dynamic. But, already for European Jews in the United States early in the century, an Americanization that required assimilation was seen as fraught with problems (as it was for other groups who seemed to be in need of Americanization). Richman's stark demand suggests the degree of cultural loss necessitated in becoming an American in this model. Not all Jews wanted to "forsake" their identities, nor did they think a strong republic necessitated such complete assimilation—especially not an American republic. To many immigrants and potential immigrants, the United States was symbolized by the Statue of Liberty, welcoming the ships that entered New York Harbor to unload their immigrant cargo at Ellis Island.[31]

The United States was known to many as the land that welcomed the scattered lowliest, the most "Other," together through her "golden door." In this volume Michael Walzer reminds us that *E pluribus unum* can be read in American as "*from* many one," but just as easily within our own national culture as "*in* many one" suggesting that, in contrast to the melting pot vision, celebrating diversity can be read as consistent with tradition in the United States. In addition, given the persistence of anti-Jewish oppression, assimilation is still not always easy even if Jewish individuals try. Instead, many Jews get caught in an uncomfortable place in the middle, sometimes trying to forsake their Jewish identity, sometimes not. In either case, Jews too often find ourselves maneuvering in a world sometimes accepting, sometimes hostile—never sure of our position, never sure when doors will be open or shut. In spite of the many accomplishments of American Jews, our precarious situation in this country arising from the multifaceted problems of assimilation provides a quintessential example of the shortcomings of the melting pot mentality with respect to the challenges of democracy and difference as well as to Jewish thriving and surviving (or, for that matter, any other minority survival).

I must remind readers that dating developments in either intellectual or cultural history is not an exact science.[32] Despite the shading and overlapping, however, it is helpful to identify the three distinct movements within the American political imagination at large with respect to the questions that difference, as it has been understood in this century, has posed for democratic theory and practice.[33] In similar fashion we must also acknowledge the interestingly pluralist phase of twentieth-century American Jewish history.

Pluralism and the "Jewish Lobby"

In the pluralist understanding, groups, however culturally diverse at home, enter into a competitive public arena whenever they want, and have the resources, to advance their self-interests. While some in the Jewish community were busy debating over and deciding the fate of Jewish education, social services, religious practice, and other "cultural" institutions in the tousle of communal "life," others were building "political" organizations to defend Jewish "interests." These "political" (read government-focused lobby) groups were ensuring safeguards against anti-Semitism through civil rights legislation, securing First Amendment promises of the separation between "church" and state, and then the protection of the builders of a Jewish homeland in Palestine, and eventually support for the Jewish state itself.

The American Jewish Congress, for example, was founded in 1918 in support of a Jewish homeland in Palestine and has come to be a primary defender of the American Jewish community with regard to the protection of First Amendment rights. In light of the way that many in this volume discuss the Christmas challenge, readers may find the American Jewish Congress (AJC) position on public holiday observance illuminating. When this predominantly Christian country displays Christmas paraphernalia everywhere, the AJC does not challenge the invisibility, marginalization, and cultural hegemony by supporting public Hanukkah celebrations and education. Instead, the AJC strategy seeks the removal of the Christmas display. We cannot lose the political point here in the midst of intense Jewish feeling concerning the commodification of a Christian holy day and/or the overwhelming cultural inundation. Rather than broadening the public arena with diverse displays, the AJC position reinforces the notion that the correct relationship between politics and culture is characterized by, to use Thomas Jefferson's phrase, "a wall of separation."

I am not saying that the AJC position is necessarily inappropriate, but that our analysis of situations we find problematic—and our discussion of what to do about them—will be aided when we clarify their ideological legacies. What makes this situation even more difficult is the complicated nature of American Jewish identity as not simply a religious group, but as a cultural, ethnic group as well. Although some have claimed that Jewish difference is religious in nature, we find even here in the Christmas challenge an important cultural expression of Jewishness. Despite a Christian tendency to categorize the Jewish people in religious terms, most Jews have tended to experience themselves as a civilization and thus even "church"–state and Christmas difficulties as reflective of our ethnic/cultural minority status. Although one could argue that Jews have always had a conception of themselves as "a people," this more expansive identity has been especially characteristic of Western Jews since their Emancipation following the French Revolution. Since then, anti-Jewish hatred largely has been known as anti-Semitism, a racial/ethnic hatred that in this case includes a religious component.

It is thus no paradox that it is the AJC, an American Jewish civic (rather than religious) organization, which became a champion in the

struggle for religious toleration and freedom. Situating the AJC position in these politically pluralist terms as they affect the American Jewish community makes all the more sense when we remember that (as
Israel Zangwill gave the United States the term "melting pot") it was
Horace Kallen, a Jewish political philosopher, who actually coined the
phrase "cultural pluralism." In this context, it cannot go unnoted that
Horace Kallen was also a founder of the American Jewish Congress.

What we have come to know as "the Jewish Lobby," however, did
not really emerge until the 1970s, when the American-Israel Political
Affairs Committee (AIPAC) became a front-running Washington interest group. Renamed in 1959 from the American Zionist Council of
Public Affairs, AIPAC was the only registered Jewish lobby until
1989.[34] As recently as 1974 few Jews outside Washington had any idea
of what AIPAC did and its budget did not exceed $20,000, half of
which went to publish its newsletter. Behind the scenes, however, the
group's director and founder I. L. Kenan was already lobbying for an
unprecedented $2.2 billion to help Israel rearm after the Yom Kippur
War. (The full impact of this figure is felt when it is compared to the
1972 figure of total aid to Israel from the United States: $404 million.)
Morris Amitay succeeded Kenan as AIPAC was deemed an increasingly successful interest group. Thomas Dine took over leadership in
1980 and was mostly responsible for the professionalization and high
profile that the group has come to be equated with today.[35]

Washington politics in the pluralist paradigm, the reader will remember, deals most effectively with monolithic, highly competitive,
self-interested groups. Thus, this "professionalization," and the con-
solidation of Jewish diversity that made it possible, was achieved at
tremendous cost to Jewish communal life. As Robert Dahl and other
pluralists were putting "interest groups" on the map of American politics, the American Jewish community itself was being transformed
into one.[36] The Jewish community as a whole—in all its fullness, history, and diversity—was increasingly identified with the pro-Israel
lobby (particularly in its 1970s–1980s AIPAC incarnation). Not only
was the complexity of our communal relationship with Israel stripped
down to an ahistorical monolith conceived as a selfish interest that we
would unquestioningly and competitively pursue in the public arena,
but the very civilization of Jewish communal life was reduced to this
pluralist specimen.[37]

Thus, just as earlier in the century the American melting pot metaphor was derived from the story of a family of Jewish immigrants, the paradigmatic "interest group" often referred to by mid/late-century pluralists was AIPAC (or the so-called "pro-Israel" or "Jewish" lobby with which it was often conflated). Again, Jewish success in this arena reflects in part our ability to "pass" as "ordinary" Americans; these developments also added to tensions between Jews and other minorities who are without such options. In this volume African American scholar Gerald Horne addresses such tensions, while Jeffrey Dekro and Nora Gold discuss the interesting issues of Jewish responsibility connected to our success by looking at the worlds of community economic development and Jewish social services, respectively.

But just as the particular trials of Jewish assimilation in the United States exposed general problems of melting pot theory, the troubles of a particular community conceived of as an interest group help expose problems of pluralism. Needing to present ourselves in an outside pluralist politics as of a singular mind, we increasingly tried to stuff a round communal peg into this square interest group hole. Expected always to be ready to fight it out in Washington in the face of external threats, we had to clamp down on internal communal diversity: in a threatening situation, "unity" is commonly demanded. We must note, however, why a politics that celebrates diversity forces us to rethink the concepts of "unity" and "threat." Constant disaster alert has been used historically to squelch freedom and diversity. "But," many respond, "Jews certainly have good reason to be on the ready: our peace and very survival have too often been threatened." The problem for Jewish life is, of course, that such a stance necessitates putting culture and honest self-exploration on hold. If this goes on long enough, Jewish life loses its vibrancy, meaning, and capacity to adapt. In trying to avert disaster from without, we risk disaster from within. It is, therefore, incumbent on a community committed to existence to challenge the common definitions of unity and danger. Multiculturalism reminds us that diversity is a strength rather than a weakness. As American Jews, we are finding that the diversity resulting from identity exploration and experimentation is essential to communal vitality.[38] The contributions in this volume by Bob Goldfarb, on integrating lesbians, gay men, and bisexuals into the Jewish community, and Ephraim Isaac, on the American Jewish community's responsibility for Ethiopian and

Yemeni Jews, are among those that seek to strengthen our community by highlighting our internal diversity.

Jews and Multiculturalism

We have noted that as pluralism was becoming a household word in the late 1960s and early 1970s, we also began to see a shift toward a politics of protest, identity, and imagination in which we root multiculturalism. Many Jews, individually and organizationally, were involved in this new form of politics. Many of the writers in this anthology, who were active at the time, were themselves workers and leaders in the American women's, civil rights, gay, and lesbian movements. Melanie Kaye/Kantrowitz will take us back to that era with the hindsight of a 1990s Jewish-affirmative perspective. In the late 1960s and early 1970s the Jewish women's, gay and lesbian, environmental, and Havurah movements also emerged. Some contributors to this volume were also involved in these Jewish movements, which jointly came to be known as Jewish renewal;[39] Martha Ackelsberg's contribution on the importance of coalitions, for example, grows out of her long struggle in both (Jewish and general) aspects of the contemporary movement for social transformation.

Jewish feminists, as Clare Kinberg of *Bridges* magazine shows us, were responding to, and helping create, an identity-based politics that had them engaged Jewishly as it had them engaged in women's movement. Progressives supportive of Israel, such as Reena Bernards, were working with non-Jewish peace activists and especially with Palestinians in their work toward a safe and peaceful Israel. Other Jews, as Naomi Nim's essay on antioppression education demonstrates, involved in civil rights work had heard over and over about internalized oppression and the need for reclaiming cultural identity; they began to apply this to their Jewish selves. As another example, when Toba Spitzer discusses how her Jewish identity was heightened through her solidarity work in Haiti, she shows us concretely how the particulars of what is sometimes inward-looking identity politics is made possible in a broader culture of exploration, so that identity politics simultaneously encourages ever-expanding coalitions. The essays in this anthology, such as Jonathan Boyarin's and Evelyn Torton Beck's different views on cultural diversity in higher education, demonstrate that the multiculturalist dialectic of sameness and difference can emerge because, in the words of Audre Lorde, we do not lead single-issue lives.[40]

In their grapplings with difference, each of the three modes discussed here—melting pot theory, pluralism, and multiculturalism—has much to teach us about politics generally and about how to secure Jewish life and promote Jewish growth and vibrancy. From this point in history, the developments appear progressive, each stage further allowing the Jewish community to flower within and to be heard without. Jews have found various ways to respond to the different climates, some better and some worse. At each stage we register our losses, we take the painful road of honestly asking ourselves who we are, what we want to be, and what we can be in a country itself so painfully stumbling along. In our current search, we are looking both inward and outward: learning more history, more about who we are in our multiplicity today, and together navigating our way into an ever more complicated future. By attending to this complex process, this anthology will provide Jews and non-Jews alike with a sense of our concerns and our visions as we grapple head on with difference.

*   *   *

As we see, Jews are increasingly applying the lessons of an emerging multiculturalism to our lives within the community as we have been struggling to figure out the role of Jewish community in a broader multicultural environment. Jews are exploring ways to engage in honest critique of our own community for narrowing the vista of Jewish life and politics; in the process we are reviving the traditions of communal identity exploration and debate. In the current multicultural round, many in this anthology ask: What is it to be a Jew if one does not fit a wealthy, male, heterosexual, Ashkenazi, urban/suburban, synagogue-affiliated model? We also, therefore, must ask: What does it mean to be a Jew in late-twentieth-century North America even if one fits the stereotypes?

Thus, part 1 of this volume explores issues of identity and difference within the Jewish community. We are increasingly realizing that one of the important aspects of our strength as a historic people has been the richness of Jewish life stimulated by our internal diversity. Clare Kinberg, Felice Yeskel, Bob Goldfarb, and Rebecca Posner discuss race, ethnicity, sexual orientation, gender, class, and religious diversity, showing that we are a strong *and* diverse people. As writers of different genders, ages, geographical regions, class backgrounds, ethnic/cultural/racial heritages, as well as sexual, religious, and political orientations, they add their voices to the multicultural chorus that is both Jewish and American democracy. Of course, this cannot be enough. We will need to hear much more on the topic and much more from groups who have been marginalized historically within our community, including more explicit contributions from/concerning Jews by choice, those who are disabled, adult single Jews, those who suffer size-based oppression, members of other sexual minorities, and the intermarried/partnered.

When our awareness concerning the complicated and multi-faceted nature of Jewish identity has been heightened, we can then discuss how Jews have worked across communities to combat stereotypes, build trust, and pursue justice. Part 2 examines some aspects of Jewish-based intercommunal work, opening with Martha Ackelsberg's essay demonstrating the significance of coalition to a multicultural politics. Melanie Kaye/Kantrowitz, Gerald Horne, Reena Bernards, and Toba Spitzer look at work between Jews and other communities such as Christians, African Americans and other people of color in the United States, Haitians, and Palestinians. These essays also demonstrate some of the limitations with dialogue, unhelpful models of solidarity, and the complexity of an identity-based politics that does not degenerate into narrow nationalism.

As education has become a central arena for multicultural debate, development as well as backlash, part 3 is devoted to exploring the difficulties and potential for Jewish life within different educational contexts outside the Jewish community. Evelyn Torton Beck provides the historical grounding of multiculturalism within the university system in the United States. Naomi Nim explores the trials of Jewish participation in more radical pedagogical encounters in workshop settings with other minorities and white/Christian ethnics. Leora Saposnik and Ellen Osterhaus bring the discussion into the realm of the public schools for children in grades K–12, while Jonathan Boyarin's contribution envisions what academia might look like if we really could include Jewish life and history.

We must also recognize that as Jews struggle for physical and cultural survival, we can be lured by false securities, externally perceived power, and access that takes a toll on our internal strengths and moral direction. Hard-working, rich in history and religious tradition, politically active, and working to make a secure place for ourselves in the face of historic fears—with a deep need for dialogue and a commitment to education, the arts, and self-improvement—as a community we have amassed much wealth, resources, organizational apparatus, and rapid modes of internal communication. However, even as we succeed, as a community we must remember to be vigilant "pursuers of justice." Given our strengths—internally related to our own vital investment in creating a world without prejudice and better able to cope with fear—we must honestly examine our responsibility to create a more just world.

The contributors to part 4 thus grapple directly with issues of Jewish responsibility in a multicultural world as well as the challenges of honestly including and responding to Jews and Jewish concerns for all those committed to democracy and justice in the emerging multiculturalist framework. Ephraim Isaac calls on the Jewish community in the United States, with its relative security and resources, to act in historic Jewish solidarity with embattled Jewish communities such as that in his native Ethiopia. Nora Gold critically addresses the impact of multiculturalism in the world of Jewish social services, while Jeffrey Dekro makes an argument for Jewish institutional involvement in multicultural community economic development. Finally, Michael Walzer struggles with the question of what it means to be an American, and arrives at the wonderfully complex conclusion that to be an American, for Jews and for all citizens, is to be constantly struggling with that very question.

In that light, this anthology is testament to the fact that, in many ways, those of us wrestling with multiculturalism are still in the process of creating a new genre of thought and action, of identity politics and relationships, justice and social change. This volume demonstrates that this is no easy task. Transformation is fraught with difficulties. In multiculturalism we are working to foster a democratic vision to the best of our—both Jewishly and generally—abilities. But with all of its potential for a more liberated world, we know that this new mode provides no simple road map to help us navigate a just route through a shifting and uncertain world. Furthermore, it offers no guarantees that we will find our way around the false peaks of privilege and over the treacherous valleys of oppression. In my involvement as a Jew in multicultural work, I am constantly reminded of the words of Rabbi Nachman of Bratslav: "Kol ha olam kulo gesher tzar m'od v'ha ikar lo lefached klal" ("All the world is a very narrow bridge and the main thing is not to fear at all"). Multiculturalist politics often feels quite dangerous. We get hurt by those we think are our allies. The chasm below us is deep and our best hope for a safe crossing is over what appears to be only a narrow bridge. We know, however, that we must explore the alternative possibilities of diversity politics if we are to overcome anti-Semitism without assimilation and if ever we are to emerge from a land where difference is "Other." We must do so even if our way sometimes feels as scary as Rabbi Nachman's narrow bridge. Multiculturalism holds great promise as a progressive form of politics. The main task—once we acknowledge the real dangers—is to cope with our fear so that we can cross anyway. This anthology, therefore, provides a portrait of where we stand in 1996 and what we hope for from the future, as Jews and as Americans, in this complex realm of multicultural politics.

Notes

1. Previously, there was a tendency within the older, Marxist-styled Left to subordinate religious, ethnic, and national questions to those of class—leaving no framework within which to address a changing but persistent anti-Semitism. Jews often opted for humanism and universalism in the hope of overcoming oppression in general, and specifically the oppression of Jews based on our particularity—anti-Semitism. This strategy often had a reverse effect—deflecting Jewish perspectives and forgetting historical Jewish legacies of struggles against oppression.

2. See Madison, Hamilton, and Jay, *The Federalist Papers* (New York: NAL Penguin, 1961), esp. #10.

3. See the political writings of Benjamin Rush and also Herzog's comments on Rush in "Some Questions for Republicans," *Political Theory* 14, no. 3 (August 1986): 473–93.

4. See early ethnic-historians such as Oscar Handlin, *The Uprooted* (Boston: Little, Brown, 1951), who focused on the alienation resulting from the separation entailed in the immigrant experience of "becoming a foreigner and ceasing to belong." Later waves of historians are critical of this view; see, for example, Rudolph Vecoli, "Contadini in Chicago: A Critique of the Uprooted," *Journal of American History* 51, no. 3 (December 1964):404–17. See feminist critiques in the exchange published in the *Journal of American Ethnic History* (Summer 1992).

5. Policies of the time instituted at the Ford Motor Company are a perfect example. Henry Ford established a school to teach English and made attendance compulsory. The commencement ceremony was a melting pot simulation in which graduates came down the "gangplank" from their "immigrant ship," dressed in their national cos-

tumes and carrying bulky baggage, into Ford's "melting pot." The teachers "stirred the contents" with "long ladles" and as the "pot boiled over" the men emerged dressed in American clothes and waving American flags. See Olivier Zunz, *The Changing Face of Inequality: Urbanization, Industrial Development, and Immigrants in Detroit*, 1880–1920 (Chicago: University of Chicago Press, 1982), pp. 311–12, in which he draws on Jonathan Schwartz's "Henry Ford's Melting Pot," in *Ethnic Groups in the City: Culture, Institutions and Power*, ed. Otto Feinstein (Lexington, Mass.: Heath Lexington Books, D. C. Heath, 1971).

6.   Israel Zangwill wrote these words in an afterword to the 1914 edition of his play, *The Melting Pot* (New York: Arno, 1975), p. 203.

7.   Reprinted from the *Chicago Daily News* as an appendix to Zangwill's 1914 edition, p. 198.

8.   Ibid., p. 213.

9.   For example, a second wave in ethnic-historiography focused on the victimization of the immigrants. See John Higham, *Strangers in the Land: Patterns of American Nativism* (New York: Atheneum, 1965), which explores the "anti-foreign spirit" of American nativism (focusing mostly on European immigrants). On the other hand, some immigrant historians suggested that the new ethnic groups used their cultures as a strength: Kathleen Neils Conzen, *Immigrant Milwaukee 1836–1860* (Cambridge, Mass.: Harvard University Press, 1976); and John Bodnar, "Immigration and Modernization: The Case of Slavic Peasants in Industrial America," *Journal of Social History* (Fall 1976):44–67.

10.   A development within the dominant Liberal ideology, pluralism broadened political analysis from a narrow focus on individuals and formal institutions to one including extragovernmental, group-based politics. Proto-pluralist A. F. Bentley, writing earlier in the century [*The Process of Government* (Evanston, Ill.: The Principia Press of Illinois, 1908)], thought that Marx had correctly understood politics in terms of group oppressions and interaction; he felt, however, that Marx's group category of class was too crude. Bentley exposed the activity of a host of groups fighting it out in politics and argued that it is group-based activity that drives American politics.

11.   Iris Marion Young, *Justice and the Politics of Difference* (Princeton, N.J.: Princeton University Press, 1990). Young provides a detailed critique of the distributive paradigm of justice. She writes, "while distributive issues are crucial to a satisfactory conception of justice, it is a mistake to reduce social justice to distribution" because (1) "this focus tends to ignore the social structure and institutional context that often help determine distributive patterns" and (2) when the distributive paradigm is extended to nonmaterial social goods, these goods are represented as "static things instead of a function of social relations and processes" (pp. 15–16). While affirming the importance of a distributive aspect of justice, she suggests a broader conception of the stuff of justice as oppression (interestingly defined beyond the terms of discrimination to include exploitation, marginalization, powerlessness, cultural imperialism, and violence) that I rely on in the following discussion of multiculturalism.

12.   The phrase actually comes from E. E. Schattschneider, *The Semi-Sovereign People* (Hinsdale, Ill.: Dryden, 1960).

13.   See Robert Dahl, *Who Governs?* (New Haven: Yale University Press, 1961). Recent writing in the field of ethnic history has focused on the challenges that racial history poses to our understandings of ethnic pluralism and assimilation. See, for example, Michael Omi and Howard Winant, *Racial Formation in the United States from the 1960s to*

the 1990s (New York: Routledge, 1994); and Ronald Takaki's work on Asian Americans, *Strangers from a Different Shore* (New York: Penguin, 1990) and, more broadly, *A Different Mirror: A History of Multicultural America* (Boston: Little, Brown, 1993), *Iron Cages: Race and Culture in Nineteenth-Century America* (New York: Alfred A. Knopf, 1979), and his more recent edited volume *From Different Shores: Perspectives on Race and Ethnicity in America* (New York: Oxford University Press, 1994).

In particular, the situation of Americans of African descent directly challenges the promise of the pluralist adaption of the melting pot view: African Americans were not seen as having a distinct culture to follow "in private," and were too different to pass for the same "in public."

14.   Some interpreted this problem of pluralism as a problem of practical politics, suggesting that pluralism, rather than being a descriptive theory of American political life, is instead a goal. In this understanding, the problem of pluralism, predominantly the practical problem that many nondominant groups remain excluded from the acknowledged political realm, is to be solved by more pluralism. What these interpreters failed to notice was that the *practical* biases of pluralist politics are rooted in *philosophical* biases found at the core of the theory itself.

On the philosophical level, note, for example, Honig's critique of Rawls: "Committed to pluralism, Rawls's liberal democracy insists that no single comprehensive vision of the good life may dominate the political space. But Rawls sees no *positive* connection between politics and pluralism. . . . Unrelated to the basic structure, it is not the subject of justice. But what if it is a *product* of Rawls's effective depoliticization of difference? What if genuine pluralism is a *casualty* of the public–private distinction that Rawlsian justice postulates as the *condition* of pluralism's possibility?" (*Political Theory and the Displacement of Politics* [Ithaca: Cornell University Press, 1993], p. 130).

15.   Numerous terms that have become part of the vocabulary of multiculturalism, such as "difference," have had much play in this era of French thought (see, for example, the writings of Jacques Derrida). Foucault, *Power/Knowledge* (New York: Pantheon, 1980), suggests that there is no truth but only constructed discourses of power through which identities come into being. In this case, then, oppression we experience based on our identities is not "natural," or inevitable and unchangeable. Multiculturalists learned that if we suffer identity-based oppression, but identity itself is a social construction, we can construct (or reconstruct) our own identities in ways we find more liberating. (This is in contrast to a postmodernist, who would call for the abandonment of the project of identity altogether.) Both groups will find interesting the work of ethnic historians who discuss the ways in which immigrant groups re-created their ethnic identities when they arrived in this country. Later works by Kathleen Neils Conzen fall into this category. See also the co-authored Kathleen Neil Conzen, David A. Gerber, Ewa Morawska, George E. Pozzetta, and Rudolph J. Vecoli, "The Invention of Ethnicity: A Perspective from the U.S.A.," *Journal of American Ethnic History* (Fall 1992):3–41, and the responses in the same volume, for example, by Fuchs, whose earlier writings focused on the assimilation model.

16.   The transformation of the Left, now designated as Old Left and New Left, spurred changes in the Right, where Old World conservative ideas based on the eighteenth-century writing of Edmund Burke were changed to "New Right," neo- (or libertarian) conservatism that was later popularized by Ronald Reagan.

17.   Nancy Fraser, in "Rethinking the Public Sphere: A Contribution to the Critique of Actually Existing Democracy," *Social Text* 25–26 (1991), uses the term "multiple

publics" in the attempt to decenter politics from a unitary sphere dominated by the state. Although I would not place the same emphasis on the contestational nature of politics, the reader will note that I share much of her perspective.

18.   Literature critically demonstrating the tendency of universalist approaches to gloss over or even to justify oppression abounds. For example, much of the feminist literature cited herein critically addresses this phenomenon. In addition, many of these contemporary writers and activists owe much to Carol Gilligan's controversial but pivotal work, *In a Different Voice* (Cambridge, Mass.: Harvard University Press, 1982).

19.   Here I draw on and rework Fraser's discussion of the role of needs in politics from "Talking about Needs: Interpretive Contests as Political Conflicts in Welfare-State Societies," in *Feminism and Political Theory*, ed. Cass Sunstein (Chicago: University of Chicago Press, 1990).

20.   This vision provides a fundamental challenge to Millian and First Amendment-style freedom (from external constraints on expression). Attention to politics in the vernacular of "raising our voices" and overcoming a silencing style of communal relations compels us to ask the question: What good is the freedom to speak if no one will listen? Politics, thus understood, is premised on the notion that our freedom of expression is meaningful only when it is consciously based on the responsibility of the citizenry to listen. For philosophical and applied renderings of this point, see Seyla Benhabib, "Afterword: Communicative Ethics and Contemporary Controversies in Practical Philosophy," in *The Communicative Ethics Controversy*, ed. Seyla Benhabib and Fred Dallmayr (Cambridge, Mass.: MIT, 1990); and Judith Plaskow, *Standing Again at Sinai: Judaism from a Feminist Perspective* (New York: HarperCollins, 1991), respectively.

21.   See, for example, Kymlicka's defense of Liberalism's claim to neutrality in response to communitarian critiques in "Liberal Individualism and Neutrality," *Ethics* 99 (1989):883–905.

22.   Despite philosophical claims to universality and objectivity, European and American colonialism (domestic and foreign) has relied, in fact, on the assumption of cultural superiority (which included the *political* ideology and way of life of Liberalism/capitalism).

23.   This insight is gleaned partially from developments of early second-wave feminism that showed women that, despite cultural pressure to be self-sacrificing, they could assert their needs and that this assertion was helpful and necessary. Feminism suggested that encouraging women to assert their needs was not "selfish" but rather helping women take better care of themselves and thereby helping, for example, the family unit as a whole. Thus, this newer theory is making room for a multiculturally needs-based politics of intergroup engagement, rather than a particularly culturally biased, competitive, interest-based politics.

24.   Citation from Martin Buber, *I and Thou* (New York: Macmillan, 1958/1987), p. 6. In response to criticism, some have attempted to disengage from universals in political theory and life (this is especially true of postmodernists). Another response has been to tangle dialectically with universals in their abstract conceptualizations, leading some to posit more contextualized universals. See, for example, Seyla Benhabib, "The Generalized and the Concrete Other: The Kohlberg–Gilligan Controversy and Feminist Theory," in *Feminism as Critique* ed. Seyla Benhabib and Drucilla Cornell (Minneapolis: University of Minnesota Press, 1987).

25.   Although many of the contributors to this volume are of Ashkenazi descent, reflecting the cultural demographics, different Eastern, African, and Sephardi perspec-

tives are represented here in an attempt to reclaim the cultural diversity of the American Jewish community. For more on particularly Sephardi American history, see, for example: Daniel J. Elazar, *The Other Jews: The Sephardim Today* (New York: Basic Books, 1989); Loolwa Khazoom, "A Bridge between Different Worlds," *Bridges* 4, no. 2 (1994/95); Joseph M. Papo, *The Sephardim in Twentieth Century America: In Search of Unity* (San Jose, Calif.: Pele Yoetz Books, 1987); selections in Melanie Kaye/Kantrowitz and Irena Klepfisz, *The Tribe of Dina* (Sinister Wisdom, 29/30, 1986); and Joanne Lehrer, "Jews, Justice and Community: An Analysis of Radical Jewish-Identified Organizing in the United States, 1880–1995," Hampshire College, Division Three, Amherst, Mass., April 1995.

26. Zangwill, *Melting Pot*, p. 215.

27. Ibid., p. 216.

28. Quoted in Maxine Greene, *The Dialectic of Freedom* (New York: Teachers College Press, 1988), p. 75. Contemporary historians now point to significant differences between the harsher demands made for assimilation by such Progressives as Henry Ford and the "gentler" approach of others such as Addams. For example, see John Higham's *Strangers in the Land*, esp. pp. 236–37; and David Kennedy, *Over Here: The First World War and American Society* (New York: Oxford University Press, 1980), esp. chap. 1. See also Allan Dawley's *Struggle for Justice: Social Responsibility and the Liberal State* (Cambridge: Harvard University Press, 1991) for his distinction between "managerial liberalism" and "progressive liberalism" of the Progressive era.

29. Philosopher of education Maxine Greene writes,

The average immigrant child had no contact with progressive teachers eager to help him/her release particular preferences and develop into a thinking person in the midst of a friendly community. Even if the child had such contact, it is doubtful whether his/her ethnic or religious distinctiveness would have been noted or valued; since the dominant concern was to usher all children into the ways of life and thinking associated with the society as it existed (*Dialectic of Freedom*, pp. 111–12).

30. Richman was a German Jew, the first Jew and first woman school principal in New York City, and served as a New York City superintendent in 1903. See the *Biographical Dictionary of American Educators*, ed. John F. Ohles (Westport, Conn.: Greenwood, 1978), 3:1099–1100. Cite from Greene, *Dialectic of Freedom*, p. 112.

31. Lady Liberty spoke the sonnet of Emma Lazerus (not insignificantly, herself Jewish):

Give me your tired, your poor,
Your huddled masses yearning to breathe free,
The wretched refuse of your teeming shore.
Send these, the homeless, tempest-tost to me,
I lift my lamp beside the golden door.

32. The roots of pluralism go back to Bentley writing at the same time that Zangwill wrote *The Melting Pot*, or perhaps even earlier to the Framers of the Constitution. Nathan Glazer and Daniel Patrick Moynihan were still grappling with the inadequacies of the melting pot vision in the 1970s. See Glazer and Moynihan, *Beyond the Melting Pot: The Negroes, Puerto Ricans, Jews, Italians and Irish of New York* (Cambridge, Mass.: MIT, 1970). Pluralism was developing as an intricate political philosophy within

the academy even as women, people of color, students, and antiwar protesters were taking to the streets, forming consciousness-raising groups and creating what we are now
calling multiculturalism. While multiculturalism is increasingly discussed and developed, many still work in the language of both melting pot and pluralist theories of
American political life.

33.   The struggle to create an alternative politics necessitates the development of
new language—hence the shading and overlapping. As multiculturalism is still taking
shape, readers may find contributors using phrases such as "true pluralism" as we all
explore new ways to express ourselves and our aspirations in a politics that celebrates
diversity.

34.   Groups often thought to be lobby groups, such as the Anti-Defamation
League, American Jewish Congress, or the Religious Action Center (which is the political arm of the Reform Movement) and more recently Americans for Peace Now's
Washington Center for Peace and Security, and Project Nishma, are in fact advocacy, not
registered lobby, groups. The Jewish Peace Lobby, formed in 1989, is the only other registered Jewish lobbying group.

35.   For a critical reading of this history, see Edward Tivnan, *The Lobby: Jewish Political Power and American Foreign Policy* (New York: Simon and Schuster, 1987).

36.   What was happening in the Jewish community can be said to parallel
Norman Jacobson's analysis of what had happened in the United States generally ("Political Science and Political Education," *American Political Science Review* 57, no. 3 [Sep-
tember 1963]: 561–69). Jacobson discussed the way in which a certain political mind-set
and framework from the founding of the American Republic created the pluralist spec-
imens of contemporary politics and academic scholarship. Bound up with AIPAC's success was the Jacobsonian self-fulfilling prophecy of pluralism.

37.   I use Mordecai Kaplan's term ("civilization") here. See, for example, *Judaism
as a Civilization: Toward a Reconstruction of American-Jewish Life* (Philadelphia: Jewish Publication Society, 1967).

38.   For more on this through the example of pro-Israel politics within the American Jewish community, see my *Cornerstones of Peace: Jewish Identity Politics and Democratic
Theory* (New Brunswick: Rutgers University Press, 1996).

39.   See, for example, Arthur Waskow, *These Holy Sparks: The Rebirth of the Jewish
People* (San Francisco: Harper and Row, 1983); Christie Balka and Andy Rose, *Twice
Blessed: On Being Lesbian, Gay, and Jewish* (Boston: Beacon, 1989); Riv Ellen Prell, *Prayer
and Community: The Havurah in American Judaism* (Detroit: Wayne State University Press,
1989); and any of the early Jewish feminist collections, such as Susannah Heschel, ed.,
On Being a Jewish Feminist (New York: Schocken, 1983); Irena Klepfisz and Melanie
Kaye/Kantrowitz, eds., *The Tribe of Dina* (Sinister Wisdom 29/30, 1986); Elizabeth
Koltun, ed., *The Jewish Woman* (New York: Schocken, 1978); and Evelyn Torton Beck,
ed., *Nice Jewish Girls: A Lesbian Anthology* (New York: Crossing Press, 1982).

40.   Audre Lorde, *Sister Outsider* (New York: Crossing Press, 1984).

A Strong and Diverse People:
Multiculturalism within
the Jewish Community

Challenges of Difference at Bridges

CLARE KINBERG

For seven years in the 1970s I worked in a lesbian collective on a newsletter that was devoted to publishing lesbian perspectives on practically everything. We did special issues on housing, food, violence, work, racism, capitalism, collectivity, sex. This was in my hometown, St. Louis, which like the many other U.S. cities I have since lived in, was almost completely segregated by race and class. Through feminism, however, and a desire to work with other lesbians, I was drawn into a community that struggled to include Black women and women from across the class spectrum—women whom I otherwise might never have met. Lesbian-feminism opened my life beyond the middle-class Jewish family and community I had grown up in. At the same time, unfortunately, I and most of the other Jewish women I knew, mostly left our Jewishness back home. Having a Jewish consciousness didn't fit in the lesbian-feminist community of the 1970s. Jews were a distinct and "Other" group. If I'd stayed closer to home I might never have had to experience Jews as an "Other" or all the insensitive and ignorant behavior that comes along with marginalization. From the writings of Black, Asian, Native American, and Latina women I've learned that other feminists who grew up in racial or ethnic communities experienced their own version of this marginality. They, too, were faced with the choice, conscious or not, of being part of a predominantly white, feminist community or staying home.

Somewhere in between Reagan's first election in 1980 and Israel's invasion of Lebanon in 1982 I was sharply reminded that the Jewish people were my "home" community. At the time I was a shop steward (Amalgamated Clothing and Textile Workers Union) at a coat factory. The company was owned by Orthodox Jews, but I was the only Jew in the union. Though my lesbianism had led me to a left-wing critique of U.S. society, which in turn had led me to union activism, I never mentioned my lesbianism to my co-workers on the shop floor. While working forty hours a week doing piecework on a sewing machine gave me a lot in common with the women I worked with, I was also terribly isolated. The isolation peaked one day as I was riding the bus to work. I overheard someone commenting on the headlines about the massacres (by Lebanese Falangists) in the Palestinian refugee camps, Sabra and Shatilla: "Never turn your back on a Jew; they'll stab you just as quick." I needed someone that I could talk to when I got to work, but I knew with sickening clarity that the understanding I needed would not be there.

As a lesbian I felt I was, politically speaking, spitting in the wind of nuclear proliferation, war in the Middle East, Reaganomics; as a Jew outside the Jewish community, I felt terrified. My own personal survival, I felt with intense conviction, was dependent on change in the way people understood the country's economic problems; changing Israel's futile reliance on military solutions to its security; creating a climate of support for lesbian identity. It was my desperate search for the possibility of participating in these kinds of changes in society, of making a political difference, which brought me home.

Despite my own denials, I was irrevocably a member of the Jewish community. I thought it was possible, even if remotely so, that my own actions could have a political effect on the Jewish 2 percent of the U.S. population. At least the Jews were a conceivable constituency. Though as a lesbian I would still be struggling for acceptance and basic rights in the Jewish community, in a profoundly *political* sense, the Jews, I knew for certain, were my people. In 1983 I joined New Jewish Agenda (NJA), an organization of thousands of Jews like myself who had visions for global social and political change and who knew that they must seek these changes from the foundation of the Jewish community.

Among NJA members I found many other essentially secular Jews whose strong identification with the Jewish people had relatively little to do with religious belief or practice, but rather was based on a historical consciousness.[1] In NJA I met Jews who were establishing a late-twentieth-century Jewish way of being in the world based on the lessons of the Jewish collective past—the ways we had organized and governed our own communities, the intellectual and spiritual quests, stories told, books written, the meals prepared and eaten, the families raised, and the social and political interactions with the other peoples of the earth.

Organizing in NJA required those of us who had been estranged from the Jewish world to think anew about the composition and structure of the Jewish community in the United States, and how a diverse group of left-wing and feminist activists could influence the Jewish community as a whole. Feminists brought to NJA what we had learned from feminist organizing. We initiated structural changes within the organization, including gender parity in all national leadership bodies, guaranteed "out" lesbian/gay representation in governance, and men's and women's caucuses. NJA's structure also insisted on geographic diversity (within the continental United States) and representation of people over age fifty-five. NJA, formulaically at least, applied a central insight of the feminist movement: the realities and contexts of our personal lives are inseparable from our political perspectives and actions.

NJA members included many women like myself who had made conscious choices to do feminist organizing within a Jewish context. For over two decades the U.S. feminist movement, particularly the lesbian-feminist part of it, has been chewing on "identity politics," that is, organizing that recognizes and values women's different (ethnic, racial, sexual) home communities. For Jewish lesbian-feminists, our home communities were too often where our parents, relatives, and neighbors lived, but not our (wandering) selves. The separations in our lives were made more conscious and visible by the pioneering work of Evelyn Torton Beck (*Nice Jewish Girls: A Lesbian Anthology*, 1982) and Irena Klepfisz and Melanie Kaye/Kantrowitz (*The Tribe of Dina: A Jewish Women's Anthology*, 1986). Some of the contributors to these anthologies, women who insisted on integrating their Jewish and lesbian-feminist identities and organizing, were members of New Jewish Agenda. However, during these years in the mid-1980s I remained intensely conscious that for the thousands of women around the country who were reading *Nice Jewish Girls* and *Tribe of Dina*, the divisions between "Jewish" and "lesbian-feminist" were profound and not readily bridged. Reading about feminist Jews and lesbian Jews was critical to transformations of consciousness, but it was still very hard to find ways of living in an active way with the new consciousness. From the late 1970s through the 1980s, there was, however, a burgeoning movement of Jewish lesbian-feminist women, in small and large cities across the country, who formed their own groups and organizations. NJA was not primarily a feminist organization, though I believe it was the only national Jewish organization at the time that seriously attempted to bring feminism and lesbian/gay issues into its core effort. Still, in the mid-1980s the multi-issue, progressive Agenda and the Jewish feminist movement were almost completely separate, like trains on different tracks.

The feminists who *had* made it to Agenda published an internal newsletter entitled *Gesher* (Hebrew for "Bridge") that attempted to connect feminists in NJA and let other members know what feminists were doing. In 1988 Jewish writers and editors Ruth Atkin, Elly Bulkin, Adrienne Rich, and I started talking about the possibilities of expanding the *Gesher* newsletter into a journal and becoming independent of NJA. Our intention was to be an explicitly Jewish participant in a multiethnic feminist movement; to connect Jewish women who are active in antiracist, peace, lesbian/gay, and Jewish renewal movements; and to make connections across generations, countries, and languages by publishing archival material and writing in different Jewish languages and in translation.

We wanted to create a forum that would address questions emerging again and again in our writing, organizing, and publishing: Who are Jewish feminists and what are we doing in our own communities? What are our goals? Who are our political allies and how do we discover them? How do we become allies to others? How can others become political allies to us? These questions, and the aspirations they imply, are embedded in the name of the independent journal we helped found in 1989: *Bridges: A Journal for Jewish Feminists and Our Friends*.

Bridges' founding editor Elly Bulkin had been, more than a decade earlier (1976–83), a founding editor of *Conditions: A Magazine of Writing by Women with an Emphasis on Writing by Lesbians*. In 1978 the *Conditions* editorial collective (which included Bulkin, Jan Clausen, and two other Jewish women Irena Klepfisz and Rima Shore) arranged a guest editorship for two African American women, Lorraine Bethel and Barbara Smith. Their volume became *Conditions: Five, The Black Women's Issue*. A few years later *Conditions: Five* evolved into Barbara Smith's much expanded volume, *Home Girls: A Black Feminist Anthology* (1983), which remains an essential collection for understanding the meaning of "identity politics" through the specific lens of Black women in the United States. The impact of *Conditions: Five* for women across racial and ethnic lines was powerful. In founding

Bridges, we hoped to create a forum for a sharpening and widening, *specifically Jewish*, lens on the conditions of our lives.

Some of *Bridges'* founding editors had done work regarding diversity primarily *within* the Jewish community. Rita Falbel, for instance, brought to *Bridges* her experience as a musician performing in different Jewish languages. On *Bridges'* masthead, the word "bridges" is printed in Yiddish, Hebrew, Ladino, and English, indicating our understanding that Jews have lived in many contexts as well as our commitment to publishing in the many languages that Jews speak. Ruth Atkin had been in the early 1980s the "women's affairs" editor for *Genesis 2: An Independent Voice for Jewish Renewal* (at the time a Boston-based Jewish student newspaper). Her familiarity with the spirited and creative transformations happening within Judaism was another door to Jewish diversity.

In *Bridges* we look seriously at who Jewish women are. We look for creative writing, artwork, essays, reports that help us put Jewish women's lives into historical, social, political contexts. We ask ourselves, and the writers and artists we publish, to notice and value particular circumstances and contexts: class, family, sexual identity, language, nationality. Our assumption is that learning in depth about Jewish women's lives will lead to connection with other women, that the deeper we explore differences among Jews and the many different facets of each Jewish woman's life, the more we will understand other women's identities and the stronger will be our basis with which to form alliances. Basically, the more respect we have for ourselves as Jews, the more respect we will have for other women's cultural and ethnic identities, the greater will be our ability to effect transformation and participate in seeking justice.

Our assumption, that learning more about Jewish experience in the world will lead to connection to others, is fraught with uncertainty. Isn't it equally possible that being drawn into the expanse of Jewish learning will lead to an inward focus? That immersion in the complex intricacies of Jewish spiritual and political experience will prove to be a satisfying end in itself? While this is perhaps true for individuals, our purpose in publishing *Bridges* is to insist that the deeper the foundation and the more sure the footing, the greater will be the ability to stretch the span and support the connections with non-Jews. We have received encouraging feedback that treating our Jewish heritage with this seriousness does foster connections with others. One African American subscriber wrote to us: "Seeing the Yiddish and Hebrew texts is an affirmation of a vibrant culture in which women and men participated. . . . The work of recovering and preserving Jewish history resonates deeply with me as one who is still discovering the meaning of being an African American."[2]

The editors of *Bridges* approach our work with another shared working assumption: publishing material that builds bridges among diverse groups cannot be done separately from recognizing and building on the diversity among ourselves. The group of women at *Bridges'* founding meeting was diverse in various ways, homogeneous in others. We were majority lesbian, from the East and West Coasts of the United States, ranging in age from thirties to sixties, all Ashkenazi (European Jews), and all from middle-class backgrounds. Our first steps to diversify—this was before we had published anything—did not reach far afield: to be relevant in more regions of the country, we sought editors from the Midwest; we expanded generationally by adding a woman in her twenties. And we prioritized building an advisory editorial board that included non-Jewish people of color and other progressive non-Jewish women and men who had demonstrated knowledge of and commitment to Jews and feminists.

Our subtitle, "a journal for Jewish feminists and our friends," was carefully formulated to state our political intentions: to be a journal that is proudly Jewish, boldly feminist, and accessible to our allies. At that first meeting we drafted *Bridges'* mission statement:

> The editors bring to *Bridges* a commitment that combines the traditional Jewish values of justice and repair of the world with insights honed by the feminist, lesbian, and gay movements. We want to provide a forum in which Jews, feminists and activists can exchange ideas and deepen our understanding of the relationship between our identities and activism. We seek writing which develops affirmatively Jewish and feminist perspectives and creates links between Jewish feminists and activists in the broad range of movements for social and economic justice and for peace. We are especially committed to integrating analyses of race and class into Jewish-feminist thought and to being a specifically Jewish participant in the multi-ethnic feminist movement.

Our mission stated that we were committed to "integrating analyses of class and race into Jewish feminist thought" because we knew Jewish participation in broad-based social justice movements depended on new thinking in relation to Jewish identity, anti-Semitism, class, and race. Still, we hadn't addressed the fact that everyone in our initial group was Ashkenazi and middle-class. Not until our second meeting, a year later, did a working-class editor, tova, join the collective. Our discussions about class were not easy, particularly for tova.

We did make progress, however, toward changing both how we work together and how we select and edit the material we publish. We made plans to add at least two more working-class or raised-poor women to the editorial group; to actively encourage submissions from working-class women; to be more conscious of the class bias in the work we consider; to have a working-class/poor women's column as a regular feature in each issue; to publish a cluster of articles on class; to consider class issues in relation to promotion and availability; and to commit the middle-class editors to discuss class with women in our communities and among ourselves.

Each of these commitments has given us much on which to reflect. For instance, when we began "networking" to find new editors we found that, even though Jews in the United States have roughly the same class distribution as other white ethnic Americans, many of the middle-class editors didn't *know* (or didn't think they knew) any working-class or poor Jews. Was this because working-class Jewish women are invisible to middle-class women? because class is so rarely discussed? because of the ways working-class women are excluded from middle-class circles? How does this relate to internalized anti-Semitism (our unexamined acceptance of the stereotype that Jews really *are* middle-class)?

The commitment to a "Working Class Words" column in each issue makes us confront these issues, as a group, over and over. For an article on how the Republican Contract with America would affect women on welfare, I contacted a Jewish woman who had mentioned in passing that she had received AFDC when her son was young. To help write the article, she immediately called up a half dozen of her Jewish friends who had also been on welfare. All of them felt, in varying ways, invisible in the Jewish community.

The contributions of working-class women have affected the

others among us as well. The middle-class editors, for example, have found that to keep up a dialogue among ourselves about class we have to start with some basic questions: What about being middle class makes it so hard to maintain a discussion about class and money? What does it mean to "own" middle-class identity? How does our class affect our editorial judgment?

Bridges now has two more working-class editors, Toby Finkelstein, and Shlomit Segal, and as a group we must remain open to fundamentally changing how we deal with money, solicit work, and make editorial decisions. As Naomi Finkelstein points out in her contribution to "Working Class Words," "It is much more difficult to 'add' a working-class perspective after a middle-class process is well under way."[3] Our specific work as editors brings us eye to eye with such questions as: How do class and class-based power inequities interact with Jewish values and experience of education, learnedness, art and literature, language, immigration, community, family? How do we as editors encourage new and thoughtful writing on these issues?

Similar kinds of issues are raised by virtue of the fact that the founding editors are all Ashkenazi, of Eastern European or Russian descent. In some ways, the most obvious, and the most hidden, of "multicultural" issues for Jews may be the differences among Sephardi (originating in Spain), Mizrachi (Middle Eastern), and Ashkenazi Jews. In our first several issues we published a song in Ladino and an article on Sephardi women's music, by Judith Cohen, an Ashkenazi woman. But this hardly did justice to the widespread misperception in the United States that Jewish culture is synonymous with Ashkenazi culture. Recently the addition to our editorial group of Debra Crespin, an Ashkephardic woman (one parent Ashkenazi and the other Sephardi), has made us more aware of how weak we've been in this area.

The particular nuances of being the daughter of Ashkenazi and Sephardi families was expressed by Ruth Behar in "*Mi Puente*/My Bridge to Cuba":

> In Cuba, my mother would have continued to be the daughter of *polacas* (Poles), and my father the son of *turcos* (Turks). My maternal grandfather was from a town in Byelorussia and my maternal grandmother was from a town near Warsaw. They learned to speak Spanish, but never lost their Yiddish accents and their ties to Yiddish culture. My paternal grandparents, on the other hand, were Sephardi Jews

from a town on the Marmara Sea not far from Istanbul. They spoke Ladino, the tender Spanish full of longing preserved by the Jews who were expelled from Spain. When I was growing up, on the first night of Passover we ate gefilte fish, matzo ball soup, and boiled chicken; on the second night we ate egg lemon soup, stuffed tomatoes, and almond squares dripping with honey.[4]

In "A Bridge between Different Worlds" Iraqi Jewish feminist Loolwa Khazzoom tells us about her fierce connection to a fading Middle Eastern Jewish culture and sharply confronts the marginalization in the United States of Jews from Arab countries. "By the time I was eight years old, I could sing the Shabbat and weekday evening prayers in the traditional Iraqi tunes; I knew dozens of Iraqi Shabbat and holy day songs by heart." Yet she wasn't allowed to use them in Ashkenazi-controlled Jewish schools or synagogues. And in her own Sephardi congregation in San Francisco, her "unique knowledge of and passion for Iraqi Jewish heritage was irrelevant" because she wasn't a boy. As a student at Barnard/Columbia in the 1980s, Khazzoom suggested chanting one prayer and singing one song during services using the Sephardi melodies. Her proposal was responded to with hostility and refusal: "'When I go to services, I want it to be the same prayers I grew up singing! I don't want it to be something *foreign*!' one student yelled."[5]

Khazzoom's essay illustrates an especially important insight we've learned from our work on *Bridges*: difficult issues of difference have been most successfully approached by writers who have explored their own multiple identities. In her essay "Tsu Got vel ikh veynen" ("To God I Cry Out," taken from a poem by sweatshop poet David Edelstadt), Aurora Levins Morales tells the stories of her Jewish and Puerto Rican grandmothers, both seamstresses—stories that lead to an awareness of today's "*maquileras* strung along the Mexican border the way old sweatshops once lined the streets of the Lower East Side."[6] Joanna Kadi, a working-class Arab-Canadian writer, reviewed a memoir by upper-class Palestinian poet Fadwa Tuqan, finding "a sorely-needed glimpse of my people/my self"[7] while at the same time wondering why Tuqan did not question how her family's wealth contributed to her success as a writer. While Kadi's review is important for what it teaches specifically about Palestinian culture, the class issues she raises cut across cultural boundaries.

Our abiding challenge is to solicit and edit work that is both grounded in Jewish identity and builds bridges. We continually experiment with new ways to ask writers and artists: What is the relationship among your identity, your people's history, your circumstances, and your politics and beliefs?

For instance, we experimented with simultaneously soliciting two reviews of the same material. We asked both African American writer Cheryl Clarke and Jewish writer Bernice Mennis to review *Making Face, Making Soul/Haciendo Caras*, a collection of writings by women of color edited by mestiza Gloria Anzaldua. Each reviewer read the collection with an eye to understanding her *own* identity. Clarke quotes a poem of Anzaldua's:

> We are the coarse rock.
> We are the grinding motion,
> the mixed potion, *somos el molcajete*.
> We are the pestle, the *comino, ajo, pimiento*,
> we are the *chile colorado*,
> the green shoot that cracks the rock.
> We will abide.

Clarke then comments: "As an African-American woman I share the Chicana/Mexicana faith that the caregivers of the land will abide/survive, though I am wary. I remember the cotton. The tobacco. The corn."[8] In her review, Mennis relates teaching *The Tribe of Dina: A Jewish Women's Anthology* while reading *Making Face, Making Soul*: The "chorus of individual voices each singing in her own style, language, voice" in *Making Face, Making Soul* led her to "listen more closely to the voices" in the Jewish women's anthology, where she finds the "persistence and depth of certain themes: The sense of uprootedness—expulsion, moving to strange lands, searching for safety, for a home; the power of history to shape us."[9]

In her review essay of two collections of African American women's literary criticism (*Changing Our Own Words*, edited by Cheryl A. Wall; and *Wild Women in the Whirlwind*, edited by Joanne M. Braxton and Andree Nicola McLaughlin), *Bridges* editor Adrienne Rich directly addresses integrating analyses of race into Jewish feminist thought. She reasons that "African Americans (like American Indians, Asian Americans, Latinos) have had, and continue to have, access to a particularly clear and undeluded view of the contradictions and failures of United States-style democracy," and points out that their "situational, experiential, accrual of insights, based on the material conditions of their lives"[10] offer a critique that American Jews have not yet, but need to, come to terms with.

For Jews, our "accrual of insights" spans two millennia, our critique of the United States includes, and is perhaps overshadowed by, our experiences elsewhere. But only in the past century have Jewish *women* begun adding their perspectives and analyses. The task we set forth in *Bridges'* pages is to inform our critique with both the writings of non-Jewish women of color *and* the unearthing of our own achievements and losses; the languages, the histories, and the values of Jewish women's lives.

In another instance we solicited two reviews from different perspectives of collections of working-class women's writing (*Calling Home*, edited by Janet Zandy; *The Common Thread*, edited by a British collective; and an issue on class from the journal *Lesbian Ethics*). The reviewers were a working-class woman, Ellie Barbarash, and a middle-class woman, Elly Bulkin. Whereas Bulkin evaluates each collection for what it offers of "political direction for women with privilege,"[11] Barbarash testifies, "I saw myself, my friends and my family described in their pages. They named me. These books reflect my triumphs, my growth, my pain."[12]

We assume that our readership includes Jews and non-Jews; Jews immersed in Jewish learning and Jews with limited Jewish education; secular and religious Jews; Jews who are, and who are not, familiar with Yiddish, Hebrew, or Ladino. We make every effort to edit work so that it is accessible and interesting to this diverse readership. We italicize and define every word that cannot be found in a standard English dictionary and to describe Jewish holidays and rituals each time they are mentioned. When we publish in Yiddish, Hebrew, or Ladino, we try to print transliteration as well as translation.

At the same time, *Bridges* is the only feminist publication that devotes substantial pages to publishing in Yiddish. We have published two complete short stories in Yiddish and in English translation and more than a dozen poems. Irena Klepfisz's forty-page essay "Di mames, dos loshn/The Mothers, The Language: Feminism, *Yidishkayt* and the Politics of Memory,"[13] based on her new translations of essays and memoirs of four Eastern European activists (all quotations are published in Yiddish and English), broke new ground in the recovery of Jewish women writing in Yiddish. In "Di mames, dos loshn," Klepfisz explains one of the central reasons that there should be such a high priority placed on the recovery of Yiddish women's writing: "we need to recognize that [*yidishkayt*] consisted of two primary components—culture and politics. In pre-Holocaust Europe and in the States, these were intertwined, in part, because political movements recognized the political nature of recording history, creating art. Like today's non-mainstream writing, Yiddish poetry and fiction were part of every political organ, and many literary journals were associated with political movements." She goes on to say that because most of us cannot read Yiddish, we have lost a whole generation's "literature, intellectual discourse, music, art, folk wisdom and custom. . . . This lack impacts greatly both on our sense of ourselves and on our ability to function politically. For example, we *know* Jews belong in multicultural organizations, but we have a hard time articulating why. If we can't explain it to ourselves, how can we expect non-Jews who oppose our inclusion to understand it?" In the century before the Holocaust, Yiddish-speaking Jews confronted, and wrote about, precisely these issues.

Bridges' unique commitment to Yiddish women's writing has highlighted one of the most subtle differences among Jewish feminists: there are those who relate to Jewishness primarily in a religious sense and those who understand Jewish identity primarily through history and politics. Hundreds of women were published in the Yiddish press over the past century, and this writing was, by definition, largely secular and political. Though women did write prayers in Yiddish, until fairly recently women were not allowed to be religiously educated enough to seriously write about religious topics. In addition, most of the Yiddish publications that would publish women were sponsored by secular, political movements—precisely the writing that Jewish feminists who look to history as their source are most interested in. Secular Jewish women are urgently concerned with learning about and from the social and political lives of these Jewish women writers and activists: their life choices, the nuances of political affiliation, their real-life experiences, and their insights on family, nation, ethics, and religion. Religious Jewish feminists, on the other hand, are busy making up for millennia of lost time. They are rewriting, expanding, and expounding upon the huge canon of texts that make up the religious Jewish heritage; reconceptualizing God and prayer; and recovering past Jewish women's spiritual experiences. Secular and religious interests are by no means exclusive and I imagine most Jewish feminists, if asked, would probably express interest in all of it.

The differences in orientation toward Jewish identity are real, however, and when writing for a diverse audience, assumptions cannot be made about Jewish readers' religious practice and knowledge, belief in God, or interest in prayer and Scripture. This is not an easy task. For instance, in an essay we solicited from Rabbi Rebecca Alpert, "Our Lives *Are* the Text: Exploring Jewish Women's Rituals," the author deftly explored the transformations that occur when religious practice emanates from a center of women's lives. Yet when we asked her to include her topic's relevance to secular Jews she wrote: "women's rituals have also created the opportunity for secular Jewish feminists to lay claim to Jewish ritual observance," even though "the Jewish element does pose problems for secular women [because it] is often defined in terms of God . . . either you force yourself to tune into them, or you are left out."[14] In this, even while Alpert is addressing different orientations, the "Jewish element" remains religious. On the other hand, when Irena Klepfisz—who has an unequivocal identity as a secular Jew—wrote in "Di mames, dos loshn" that commitment to Jewish secular and cultural continuity "must benefit the observant Jews as well—it [*yidishkayt*] is their legacy as much as it is the secularists," one reader responded that to make the distinction between observant and secular is to "fight a fight that doesn't exist anymore." Jewish feminists, it seems, are still searching for definitions that make distinctions but do not exclude for language that can hold meaning for all of us.

This search, we believe, must include acknowledgment of differences. For *Bridges'* second issue we solicited two reviews that attempt to both highlight and bridge these differences. In the first instance we asked Ruth Kraut, a religiously oriented *Bridges* editor, to review *We Rejoice in Our Heritage: Home Rituals for Secular and Humanistic Jews* by Judith Seid.[15] We hoped to prompt new understandings of secular Jews' attitude toward and use of religious tradition. In the other review we asked historian Lori Ginzberg to review Judith Plaskow's *Standing Again at Sinai: Judaism from a Feminist Perspective,* a book that is structured on basically religious concepts and categories, Torah, Israel (community), and God.[16] We wanted to know what the reconstruction and reinterpretation of patriarchal religious traditions mean to a secular Jewish historian. We expect this to be an ongoing dynamic in *Bridges'* pages.

While we obviously seek work partially based on the contexts from which a woman is writing, we do not propose any single definition of feminism or Judaism. Our goal for *Bridges* is to create a forum in which diverse women speak for themselves and engage in dialogue with each other. One of our central questions remains: How can non-Jewish women be allies to Jewish women? What are the insights non-Jewish women take from our experiences? What will be the sound of non-Jewish voices that take our lives as seriously as we do? For the future we plan to solicit more non-Jews to review books by and about Jewish women.

As I write these final lines about creating more connections of understanding and support between Jewish and non-Jewish women I am reminded of the complex reasons I joined New Jewish Agenda in 1982 and eight years later helped found an independent Jewish feminist journal. My political urgency; my joy and passion in being a lesbian; my joy and passion in being Jewish; Reagan's attack on unions and low-income workers; war involving Israel, Palestinians, and Arab countries; the gathering winds of the specifically homophobic religious right—these complex factors and many others led me to both a deep critique of U.S. society and personal isolation. Helping build Jewish feminist organizations that value diversity has definitely ended my isolation, but progress on the political goals has been elusive. While I think *Bridges* is contributing, however slightly, to reshaping the definition of Jewishness, we've barely begun on the objective of building alliances with non-Jews that could affect political values and priorities of society at large.

We will continue to work from our assumption that learning more about Jewish experience in the world will lead to connection to others. We know that Jews are not all middle-class or all white. We know that Jews are from Asian, Middle Eastern, African, and European cultures, that Jews have mixed heritages of all sorts. Knowing who we are as Jews in our complexity and difference is necessary for us as well as for our allies. The questions remain, as urgent as ever: Who are Jewish feminists and what are we doing in our own communities? Who are our political allies? How do we discover them? How do we become allies to others? How can others become political allies to us?

Subscriptions to *Bridges* are $15/one year/two issues. Send all subscriptions and corresponence to Bridges, PO Box 24839, Eugene OR 97402. 503–935–5720.

Notes

1. I feel I should make it clear that activists came to NJA with various motivations, some of which were religious in nature.

2. Cheryl Clarke, "Letters," *Bridges 2*, no. 2 (1991):8–9.

3. Naomi Finkelstein, "Celebrating Differences, or the Difference Between Pain and Oppression," *Bridges* 4, no. 1 (1994):60.

4. Ruth Behar, "*Mi Puente*/My Bridge to Cuba," *Bridges* 4, no. 1 (1994):64.

5. Loolwa Khazzoom, "A Bridge Between Different Worlds," *Bridges* 4, no. 2 (1994–95):49–56.

6. Aurora Levins Morales, "Tsu Got vel ikh veynen," Bridges 3, no. 1 (1992):76.

7. Joanna Kadi, "Finding Glimmers," *Bridges* 3, no. 1 (1992):166.

8. Cheryl Clarke, "Making Face Making Soul From Two Perspectives," *Bridges* 2, no. 1 (1991):131.

9. Bernice Mennis, "Making Face Making Soul From Two Perspectives," *Bridges* 2, no. 1 (1991):134.

10. Adrienne Rich, "Words Out of the Whirlwind," *Bridges* 1, no. 2 (1990):112.

11. Elly Bulkin, "Reading Class: Lessons on Privilege," *Bridges* 3, no. 1 (1992):153.

12. Ellie Barbarash, "Naming Ourselves, Telling Our Stories," *Bridges* 3, no. 1 (1992):126.

13. Irena Klepfisz, "Di mames, dos loshn/The Mothers, The Language: Feminism, *Yidishkayt* and the Politics of Memory *Bridges* 4, no. 1 (1994):12–47.

14. Rebecca Alpert, "Our Lives *Are* the Text: Exploring Jewish Women's Rituals," *Bridges* 2, no. 1 (1991):73.

15. Ruth Kraut, "New Rituals for Secular Jews, and Others, Too," *Bridges* 1, no. 2 (1990):128–130.

16. Lori Ginzberg, "Feminists at Sinai," *Bridges* 1, no. 2 (1990):126–27.

Beyond the Taboo
Talking about Class

FELICE YESKEL

Am I working-class enough to be writing this? Echoes of the question, Am I Jewish enough? What does it mean to be a Jew? What does it mean to say I'm working-class? I have so many feelings about being public about this identity: confusion, shame, pretension. Why couldn't the editors find someone who has it all worked out and feels clear, comfortable, and proud about being working-class? Why couldn't they find someone who came from the tradition of proud Jewish union organizers? Why couldn't they find someone who has more answers than questions?

These were the words I wrote six years ago, as I sat down to write a chapter on being a Jewish, working-class lesbian for *Twice Blessed: On Being Lesbian, Gay and Jewish* (Beacon, 1989). Although the final version of my piece excluded this expression of ambivalence, I wish I could say I've resolved my class identity confusion or that the issues connected to class in my life have become less emotionally loaded. But the same feelings and questions return as I contemplate writing this essay. My Jewish working-class experience is one of class dislocation, of "passing," of biculturalism, and of mixed messages.

Many of us grow up unaware of the impact our class situation has on our lives. There is so much class segregation in U.S. society that we are often adults before we come in contact with people from substantially different classes, except through the make-believe worlds of TV and movies. My innocence on this score, however, ended quite early as I negotiated the class tensions between my parents—on one side, my immigrant, working-class father; on the other, my U.S.-born, upwardly mobile, lower-middle-class mother. Years later I dedicated my dissertation to "my father who wouldn't have cared" and to "my mother who if she hadn't wanted me to be a doctor so badly, I probably never would have written this." Two voices in my head, two world-views, two value systems, an inner war. A mixed-class heritage.

This early experience of different class perspectives was, however, minor compared to the whole range of class experience. My class horizons broadened considerably when at age five I was shipped off to an "elite" public school, Hunter College Elementary, filled with middle- and upper-middle-class kids. I will always remember the shock of going home with one of my classmates to her Park Avenue apartment, which had a doorman out front. We walked through a marble lobby, took an elevator to her private floor, and entered a "foyer" that could have contained my family's entire two-bedroom apartment. "Do better than us," was the message from my mother. "Make something of your life." Sent off into a different world each day, I learned to speak differently from my family, to blend in, and to hide where I came from. So began the process of my class assimilation. However, while I may have succeeded in blending in externally, it didn't really work for me personally. Although I was able to negotiate through the terrain of school fairly smoothly, I never felt like I belonged in this new land, and I didn't really want to. But I no longer fit in at the home I had learned to be ashamed of. I found myself caught between two class cultures, the one at home and the one at school, and I have never felt truly at home anywhere since.

I get nervous as I write this; I imagine folks who are "really" working-class (who didn't get an "elite" education and the cultural conditioning and upper-middle-class expectations that were part of the indoctrination), getting angry while reading this and wondering where I come off thinking I'm working-class. Is it similar to the anger I feel at downwardly mobile, middle- and upper-middle-class folks, who always seem to pay at the low end of the sliding-fee scale because of the choices they've made? I am sometimes in awe of their sense of entitlement, which allows them to expect help because they feel like working part-time or taking the year off to travel abroad. Or who think they're poor when really they're just broke, unaware of the difference between a cash flow emergency and persistent, inescapable deprivation. Or who think that folks who are concerned with making money or saving for retirement are concerned with trivial matters. Of course, it is a bit easier to be concerned with more "lofty" goals when you are being financially subsidized by family money. If your parents have set up trust funds for their grandchildren, it may be far easier to follow your dreams than to deal with the compromises providing for a family necessitates. My life, in various movements for social change over the past twenty years, has been filled with such middle-class, upper-middle-class, and owning-class self-exiles who espouse simple living, but who usually have the privilege of going back home to their families for help whenever they tire of things being quite so simple. On the one hand, such attitudes make me angry. On the other, I appreciate that these folks can take leadership in rejecting materialism as the panacea it's cracked up to be. For those of us who have never had much (and have felt on the outside because of this reality), saying "no thanks" without ever having had the choice of having can be a real leap of faith. It is quite a different story for those who have grown up with such material privileges to reject them.

All this certainly raises the question, What do we mean by working class? There are many theories about social class from disciplines like sociology and economics, which define class differently. In some theories the amount of income you make puts you in a particular economic strata or class; the focus here is on wealth. In other theories, the type of work you do is the distinguishing feature determining what color collar (blue, pink, or white) you wear, and therefore to what class you belong; the focus here is on status. In traditional Marxist and Neo-Marxist theories your relationship to the means of production is the determining factor; the focus here is on power.

However, in our actual lives our class situation is far more difficult to identify than it appears in these theories. In my experience, social class seems to be comprised of the wealth, status, and power we have relative to others in society. Typically when we have one of these, for instance wealth, we tend to also have others, that is, status and power. When we have status, we tend to have power and wealth. When we have power, we usually have wealth and status. While these factors tend to go together, there are exceptions. Drug dealers may have money, but not status. Members of the clergy may have status and power, but not wealth.

Our felt experience of class, our subjective experience, often depends on with whom we compare ourselves. Class is a relative thing. If we create a class spectrum, from those who have the most (wealth, status, and power) to those who have the least, our felt experience will depend largely on whether we primarily look up to those who have more or down on those who have less. Because most of us grow up in a fair amount of class segregation, we know only a small portion of the whole class spectrum. My years at Hunter College Elementary School brought me in contact with many who had far more than my family did. In comparison, I felt relatively poorer. When I visited my cousins in rural South Carolina, and saw the conditions of Blacks living in the "other part of town," with no running water, no paved streets or sidewalks, and no electricity, I felt relatively rich. If my actual situation had been the same, minus the exposure to the world outside my neighborhood, my experience of class would have been quite different.

There are many signifiers of power, status, and wealth, many different class indicators. Some of the more common ones are as follows: *education*—how much and what kind (private, public, parochial, boarding, private tutors); *housing*—if, how many, what kind, what neighborhood, area of the country, countries of the world, how large, what materials were used, owned (for how many generations?); *work*—is it a necessity or hobby, how much, if any, control over working conditions; *source of income*—hourly wage or salary, profits from investments, income from property, AFDC; *leisure time activities*—is there any, travel abroad, playing in the streets, museums, hunting, skiing, bingo, country clubs, bowling, tennis, opera, ballet, symphony, travel; *stuff*—any, how much, what kind (designer jeans and sneakers or the generic brand), the latest model or used; *language*—which one(s), accent (which one), vocabulary, pronunciation; *access to money*—how much, what sources (regular paycheck, trust fund, family or friends, self-reliant); *dress*—how much, what kind (polyester or cotton/wool/linen), what style (designer, thrift store specials, this year's or last decade's); *care of the children*—older siblings or relatives, live-in help, day care, boarding school; *values*—logic and analytical thinking equated with intelligence, intuition and gut instinct equated with intelligence, politeness, niceness, and indirectness are necessary to earn respect, toughness, loudness, and flashiness bring respect, work hard and save to get ahead, spend and share what you have because it won't amount to much anyway, uncomfortable or mistrustful of openly expressed feelings, uncomfortable or mistrustful of indirectness, being in touch with emotions is best.

Based on a number of these factors I come from a background that was, at least in part, working-class. Neither of my parents was college-educated. My father did manual labor. When I was younger he was a "bagman," a dealer in used burlap and cotton flour sacks. When I asked him what I should say when people asked me about his occupation, he said, "Tell them I'm a peddler." He came home each night covered with flour and sweat. Later he worked in the shipping department of a men's clothing manufacturer. My mom also worked; she sold advertising over the telephone for the Yellow Pages. We rented a small apartment in an "okay" neighborhood in New York City; most leisure time was spent visiting family. For vacations we visited relatives, or occasionally went to a small hotel in the "Borscht Belt" with relatives for the weekend. One summer I worked at a bungalow colony that my aunt and family stayed at. During the week it was only women and children, playing canasta or mah jong; on the weekends the men came up and played poker or pinochle. My parents read the *New York Daily News* or the *New York Post* rather than the *Wall Street Journal* or the *New York Times*. The amount of money and the relative status and power my parents had put us in the working class.

On the other hand, there was my mother's denial of the differences between us and middle- and upper-middle-class people, and her typically Jewish insistence on getting me a good education, exposing me to "culture," and teaching me about the "finer" things. One thing that makes the issue of class especially confusing for working-class Jews is that Jewish culture or values often resemble or overlap with middle-class culture or values. Three areas of overlap, in my case, were education, materialism, and "culture."

First, my mother made sure I got a "good" education. Where she originally heard about Hunter College Elementary School, a free public school for "intellectually gifted" children, I don't know. I do know that the process of getting me into the elite public school required persistence and effort on her part. In order to be accepted by Hunter I had to undergo many rounds of testing, IQ tests, psychological tests, and interviews, all over the city of New York. My parents were also required to write my autobiography (not too daunting for a five-year-old) and other essays. This responsibility fell on my mother. All this took place during the same time my father was developing a brain tumor and experiencing some major behavioral changes. My father was successfully operated on in August 1958. A month later, at the age of five, I started Hunter. It is clear to me that had my mother had any less desire and dedication to my getting the "best" education (as defined by the mainstream culture at the time) I would have gone to my local elementary school, P.S. 20.

In addition to providing me with the "best" education possible, my mother made sure I was exposed to and immersed in "middle-class culture." Since assimilation (i.e., "passing") was my ticket out and toward success, it was necessary for me to become proficient in the ways of the middle class. So she made sure I had violin and dancing lessons, which I took at the Henry Street Settlement. The Henry Street Settlement, founded in 1909, was one of many settlement houses set up in the early 1900s to help the masses of immigrants assimilate to the United States. They taught English and helped the "greenhorns" learn the ways of their new land. The Henry Street Settlement, on the Lower East Side of New York, was founded by Lillian Wald, a Jewish woman, and initially served the large number of Eastern European and Russian Jewish immigrants. It is ironic that a generation or two later I was basically undergoing the same process at the same settlement house that my great-grandparents and my grandparents had gone through. In order to assimilate into the U.S. culture back then, they needed to learn English and how to dress appropriately and according to current U.S. fashion. In the 1950s my process of assimilation (and upward mobility) involved learning to play the violin and perform ballet. I remember my mother telling me that every "well-bred" young lady knew how to play an instrument and knew ballet.

Under my mother's tutelage I spent countless hours in museums (free at that time), learning art appreciation. She took me to concerts and Broadway shows as well. I learned which fork you were supposed to use to eat salad, where these various forks were to be placed on the table, and the importance of table manners. When I was quite young my mother tried to bribe me with the promise of a meal at a famous New York restaurant, "The Top of the Sixes," if I learned to eat "correctly." She took me clothes shopping at discount stores (Klein's, Mays, or Loehman's), but she made sure to read the labels and buy only things that could have been (or once were) for sale in the fancy Fifth Avenue stores. Somewhere along the line I lost whatever Jewish accent I may have had. I don't remember how this process occurred; just that I began to speak differently than many members of my extended family. I would feel pleased when I met someone who would not believe that I was from New York City because, as they said, "You don't sound like you're from New York."

Although I never much took to any of this, I did learn enough to pass in the middle class. In short, I was a working-class kid who acquired tons of class privileges. Therefore, the confusions concerning my class identity: Did I achieve enough privileges so that it makes more sense to say I grew up middle-class? And even if it was true that I grew up *solidly* working-class, does that identification make any sense now, for someone with a doctorate? My white skin along with all the training I received enabled me to "pass," even though inside I feel like an impostor. I find, now, that I resonate most to other working-class people of whatever religious, racial, or ethnic background: African American, Italian, Cuban, Irish. It seems you can take someone out of the working class, but can you take the working class out of the someone.

Clearly, the nightly reruns of the "Beverly Hillbillies" are a testament to the resilience of one's class of origin. Having acquired large amounts of money may make the Clampets rich, but it does not make them upper-class. They remain hillbillies, much to the consternation of their neighbors. Many Hollywood movies play with cross-class issues, either à la Eliza Doolittle, or the more contemporary "Educating Rita," or in the case of the upper-class person who loses class privilege and doesn't have the skills to survive on the street as in "Trading Places." What do these cultural symbols teach us about class, and what do we mean by class? Is it just money or wealth? education? status? power? choice? connections? values? all of the above?

Using whatever theory, taking into consideration all of the factors, and given all of the complications, one question looms large for me: To the extent that I have privilege with respect to class, how do I live in an ethical way? I have obsessed for years about the question, What is my fair share? I wonder if it is my particular mixed-class background, or bicultural class experience, or current situation that leads me to dwell on this particular question. Perhaps it is my Jewish cultural heritage and religious values. Does anyone else wonder what their "fair share" is, or ruminate on what lifestyle choices to make, or what level of consumption to strive for *or* to engage in? I can spend endless hours debating whether it's okay to buy an appliance that I want, or if I should buy a couch (that I currently can easily afford), when others go hungry. Is this conscientious class angst, ethical self-reflection, personal neurosis, Jewish guilt, or all of the above? When I raise these questions with my friends and acquaintances I feel like I'm breaking a taboo. It seems no one wants to think about these questions too carefully. To do so might raise feelings of anger, guilt, shame—and necessitate changes.

I have experienced the same dread when I have asked questions that have to do with class issues within a Jewish context. The progressive Jewish community is currently actively engaged in dialogue and, in many cases, action about the diversity within our community on issues of gender, sexual orientation, intermarriage, Jewish lineage, and ethnicity. There is, however, virtual silence on the class differences among us. In regard to that silence, it is important to note that the Jewish community is no different from the wider society.

I have experienced this nonrecognition and nonembracing of class concerns within the Jewish community in a variety of ways: while serving on a committee to reconsider the dues structure for my temple; in determining which organizational fundraising strategies to employ; in deciding what type of work should be financially compensated within the synagogue; when raising questions about *tzedekah* with Jewish feminist groups; and in personal conversations with friends. While I have been raising these concerns for many years, through teaching courses at Elat Chaim (a Jewish Retreat Center) or at the Reconstructionist Rabbinical College (RCC), I know of only a few others within the Jewish community who are similarly engaged.

For instance, let us look at the practice of *tzedekah*. *Tzedekah* is one of the central *mitzvot* in Jewish life. Every year during Rosh Hashanah and Yom Kippur davening Jews repeat, "*Teshuvah, Tefilah,* and *Tzedekah;*" repentance, prayer, and *tzedekah* are the three things that can improve our lot as we face our judgment. *Tzedekah* comes from the Hebrew root, *tzedek,* which means justice or righteousness. So if *tzedekah* is closer to justice or righteousness than to charity, doesn't that mean we must ask questions about what's fair and what's just? Unfortunately, these questions typically remain unasked. Dialogues about class differences, privilege, need, and the like within a framework of justice and fairness aren't the norm in the ways in which our communities have commonly interpreted and practiced *tzedekah*. Most traditional interpretations of the *mitzvah* of *tzedekah* (to give 10 percent of our annual income) have led to the creation of a significant social safety net; we try to make sure other Jews don't fall through the cracks.

We see this as our responsibility as Jews, as members of a Jewish community—to provide the basics (food, shelter, clothing, etc.). This is no small commitment in these days of cutting welfare benefits, blaming the poor for their situation and for our budget deficit. We don't, however, seem to ask why there is such an inequitable distribution of resources in the first place, why we allow the inequity to remain, or who is a "normative" Jew with respect to class.

While we struggle to rid ourselves of the assumptions that Jew equals male, heterosexual, married to another Jew, white, or Ashkenazi, we don't seem to struggle to remember that Jew doesn't necessarily mean middle- or upper-middle-class. This unchallenged assumption perpetuates the invisibility of the identity of Jews at both ends of the class spectrum—owning-class Jews as well as poor and working-class Jews. This invisibility insures silence about class issues and in turn serves to keep the current vast inequities unchallenged.

We also don't seem to discuss the relative class privilege we have as a Jewish community compared with other communities. Lawrence Bush and Jeffrey Dekro in *Jews, Money and Social Responsibility: Developing a "Torah of Money" for Contemporary Life* (1993) report Steven M. Cohen's (a leading demographer of Jewish life in the United States) finding that "One third of multi-millionaires [in the United States] are Jews, and Jews are 40–50% of elites in professions such as medicine, law, and the media." When I read this I was flooded by a variety of feelings. While I have attended my share of Bar/Bat Mitzvahs and weddings at large, suburban synagogues, when I read these statistics I still felt surprised by how many Jews were in the upper part of the class spectrum. After my initial feelings of surprise, I felt nervous; this information was just too close to the prevailing stereotypes about Jews. This information felt dangerous. I was scared about what anti-Semites could do with these statistics. My internalized anti-Semitism surfaced as I began to wonder if those stereotypes were in fact true (rich, cheap, selfish, clannish, vulgar, pushy, smart); I felt ashamed and guilty. Finally, I felt determined to help myself, my friends, and the wider Jewish community take responsibility for this enormous amount of class privilege and resources we hold relative to others. While Jews may be exceptionally philanthropic, I felt a real need to promote Jewish giving (identified Jewish giving) beyond the Jewish community as one way to take responsibility and to pursue justice. Over the past few years a number of groups and organizations have been created that share this mission, including the Jewish Fund for Justice, Mazon, the Shefa Fund, the American Jewish World Service, and, in Israel, the New Israel Fund.

The first step in getting the Jewish community to take greater responsibility is through education about the current situation. I began by initiating conversations with my close Jewish friends and simply reporting what I had read. I was amazed at the unanimity of the reactions I received. Overwhelmingly my friends tried to deny the truth of the information: comments like, "It must be wrong," "You know statistics always lie," "Who is spreading this anti-Semitic stuff?" After I told them where I had read it, the denial was more difficult for them to maintain. I also shared that of the four hundred richest Americans listed by *Forbes* magazine annually, 25 percent are consistently Jews. Given that Jews comprise only about 3 percent of the population we must face that as a group we are significantly overrepresented among the wealthy. A higher percentage of Jews have made it and have reached the "American Dream." For some significant portion of the Jewish community, the *Goldena Medina* (Golden Land) has become a reality.

This information can be viewed through a number of different frameworks. The framework of anti-Semitism is one that I alluded to earlier, and is one of the scariest ones to me. The overrepresentation of Jews among the more privileged can be attributed to an international Jewish conspiracy, crooked business practices, cheapness, and so on. I have heard many Jews take enormous pride in Jewish economic success and attribute it to the greater intelligence of Jews, to the fact that Jews are harder-working, to the truth that we do better at looking out for our own. This perspective is also worrisome to me. These Jews point to the fact that other immigrant groups didn't succeed economically as well as the Jews as proof of Jewish superiority. Explanations that account for this phenomenon that neither make the Jews better or worse, but are rooted in the particular historical conditions of Jewish life make the most sense to me: the high literacy rate among Jews, along with the Jewish religious emphasis on study, allowed Jews to excel in the professions; the frugality and nonostentatiousness of early immigrants due to their fear of lower-class violence in pogrom-ridden Europe allowed the amassing of capital necessary to entrepreneurial success; the communal self-sufficiency that was necessary for the survival of European Jewish communities during the feudal period resulted in Jews acquiring many skills that were useful to their economic success in the United States.

While it is important to acknowledge this reality of disproportionate Jewish economic success with neither boasting nor blaming, and to take responsibility for this privilege, it is equally important to remember that this reality is not the reality for all Jews. In fact, according to the Council of Jewish Federations' 1990 National Jewish Population Survey, 70 percent of American Jewish households earn under $50,000, and about 10 percent (compared to 13 percent of the general population) live at or below the poverty line. Due to mainstream stereotypes of Jews = rich, and the acceptance of this stereotype by many Jews as well, many poor and working-class Jews remain invisible at the best, or nonexistent by definition at the worst. This presumption of middle-class or "better" status as normative for Jews in the United States has led to alienation, shame, and self-blame among many poor and working-class Jews.

Just as we don't discuss the many poor and working-class Jews among us, and our relative privilege compared to others, as a community we don't discuss the relationship between improved class status and assimilation. We don't discuss what we as individuals and as a community have lost as we have "made it" in the United States. While assimilation often brings class privileges—safety, security, greater access to institutions, greater respect, and increased choice—it also costs. In the short run it often costs us our culture, that which makes us uniquely who we are—our religious practices, our food, our clothing, our language(s), our art, our styles of communication, our physical appearance, and our names. We may be allowed to become a part of the dominant culture but not as ourselves, not as Jews. For the many Jews in the United States of Ashkenazi background, our white skin has enabled us to melt in the "great melting pot." Our response to other communities, especially communities of color, has been mixed. Their calls for multiculturalism as a means of not having to give up their unique cultures to succeed economically have been met with both support and condemnation from Jews. Perhaps the refusal (or inability) of other communities to give up their culture(s) reminds us of our own painful loss.

Our self-negation is not only enforced by the dominant Gentile culture, but often by other Jews pursuing assimilation and invisibility as coping and survival strategies. These Jews may become fearful and discounting, as well, when other Jews act "too Jewish" (Jews with stereotypically Jewish accents or religious Jews whose practice makes them stand out). This process parallels the process of immigration, where Jews who were more "Americanized" often were most critical of the "greenhorns." Often, but not always, the "too Jewish" Jews are those farther down on the class spectrum, poor and working-class Jews. This is destructive of our sense of community. When we distance and dissociate from other Jews, because of our fear of being identified with them, it is hard to maintain a sense of connection and community.

For us as Jews, issues of safety and security are often paramount. Money seems to equal security. When we assimilate we trade our culture, our identity, and our sense of community for potential security. Unfortunately, underneath this surface of relative safety and security in the United States exist many anti-Jewish attitudes and stereotypes. It often takes only a small stimulus to evoke them. When there are economic and political crises, Jews are often targeted as the problem and used as a scapegoat for society's socioeconomic problems. This pattern was true in the pogroms of Europe, the ravages of the Holocaust, and the rhetoric of right-wing hate groups during the economic downturns of our time. The rise of anti-Jewish rhetoric and violence in the Midwest during the crises in the farming community was a response to farm foreclosures. "Jewish bankers" were blamed, although much of the banking industry is notoriously anti-Semitic. The ruling class, aided by these preexisting anti-Jewish beliefs, encourages other oppressed groups (i.e., people of color, poor and working-class whites) to direct their anger against the Jews rather than against the true power holders, their real oppressors. Jews have tried the strategy of siding with the interests of those in power rather than with the interests of the disenfranchised majority. It is a strategy that has failed us. Jewish history is full of such examples; the relatively secure class position of many Jews in pre-Nazi Germany was no protection from centuries of ingrained anti-Semitism. We must break the barriers of silence and talk about how the issues of money and class affect our relationships with each other as well as our relationships with communities of non-Jews.

Such silence is not the only response. There has always been a strong progressive part of the Jewish community that has dealt with issues of class. From the early union activists in this country, to the many

Jews involved in the Civil Rights struggle, to the Bolsheviks in Russia, Jews have often identified with and struggled in solidarity with the masses of "have-nots." As we, as a community, "make it," we must be careful to not stray from this part of our history and tradition. My personal experience in over twenty years of movements for social change makes me concerned. In the 1970s those of us active in progressive movements for social change (often peopled with Jews, although not very Jewishly identified) seemed to endlessly challenge (often without much understanding or compassion) each other on our lifestyle choices, such as how we made our money or what we consumed. Tired of having every decision scrutinized, the swing in the 1980s seemed to be toward a "there's no one right way, so do your own thing" type of isolated individualism. Neither of these paths has worked for me personally or for our community.

The questions that I have about class, about money, about resource use, about work and lifestyle choices are not things that I believe I can or should figure out alone. Class is a relative thing; there are not many hard and fast lines. I want a community with others from a range of class positions (backgrounds and current situations) with whom to think, question, argue, and be mutually accountable. Since how I understand and feel about my class position is based on whom I use as a reference, I know I need these multiple perspectives to have a truer context for my own choices. I hope we have learned from the 1970s and will challenge each other in respectful and loving ways. I hope we have learned from the isolation and fragmentation of the 1980s that we need each other. I hope those of us who work for social change in the 1990s and beyond will find ways to create mixed-class communities, both within the Jewish community and with the wider communities of which we are part, so that we can deal with class differences and class issues with *directness* and with *compassion*.

I believe that "there can be no peace without justice," and that this includes economic justice. Currently in the United States there is a growing gap between the rich and everyone else. Over the past fifteen years the share of wealth owned by the top one percent doubled from 19 percent to almost 40 percent. The wealthiest one percent of the population now has more wealth and assets than the bottom 92 percent of the population combined. Simultaneously a growing number of U.S. families are falling into poverty. One in five children in the United States will now grow up in poverty. The average U.S. family is on a treadmill, working harder for less money and having less free time. In fact, no other industrialized nation in the world has such a wide disparity of wealth and poverty. This creates economic insecurity for growing numbers of low- and moderate-income Americans. As a nation we are drowning in the federal debt. Our community institutions are falling apart—our schools, libraries, parks, highways, and streets suffer from lack of government investment. In short, the quality of life for most Americans has declined. This imbalance of wealth is a disaster for our nation's economy, democracy, and culture.

We all, even the rich, suffer in a society that generates rage, violence, illness, and despair, because of its vast inequalities. As Jews this situation should give us cause for great concern. First of all, we are overrepresented in the small group whose share of wealth continues to escalate while others' falls. Charity will not address this massive problem; *tzedekah*, justice, is what is needed. Second, when economic insecurity grows and despair increases, anger increases and violence escalates. Scapegoats are created to distract people from the real causes of their problems. Currently immigrants, welfare recipients, single mothers and gays and lesbians (who undermine the nuclear family), and people of color are the targets of misplaced rage. Jews have always been a convenient scapegoat. Given the current situation, we are vulnerable. I believe it is in our best interest as Jews to take leadership in addressing the real causes of our economic crises.

I, personally, have begun to turn my full attention to this fundamental problem. I, along with a number of others, have started an organization called the Share the Wealth Project. We are deeply concerned that the concentration of wealth is hurting our nation, and we are organizing to revitalize the United States through a more fair distribution of wealth. We are working to meet this goal through popular education, advocacy and political action, local action, and the development of materials and resources. We publish a quarterly newsletter, *Too Much*, and we have begun to set up local Share the Wealth chapters across the United States. As I do this work, I feel very much that I am part of a long line of Jewish activists concerned with justice, and I feel that I am living out my understanding of the *mitzvot*.

We talk a lot about environmental sustainability as a necessity for our survival on this planet. We must begin to talk about social sustainability (which must include social *and* economic justice) as a necessity for our survival as a human community. I hope that we will insist that our communities and institutions (both Jewish and other) take even greater leadership in providing a process for creating economic justice, accountability, and social sustainability.

Acknowledgments

I would like to thank Fai Coffin, who first suggested to me that I might be working-class; Chuck Collins, my comrade at Share the Wealth, for inspiration; and Felicia, my partner, for loving and believing in me.

Note

The address for the Share the Wealth Project is 37 Temple Place, Third Floor, Boston, MA 02111 (617) 423–2148.

Key Resources of General Interest On U.S. Class Issues

Bartlett, Donald L., and James B. Steele. *America:What Went Wrong?* Kansas City: Andrews and McMeel, 1992.

————. *America:Who Really Pays Taxes?* New York: Simon and Schuster, 1994.

Batra, Ravi. *The Great Depression of* 1990. New York: Dell, 1985.

Bluestone, Barry. *The Deindustrialization of America.* New York: Basic Books, 1984.

Brouwer, Steve. *Sharing the Pie:A Disturbing Picture of the U.S. Economy.* Carlisle, Pa.: Big Picture Books, 1992.

Bush, Lawrence, and Jeffrey Dekro. *Jews, Money, and Social Responsibility: Developing a "Torah of Money" for Contemporary Life.* Philadelphia: The Shefa Fund, 1993.

Coleman, Richard P., and Lee Rainwater. *Social Standing in America: New Dimension of Class.* Nashville, Tenn.: Apex, 1992.

Crittenden, Ann. *Killing the Sacred Cows: Bold Ideas for a New Economy.* New York: Penguin, 1993.

Demott, Benjamin. *The Imperial Middle:Why Americans Can't Think Straight about Class.* New York: William Morrow, 1990.

Domhoff, G. William. *Who Rules America Now? A View for the 80's.* New York: Simon and Schuster, 1983.

Ehrenreich, Barbara. *Fear of Falling:The Inner Life of the Middle Class.* New York: Harper, 1989.

Galbraith, John Kenneth. *The Culture of Contentment.* New York: Houghton Mifflin, 1992.

Geoghegan, Thomas. *Which Side Are You On? Trying to Be for Labor When It's Flat on Its Back.* New York: Farrar, Straus, and Giroux, 1991.

Greider, William. *Who Will Tell the People:The Betrayal of American Democracy.* New York: Simon and Schuster, 1992.

hooks, bell. "keeping close to home: class and education." Chapter 11 of *Talking Back: thinking feminist, thinking black.* Boston: South End Press, 1989.

Inhaber, Herbert, and Sidney Carroll. *How Rich Is Too Rich? Income and Wealth in America.* New York: Praeger, 1992.

Jones, Jacqueline. *Labor of Love, Labor of Sorrow: Black Women, Work, and the Family from Slavery to the Present.* New York: Vintage, 1985.

Kozol, Jonathan. *Savage Inequalities.* New York: Crown, 1991.

Lapham, Lewis H. *Money and Class in America: Notes and Observations on the Civil Religion.* New York: Random House, 1988.

McKenney, Mary. "Class Attitudes and Professionalism." In *Building Feminist Theory: Essays from Quest.* Edited by Charlotte Bunch. New York: Longman, 1981.

Mogil, Christopher, and Anne Slepian. *We Gave Away a Fortune: Stories of People Who Have Devoted Themselves and Their Wealth to Peace, Justice, and a Healthy Environment.* Philadelphia: New Society Publishers, 1992.

Peterson, Wallace C. *Silent Depression: The Fate of the American Dream.* New York: W. W. Norton, 1994.

Phillips, Kevin. *The Politics of Rich and Poor: Wealth and the American Electorate in the Reagan Aftermath.* New York: Harper, 1990.

Pizzigati, Sam. *The Maximum Wage: A Common-Sense Prescription for Revitalizing America—By Taxing the Very Rich.* Nashville, Tenn.: Apex, 1992.

Rose, Stephen. *Social Stratification in the United States: The American Profile Poster.* New York: New Press, 1992.

Rubin, Lillian Breslow. *Worlds of Pain: Life in the Working Class Family.* New York: Basic Books, 1976.

Ryan, William. *Equality.* New York: Vintage, 1982.

Schor, Juliet B. *The Overworked American: The Unexpected Decline of Leisure.* New York: Basic Books, 1992.

Sennett, Richard, and Jonathan Cobb. *The Hidden Injuries of Class.* New York: Vintage, 1972.

Slater, Philip. *Wealth Addiction.* New York: Dutton, 1980.

Wachtel, Paul. *The Poverty of Affluence: A Psychological Portrait of the American Way of Life.* Philadelphia: New Society Publishers, 1989.

Zinn, Howard. *A People's History of the United States.* New York: Harper Colophon, 1980.

Klal Israel[1]

Lesbians and Gays in the Jewish Community

BOB GOLDFARB

Jews have millennia of multicultural experience. Even before the destruction of the Temple, Jews were continually aware of the differences between their values and those of the strangers that lived among them. In the Diaspora, Jews have had to define themselves both as Jews and with respect to the dominant cultures in which they lived, resulting in an ongoing dialogue with other cultures and other values.

To a great extent, Jews have survived and thrived since antiquity through distinctive ways of thinking and living. Jews have believed that our destiny is not the same as others', and that our values in some ways differ from those of other peoples. But because we do not insist on converting these peoples to our own views, we have found practical ways to live among foreign ideas while preserving our own culture.

The successful encounters between Jewish culture and other civilizations have yielded profound means of moral thought and action. Maimonides lived in an Arabic culture and was strongly influenced by Aristotle—and wrote some of the defining texts of Jewish thought. Leo Baeck, the leader of Liberal German Judaism in the first half of this century, was influenced by German philosophy as he set forth *The Essence of Judaism*.

Less successful encounters between value systems can result in self-righteousness, condescension, and inflexibility. Instead of learning how to understand and live with those who hold alternative views, some people retreat to an arrogant confidence in their own rectitude and superiority, attitudes that are all too common in contemporary discourse. The resulting polarization sets Jews against others, and sometimes pits Jews against Jews.

The question is, Which of these will be the model as institutional Judaism responds to the claims of lesbian and gay Jews? At one end of the ideological spectrum, some Jews categorically reject any consideration of the issue as the product of foreign values: they believe the Torah[2] proscribes homosexuality, so nothing further need be said. At the other end, some gays and lesbians believe it is self-evident that they constitute a significant group within the Jewish community, and that their status is questioned only because of bigotry. At both extremes, this is self-righteousness par excellence.

In the middle ground between these extremes, synagogues and Jewish communal institutions sooner or later will need to respond to lesbians and gays; Jewish homosexuals will have to take into account the teachings of the tradition in defining their place within those institutions. For all of us the challenge is for the Jewish community, and its lesbian and gay members, to learn from each other. As in the encounters between worldviews in Jewish history, we can find ways of living together that preserve timeless Jewish values—the shared responsibility of Jews for one another, the importance of moral action.

Gay and lesbian Jews have approached Jewish institutions with several hopes. Like the non-European cultures seeking recognition by Western societies, we Jews want to change the perception of ourselves as the "Other," so we will be seen as real people who cannot a priori be excluded or marginalized. Beyond being recognized, we want to be enfranchised as members of the Jewish community with talents to share and needs to be met. In the end, we want to live with the respect and friendship of other Jews.

This discussion is emotional largely because it is concerned with sex. It is also concerned with change, but if change alone caused all the controversy, there would be equal passion, for instance, about the Conservative movement's rewriting of the traditional liturgy. After thousands of years, the prayers to restore the sacrificial order and rebuild the Temple have been revised or discarded; historically and ideologically that is a far more radical departure for Judaism, but few people talk about it. Yet issues affecting lesbians and gays are in the news practically every week. The reason these discussions come around to sex is that heterosexuals usually define us simply in terms of sexual activity. When well-meaning Jews say, "I don't care what you do in the privacy of your own bedroom," they miss the point: being gay or lesbian is a fundamental component of one's identity. It affects one's personality, friendships, family, and social activity in a far-reaching way. Homosexuals who want to be part of organized Jewish life are not looking for an endorsement of a way to have sex. Rather, we expect to be recognized as part of the Jewish people.

The dialogue should begin with the recognition that Jewish lesbians and gays are particular kinds of human beings, created by God with a purpose; we are not lapsed or flawed heterosexuals. Blacks and Native Americans have been regarded as imperfect versions of white people; Jews have been seen as incompletely realized Christians. Such self-centered perspectives have given way to a broader acceptance of the variations among humanity. Homosexuality is not stunted or perverted heterosexuality; gay and lesbian Jews are not deformed or depraved Jews.

It is equally important for lesbians and gays to avoid characterizing as "homophobic" Jews who favor anything less than complete, immediate parity for homosexuals, and for same-sex relationships. Even those Jews who sympathize with our goals can be constrained by their personal history or their situations, and any real dialogue requires an understanding of those constraints. Demands for complete and immediate change are unlikely to succeed because they ignore the complex needs of others. Polarization is almost always unhelpful.

A more problematic form of intransigence can take place among traditional communities that feel assaulted by unwelcome trends in the larger society. A traditional Jew may dismiss demands for the recognition of lesbians and gays as a surrogate way of protesting all the unwelcome changes in society at large. Ironically, Jewish tradition does not condone singling out homosexuals for ill treatment; the animus against homosexuality has its roots in other religious traditions that inform our secular culture. A Jew who endorses antigay actions is electing foreign values over Jewish ones, and drives a wedge between Jews besides.

Some Jews are honestly troubled by gays and lesbians in the synagogue because they believe that the Torah condemns homosexuality. But that is not the only possible response for a Jew who takes Torah seriously; we need not give the text a fundamentalist reading. For instance, God told Adam that he would eat bread in the sweat of his face—that is, humanity would have to work hard for a living—but no one takes this as a prohibition of labor-saving devices.

A strong case can be made that the Torah is actually silent on the subject of homosexuals. The usual passage cited as proof that homosexuality is unacceptable, in the Holiness Code of Leviticus, says that for "a man" to lie with a man as he would lie with a woman is an abomination. The most sensible reading is that *heterosexual* men may not lie with other men, because to do so violates the boundaries of the category of which they are a part. The Holiness Code similarly pro-scribes planting two different kinds of seed in the same furrow, or yok-ing two different kinds of animals together, or mixing two different kinds of fabric. Its overwhelming concern is preserving perceived nat-ural categories. That, and not homosexuality, is its real subject. The very idea of homosexuals as a class of people has only existed for the past 150 years. Until the past century, sex between two men was un-derstood as an unnatural act because men were "supposed" to have sex with women; there was no concept that some human beings (i.e., ho-mosexuals) naturally formed sexual and emotional relationships with members of the same sex. Reading homosexuals into Torah is there-fore anachronistic.

This interpretation distinguishes between the Torah's prohibition of perversion and the community's responsibility to a class of people not mentioned in the Torah. It does not overturn a Torah prohibition; it more narrowly defines the boundaries within which that prohibi-tion applies. This reading enables Jews to read Torah so as to serve God with greater understanding than before. It also illustrates how the in-terplay between traditional Jewish thought and secular learning can lead to an interpretation that addresses contemporary issues in the framework of timeless Jewish values.

These halakhic[3] questions are of less practical importance for Jew-ish institutions, and for individual gay or lesbian Jews, than the con-crete issues of how to live together. Virtually no synagogue would categorically exclude homosexuals from attending services, for in-stance. Their tolerance might be similar to their tolerating Sabbath violators or thieves—a grudging acceptance of gays as members of the community without any endorsement of their behavior. But that minimal acceptance provides a starting point for a wider consideration of how we can live within the Jewish community.

For individual communities, the question is usually phrased in terms of where to draw the line. Will a congregation allow a lesbian to teach Hebrew school? Will it call a gay man to the Torah? Will it allow a homosexual to run for the board? Will it interview gay and lesbian candidates for rabbi and cantor? Will it allow its clergy to perform a commitment ceremony for two men or two women? The whole notion of drawing a line is problematic for gays and lesbians, of course, because it means that our differences are regarded as relevant to these decisions; the only question is how relevant. For many Jewish homo-sexuals there is no good reason to make distinctions based on sexual orientation. That is not intended as an extreme position, put forward in the hope of obtaining moderate concessions as a compromise: it is simply the way we think our communities ought reasonably to function. Raising the issue should not be seen as inherently a provo-cative act, but rather as a concern of Jews who care about Jewish institutions.

Likewise, resistance to this view should not be taken as always aris-ing from ignorance, fear, or prejudice. Most Jewish communities see this principle as too radical to absorb all at once; many believe as a mat-ter of conscience that Jewish institutions ought to promote family life, and that according equal status to gay and lesbian relationships is destructive of Jewish values and ultimately of the Jewish people. That, too, is a vision of how our communities ought to function, and it deserves the respect even of those who are committed to a different view, if we are to find a way to live together.

Gays and lesbians who are not ready to respect such ideas ought to beware of stereotyping more traditional views as simply narrower, less tolerant precursors of their own. Consider the experience of Jews among Christians. Many Christians have believed that Judaism is a collection of outdated notions superseded by the later revelations of Christianity. This leads to impatience with and disrespect for Jews by such Christians. It is just as great a mistake for gay and lesbian activists to believe in the certitude of their own views because those views are more recently arrived at. The effect of such a view is to take away all re-spect for the other participants in the dialogue, and to replace it with a smug arrogance that is contrary both to the spirit of multiculturalism and to the Jewish values of concern for the entire Jewish people. It also promotes polarization instead of cooperation.

Jews who want to preserve the peace of the community can work together on pragmatic issues, even when they do not agree philosoph-ically. In practical terms, this means arriving at ways that gays and les-bians can take on roles in Jewish community life, even if the theoretical or halakhic issues remain unresolved. A look at the current state of af-fairs will help set the stage for specific proposals of what can be done.

By now there are numerous examples of synagogues that have successfully embraced lesbians and gays. Contrary to stereotype, these are not limited to New York and San Francisco, or to Reform congre-gations. Temple Emanu-El of Tucson, Arizona, has reached out to this community for years. Valley Beth Shalom, a Conservative congregation in suburban Encino (Los Angeles), California, has its own lesbian/gay havurah. In fact, there are enough conspicuous examples of the acceptance of homosexuals in the Jewish community that some Jews may feel there is no reason to make more of an issue of it. There may even be some impatience with activists, out of a belief that so much has been accomplished that we no longer have a basis for complaint.

The reality on the congregational level is that some rabbis still denounce homosexuality from the bimah.[4] Most rabbis will not consider performing a gay or lesbian commitment ceremony. At the Jewish Theological Seminary, students in the Rabbinical program cannot be openly gay or lesbian. In the Reform movement, several openly gay and lesbian rabbis were ordained by Hebrew Union College in 1994 and placed with congregations; some students in the rabbinical program, and a number of recently ordained rabbis, however, are reluctant to identify themselves openly as gay or lesbian for fear of damaging their career prospects. In short, lesbians and gays still face second-class status in much of Jewish life.

To be sure, the needs of gays and lesbians have been recognized to some degree by the different movements. The Reconstructionist movement is the youngest and smallest, and it has moved the farthest: its seminary's policy is to admit gays and lesbians without discrimination, and gays and lesbians have taught there. Its version of the grace after meals includes wording to bless a beloved partner, which implicitly recognizes gay relationships.

Hebrew Union College, the seminary of the Reform movement, does not officially encourage openly gay applicants, but its classes include a number of lesbians and gays. The Reform movement's leadership, with some conspicuous exceptions, has spoken out in favor of equal rights. The rabbis who lead the Conservative movement, while endorsing full civil rights for homosexuals in secular society, have been slow to accept anything more than opening their synagogues to lesbian and gay members. The Rabbinical Assembly has, however, been discussing the issue, and a sizable number of Conservative rabbis have associated themselves with a group called *B'tzalmenu*,[5] supporting a greater role for gays and lesbians within the movement. Among the Orthodox, homosexuality is most sympathetically treated as a private failure; to raise the subject explicitly is usually to bring about ostracism and condemnation.

These institutional policies are only part of the story, and they are somewhat removed from the daily lives of most Jews. Here are a number of practical steps that can be taken for individual communities to respond to their lesbian and gay members. These suggestions do not constitute a political agenda: without requiring adherence to any particular view of homosexuality, they set forth ways of dealing with unresolved issues that have come to the fore as lesbians and gays have become more visible in Jewish life.

Youth Education. Adolescence is a trying time for anyone, particularly because of the need to come to terms with sexuality. Boys and girls who suspect that they are homosexual can face particularly severe challenges: besides understanding their emotional needs and sexual urges, they have to deal with social, legal, and religious issues that heterosexuals need not address.

They may feel even more isolated and uncertain than most teenagers because they see their peers using gay epithets to taunt one another. If they follow current events, they see society's ambivalence about—if not outright rejection of—homosexuality. They can come to feel that they are failures who can never lead productive lives. As a result, gay and lesbian teens are much more likely to commit suicide than their heterosexual peers.

Teenagers who harbor fears about their sexuality need someone to talk to, and they need concrete information about what homosexuality is and what its implications can be in both Jewish and secular contexts. Whatever a congregation or a school may wish to teach about the centrality of family or about sexual norms, it must also offer counseling to girls and boys whose fears about sexuality threaten to overwhelm them. If our institutions act as if there are no gay or lesbian Jews, they may leave young people who are troubled by their sexual feelings with nowhere to go, except away from Judaism. The tragedy of teenage suicide can largely be avoided if it is addressed early.

Membership Outreach. Some leaders of Jewish institutions have lamented the existence of gay and lesbian synagogues, believing that homosexuals ought to remain within mainstream institutions. Yet in most mainstream congregations, gays and lesbians are at best invisible and at worst are explicitly given inferior status. This effectively excludes homosexual Jews from most synagogues, which is a considerable loss to Jewish continuity and to the vitality of these institutions.

For people who regard homosexuality as a conscious choice, living one's life as a gay or lesbian is understood to be a rejection of conventional values in general and Jewish values in particular. Gays and lesbians usually do not experience their sexuality as a choice, however. Being homosexual is not at all inconsistent with a strong sense of Jewish identity, and many lesbian and gay Jews feel emotionally and spiritually close to Judaism. Usually it is the heterosexual community that cuts these Jews off from their roots by denying them full participation in synagogue life.

Sometimes synagogues claim that they are merely following Torah teachings when they discourage gays and lesbians from joining or prevent them from enjoying the same status as other synagogue members. Yet some congregations seem far more tolerant of, say, adultery among their membership than of homosexuality, despite the fact that adultery poses a far greater threat to the family and is a more serious offense under Jewish law. In such circumstances, antigay policies are clearly the result of bias, not of an identification with Jewish values.

It is understood that congregations consist of human beings whose behavior deviates from the norms of the Torah. (On the eve of Yom Kippur, the *Kol Nidre*[6] prayer is preceded by a formal request by the cantor for permission to pray among sinners.) There is little halakhic basis for excluding individual Jews from a congregation a priori. In that spirit, even congregations who continue to view homosexuality as deviant should welcome lesbians and gays as they would any other Jews.

Congregations should also recognize that they often promote the idea that gays and lesbians do not exist: they assume that everyone will marry heterosexually and have children, and they structure their education programs, their social activities, their membership policies, and their governance around that assumption. This tacitly tells homosexuals that they are unwelcome, even in places that do not actively discriminate against gays.

Some lesbian and gay Jews have founded or joined their own synagogues as a result of such conditions at synagogues they otherwise would join. Others have joined gay/lesbian congregations for social reasons, or to meet a future lover. Whatever the reason, they have chosen to reaffirm their Jewish identity through this means. They can also enrich more broadly based congregations, if only they are invited to do so.

Outreach for Lay Leadership. Gay and lesbian Jews have a great deal to offer to Jewish institutional life: many of us have skills as teachers, as leaders, and generally as active members and supporters of synagogues, Federations, and Jewish Community Centers. However, whether it is acknowledged or not, many institutions place barriers before Jews who want active roles if those Jews are homosexual.

Sometimes this discrimination grows out of caution or conservatism—the fear of offending major donors, anxiety about losing members who do not want to associate with gay people, or simply a concern for public image. Such discrimination is, sadly, nothing new; a century ago, German-dominated Jewish organizations had similar fears about the newly arrived Jews from Eastern Europe. Nowadays most kinds of discrimination—based on age, sex, socioeconomic class, political affiliation, national origin—are untenable, but the bias against lesbians and gays in many places is active and even promoted.

The result of this kind of discrimination is to deprive Jewish institutional life of the contributions of many talented people. At a time when one of the most frequently articulated concerns in the community is Jewish continuity, it is especially foolish to drive people away from the Jewish community and its institutions. Organizations would do well to encourage the active participation of gays and lesbians, and to work actively to attract gay people to join them.

Membership Status. If lesbians and gays are welcomed at synagogues and Jewish communal institutions, the question of membership status will inevitably come up. Will a lesbian couple, or two gay men who live together, be allowed to join as a family?

Despite the challenges by some gay activists to traditional notions of monogamy and family, Jewish organizations, like society at large, have an interest in promoting the family unit. Families represent stability, commitment, and mutual caring and support; they implicitly stand in opposition to self-centered gratification and to living only for the present. Organizations that refuse to accept lesbian or gay couples are implicitly rejecting family values, specially when those couples have children.

The argument is sometimes made, of course, that Jewish values require endorsing only families headed by heterosexual couples, because they bear children, and therefore family status must be denied to gay or lesbian couples. If discrimination is justified by the need to promote Jewish family values, then by extension, sanctions would need to be applied against any couple that does not have children. Of course, lesbian and gay couples sometimes do have children, and this reasoning would not apply to those that do. As to the more general case, the first commandment in the Torah is the injunction to be fruitful and multiply; in order to promote the observance of this commandment, organizations could reason that they are obligated to charge higher fees to members who have not yet fulfilled it. In practice, they do not; they only charge higher fees to homosexual couples. That inconsistency is not the product of Jewish values but of prejudice. The ratification of that prejudice in membership rules should not be perpetuated.

Clergy. The most controversial instance of the discrimination against lesbians and gays in Jewish life is probably in policies affecting the choice of rabbis and cantors. Even those who support full participation by lay people in Jewish life sometimes balk at endorsing nondiscrimination in the hiring of clergy.

People have different reasons for hesitating on this issue. Some distinguish between the private rights of individuals and the public role of the cantor and rabbi, feeling that the clergy ought to be representative of the community in a way that gays and lesbians are not. Others believe the clergy ought to exert leadership, serving as examples that congregants can imitate, and that homosexuality is not a quality to be imitated. Still others hold that anyone who receives ordination ought to be particularly conscious of *mitzvot*,[7] and should be held to a "higher" standard.

These ideas may be advanced without malice, but they grow out of secular culture or personal bias rather than from traditional Judaism. In our tradition, rabbis are not high priests or patriarchs: they are teachers. The Roman Catholic Church requires that its priests be celibate, but Judaism has no comparable requirement that rabbis suppress their sexual nature. These arguments also imply that the rabbis and cantors who currently serve congregations are, in fact, role models, and that bringing gays and lesbians to these positions would result in a lowering of standards for the Jewish clergy. The reality is that our clergy, like the rest of us, are flawed in various ways. There are undoubtedly many ways in which the standards for rabbis and cantors could be strengthened. To single out sexual orientation as the one area where qualifications for the clergy are to be scrutinized suggests an unnatural interest in sexuality more than a genuine interest in maintaining professional standards for cantors and rabbis.

The barriers to gays and lesbians serving as cantors and rabbis were erected by some of the national organizations of the different movements. It is worth asking why they take up this issue in particular. The national organizations limit the choices of their member congregations only for the most compelling reasons. Singling out sexuality, and circumscribing the right of member congregations to hire homosexuals in professional positions, distorts Jewish values by focusing on an emotionally charged issue instead of considering how best to maintain excellence among the clergy.

Some congregations prefer rabbis who make social action a priority; others prefer a scholar in the pulpit. Some communities want their clergy to share their members' background; others look for someone who brings a new perspective to the community. There are also preferences with respect to age, pulpit style, and many other factors. The prevailing practice is for congregations to make these decisions for themselves. The wisest course is to allow congregations to hire whom they wish, without circumscribing their actions by restricting the candidates for these jobs according to sexual orientation.

Subgroups. Synagogues and communal organizations often encourage their members to form subgroups centered around common background or interests. Many congregations and community centers have groups for the elderly and for teenagers. The Sisterhood, or athletic teams, might similarly attract people who want to get together to participate in specific kinds of activities.

It makes sense for such organizations to foster the creation of activities for lesbians and gays as well. The purpose is not the superficial one of creating symbolic equality. As with other subgroups, the idea is to bind members more tightly to the organization by making it a place where members want to spend more of their time.

At community centers and synagogues that have groups for lesbians and gays, the members typically get together for meals, speaker programs, films, and the like. By creating a Jewish context for such activities, these groups enable us to be part of the Jewish community through social activities, instead of forcing us into the secular world.

These activities also enhance the likelihood that lesbians and gays will form stable social and personal relationships within the Jewish community. Anyone concerned with Jewish continuity should want to encourage gay and lesbian Jews to spend time with other Jews instead of building their social lives primarily or exclusively in the non-Jewish world.

Some in the Jewish community are afraid that creating such groups is tantamount to an "endorsement" of homosexuality. Forming a gay and lesbian group does not imply support for homosexuality any more than the existence of a men's club constitutes an endorsement of masculinity. It simply recognizes that lesbians and gays often have common interests and concerns, and that they have an understandable basis for doing things together.

All of these suggestions are based on the premise that Jews can and should find ways of living together even when they disagree. When Jewish organizations resist proposals of this kind, they should ask themselves whether they are treating gays and lesbians as part of the Jewish community or as outsiders seeking recognition and acceptance. All too often their words and actions imply that Jewish institutions need to protect themselves from hostile intentions on the part of gays and lesbians—as if we are not already part of the public that those institutions were created to serve. If all Jews are responsible for one another, our communal organizations must regard lesbian and gay Jews as an inseparable part of the Jewish people. When they separate themselves from this, or any, part of the Jewish people, they create strife and discord and thus undermine Jewish unity. That is far more serious than any position on sexuality.

These steps are urgent because the need to strengthen the Jewish community is urgent. At a time when the rate of intermarriage is higher than ever and when the pressures of assimilation are stronger than ever, it is foolish as well as counterproductive to turn Jewish homosexuals away from the community when working together can be so beneficial to all.

Unfortunately, some of our institutions impose serious obstacles to such comity and mutual support. As recently as April 1995 one major national Jewish organization rejected an applicant for employment solely on the ground that he is gay. Although he has spent his whole life involved in the Jewish community, and has served with distinction in positions identical to the one he applied for, he was told by his prospective employer that the organization's goals were incompatible with hiring a homosexual. What's more, as a religious organization, the employer claimed immunity from laws against discrimnation on the basis of sexual orientation.

When a major national Jewish organization invokes its immunity from the civil law in order to be able to practice this sort of discrimination, it shows how far it has strayed from the Jewish ideals of pursuing justice, acting in righteousness, and protecting the defenseless. This is the price of promoting divisiveness, of separating one group of Jews from another. When such animus accompanies an action, it is no longer a matter of disagreement on a matter of conscience; it is an act of malice. Perverting Jewish teachings leads to perverting justice, and no one gains.

Unfortunately, this is not an isolated case. As simple as it is to include lesbians and gays in mainstream Jewish life, there are individuals who resist that opportunity, and instead use their positions to further their private prejudices, even when their views conflict with the pursuit of justice. Such individuals threaten Jewish values far more than do lesbian and gay Jews.

To live by Jewish values is to learn how to apply the teachings of our tradition to our own lives. The book of Leviticus is not the last word on Jewish sexuality, any more than Biblical language assuming slavery or polygamy is the ultimate Jewish law on keeping slaves or having multiple wives: Rabbinic law rejects these practices for Jews. The Rabbis and commentators, grappling with the Torah passages on homosexual acts, often emphasize not the sex act or the human relationship, but the "wasted seed." The Rabbis condemn the vain discharge of semen as more serious than any other sin mentioned in the Torah because it is like taking a life—but of course that can be the result of birth control or masturbation, as well as a homosexual act.

Following those sources, abridging the role of homosexuals in the Jewish community is no more justified than imposing sanctions against those who masturbate or practice coitus interruptus. Jews who believe that their bias against lesbians and gays comes from the Torah may be faithful to the Jewish tradition in the same way as the followers of Shammai:[8] it's a valid opinion, but it's not a Jewish way to live.

The reality is that Jews who oppose equal status for gays and lesbians, far from being true to the Torah, are embracing prejudices long held by the dominant culture. (Jewish commentators, by contrast, mostly have not emphasized this issue.) The Talmud teaches that all Jews are responsible for all other Jews—that we form one community, *klal Israel*. It is this, not a narrow misreading of Torah verses, which is the real Jewish teaching that applies to the issue of gays and lesbians.

Secular society has no comparable imperative toward inclusion, reconciliation, and mutual responsibility. Indeed, the debate in the Western world between once-prevalent values and the alternative values argued by multiculturalists at times seems irreconcilable and even apocalyptic. In Jewish life we can furnish an example of overcoming different outlooks for the sake of community as gays and lesbians are integrated into Jewish life, searching for compromise and just solutions to deep and basic questions. It is within our reach to strengthen both our institutions and our values, as well as our respect for one another. *Ken y'hi ratzon.*[9]

Notes

1.   *Klal Israel* refers to the community of the entire Jewish people.
2.   Torah literally means "teaching" or "instruction." More specifically, Torah

refers to the first five books of the Bible. The term is also used broadly to refer to all of Jewish law.

3.   "Halakhic" means pertaining to halakha, the evolving body of Jewish law considered binding on traditional Jews.

4.   The bimah is the synagogue pulpit. Literally, the term means "stage."

5.   *B'tzalmenu* literally means "in our image."

6.   *Kol Nidre* is Aramaic for "all vows." It is the focal prayer of the Day of Atonement—the most serious service of the liturgical calendar—for Ashkenazi Jews.

7.   *Mitzvot* (plural of *mitzvah*) are halakhic commandments, 613 of which are found in the Torah.

8.   Shammai was a first-century exegete whose stern, narrow interpretations of Jewish law did not prevail. The more humane and tolerant views of his contemporary, Hillel, were ratified (with only six exceptions) as halakha by succeeding generations.

9.   *Ken y'hi ratzon* means "May [God's] will be thus."

Ashkenazi, Sephardi, Quebecois
Jewish Politics in Multicultural Canada

REBECCA POSNER

The relationship of official multiculturalism in Canada to the Jewish community in Quebec is particularly interesting given the formal multiple identity—Ashkenazi and Sephardi—of the local Jewish community. Since the late 1960s the federal government's policy of official multiculturalism has been at odds with the nationalist political movement in the province of Quebec. The situation has created tensions between the nationalist francophone majority in the province (which is seeking to solidify its cultural base) and the various minority groups currently living here. Thus, the question of sustaining Jewish identity in Quebec is delicately interwoven with the larger questions of identity in the province. Despite the negative publicity, which has so often surrounded the question of the future of the Jewish community in Quebec, members of the Jewish community still sustain a distinct Jewish identity in this transforming province.[1] Jewish attitudes toward multicultural policies are, however, complex.

Official multiculturalism was adopted by the federal government in 1971, two years after the government declared that Canada had two founding peoples, the French and the English. Both resolutions were attempts by the federal government to halt the impetus for Quebecois nationalism; however, they actually had the opposite effect. In Quebec, francophone politicians felt that official multiculturalism threatened their distinct status as one of the founding nations of Canada. They wondered, If all cultures are equal, how can there be only two official languages? It is easy for the English to assimilate the many influences and heritages of other cultures. However, in an ocean of 250 million English-speaking people, there seemed little chance for the cultural survival of 6 million Francophones. For many people in Quebec, therefore, raising multiculturalism to a constitutional question threatened the idea of a distinct Quebecois culture. In light of this

concern, Quebec adopted its own distinct approach to ethnic pluralism in 1990, calling it "interculturalism." The aim of this program was
to foster interrelationships among all the different cultures, with the
larger goal of creating a unified Quebecois culture. This is quite distinct from the federal approach, which emphasizes the preservation
and promotion of all cultures with no explicit program to integrate
these cultures into a particular Canadian culture.

Over the years, these diverging visions became recurrent themes
in the conflict between French Québéc and English Canada. In Quebec, minorities find themselves caught in the terrain of this complex
identity struggle.[2] Simply put: Are they Canadians, Quebecers, or
something else? So it is within this often perplexing political maze that
the Jewish community negotiates its identity. As Quebecois society
changes, where do the Jewish community's allegiances go? In what
way must it engage in the struggle for self-preservation and to what
end? Is it possible to be Quebecois (the French Canadian word for the
people and culture of Quebec) if one is not French Canadian?

The Jewish Experience in Quebec

To understand the Jewish position today, it is important to briefly
review Quebec's Jewish history. Although there had been a small Jewish presence in Quebec for two hundred years, the late 1800s saw the
first massive influx of Jews into the province. Between 1901 and 1913
this economically impoverished group of immigrants, fleeing hard-
ship and religious persecution in Eastern Europe, expanded the
province's Jewish community from seven thousand to sixty thousand.
Settling mostly in bustling Montreal, around St. Laurent Boulevard
("The Main"), they lived side by side with other immigrants and
French Canadians.

During the 1930s Ottawa slammed its doors shut to all but eight
thousand Jews from Nazi Europe. Canada's immigration policy is
widely viewed as having been worse than that of any other Western
country at the time. The minister of immigration at the time is said to
have characterized the policy toward Jewish refugees as "none is too
many."[3] In the French Canadian context a more overt anti-Semitism
manifested in the 1930s with the "achat chez nous" campaigns and the
large fascist, anti-Semitic party led by Adrien Arcand. In Anglo society

a more covert anti-Semitism existed in the form of restrictions on Jews entering Anglo institutions; for example, McGill University still had a quota in the late 1950s.

In 1947, and in the wake of the Holocaust, Ottawa opened its doors to thousands of European Jews. From the nightmare of Europe, these survivors stepped into a thriving, vibrant culture. Despite the anti-Semitic sentiments in some parts of French society, the two communities lived and worked together closely. There were even some cultural inroads made like the Yiddish and francophone theater, which shared the same stage at the Monument National.

Within the Jewish community, integration services were offered; Allied Jewish Community Services offered health and recreation services, as well as immigrant reception support. The Montreal Jewish community expanded to one hundred thousand, and became the center of Jewish culture in Canada. The community continued to grow throughout the 1950s and 1960s. Although the Jewish community remained alienated from both French Catholic society and the Anglo-Protestant population, anti-Semitism in Quebec—as well as in the rest of Canada—began to diminish in the aftermath of World War II.

During the 1960s significant changes took place in many areas of Quebecois society. The Quiet Revolution, as it is known, caused a social transformation throughout the late 1950s and into the 1960s. It was characterized most distinctly by a rethinking of the role of the Catholic Church in Quebecois society and as a reaction against the cultural and economic anglophone hegemony.

This Quiet Revolution ended in October 1970 with "The October Crisis," the first peacetime state of emergency declared in Canada. Its purpose was to crush the Fronte de la Liberation du Québec (FLQ), young francophone Marxist revolutionaries who used terrorist techniques to put forward their nationalist-separatist objectives. By 1970 the FLQ were responsible for the hostage taking and murder of Quebec's transport minister, Pierre Laporte, as well as a string of bombings.

The events surrounding "The October Crisis" caused a wave of fear in the Jewish community: while the FLQ focused their threats on the anglophone establishment, they clearly lumped the Jewish community in this group. Jewish institutions reported a rash of threats made against them by the FLQ, and in some cases community schools were closed temporarily. These threats only further supported Jewish fears of the nationalist movement. These fears must be viewed in light of several important factors that characterize the Jewish community in Quebec. First, Holocaust survivors make up a full third of the Jewish community in Montreal. Thus, this is a population that has firsthand experience of nationalism taken to the extreme. In addition, Adrien Arcand's Fascist Party of the 1930s, which sprang from Quebec, also defined itself strongly by its nationalism and anti-Semitism. These two factors made Jewish worries concerning the resurgent nationalist movement a complicated and understandable reaction.

The nationalist movement that emerged in the 1970s, however, was a very different brand from the one that existed in the 1930s; the objectives of the 1970s group were more politically focused on the issue of independence from Canada, and they were not blindly defined by racial determinism. By the late 1960s this new strain of nationalism found its parliamentary voice in the Partí Quebecois (PQ). Under the tutelage of its charismatic leader, Rene Levesque, the PQ won the 1976 provincial elections.

The victory of the PQ had alarming repercussions on the Jewish community of Quebec: five thousand members of the community left Quebec in 1976.[4] By 1980 that number had risen to ten thousand. For many Jews, a future in Quebec was being threatened by this new group of political leaders whose long-term goal was to separate from the rest of Canada.

Many Jewish leaders today are careful to point out that the PQ is not an anti-Semitic party. Allan Rose of the Canadian Jewish Congress reminds us that the PQ gave generously to the Jewish community and tried to ease Jewish apprehensions about the PQ. Still, there remain some misgivings in the larger Jewish community. Members of the PQ had made unofficial comments about Zionism and the PLO that alarmed the Jewish community.[5] For example, certain members publicly supported the UN resolution that equated Zionism with racism. Although Levesque decidedly distanced himself from these sentiments and publicly condemned these comments, Jewish misgivings about the party were not assuaged. A full three years after his election, in a speech Levesque gave calling on the Jewish community to join the PQ program, he was heckled for referring to "Quebecois" as "us" and to "Jews" as "you." "We are not foreigners, you know!" someone shouted.

Levesque's introduction of Bill 101, which essentially bans the use of English in public and commercial advertising, has been criticized for overriding individual rights with collective rights. For the Jewish community, Bill 101 meant that, among other daily effects, the "funds to Jewish day schools were now tied to the number of hours taught in the French language. Since Hebrew, Yiddish and English were already being taught, Jewish educators felt badly strained."[6] Advertising and business relationships were affected as well—also a cause for concern to the Jewish community. Other Jews accepted the bill as a move toward changing Quebec into a French-speaking province. As Jewish historian David Rome said, this move can be seen as more appropriately reflecting the majority culture, which is 80 percent francophone.[7]

However, the transformation was not an easy one. In North America, Jewish identity generally has been intertwined with the English language. Speaking English was the link to Jews elsewhere in Canada and the United States, and as such became an integral part of the Montreal Jewish identity. Also, until recently, the Jewish community was a mostly English-speaking community whose schools were part of the Protestant school board and not the French-speaking Catholic school board. The alliance with the Protestant Anglo-school is a result of a complicated history, but one important factor is that immigrant Jews were not admitted into French Catholic schools. The adoption of English by the Jewish community had become for Jews, like French Canadians, an expression of identity and a symbol of their freedom.

Diversification of the Jewish Community

A singular phenomenon that has transformed the Jewish community, both creating a bridge in the cultural rift and causing tension, was the immigration of French-speaking Sephardi Jews that began in the late 1950s. Fleeing postcolonial wars in Middle Eastern countries and anti-Zionist sentiment following the declaration of Israeli independence, many of these Jews settled in France, Israel, and North America. In North America many of the French-speaking emigrants came to Quebec because of its francophone community. By 1981 the Sephardi community in Montreal numbered twenty thousand, a large majority of whom were from North Africa.

The arrival of French-speaking Jews presented a tremendous challenge to the Jewish community, and it began to reexamine what it meant to be a Jew in Quebec. Initially, Sephardi integration was facilitated by Jewish Immigration Aid Services, as was that of the earlier groups of Jewish immigrants. The established community advised Sephardi Jews to learn English and to enter the Ashkenazi school system. They assumed the newcomers would also adopt English as their language.

Tensions rose in the early 1970s between these groups, leading ultimately to significant misunderstandings. The newcomers felt that the established anglophone Jewish community was reacting to them with hostility.

Although there has always been tension within minority groups when a new influx of newcomers arrives, the situation in Quebec has exacerbated these divisions. The social transformation as a result of the separatist and nationalist Quebecois movement has aroused a certain fear and instability in many minority groups in Quebec. Thelma J. Wallen notes that "many of the basic problems which affect visible ethnic minorities relations in Canada can be attributed to the deep gulf or division in the balance of power in a united organizational force between the French and English."[8]

In the mid-1960s the Sephardi community, responding to its alienation from the English-speaking Ashkenazi community, set out to create its own institutions. In 1966, for example, the Association Sepharade Francophone (ASF) was established. The ASF spearheaded significant developments in the lives of Sephardi Jews in Quebec. For example, in 1972 L'Ecole Maimonedes, a French Jewish day school, was established. The Association of Jewish Day Schools (ADS), an anglophone Jewish organization, greeted these developments coolly. Still reeling from the Ministry of Education's demand for more French-language instruction in the English Jewish day schools, the ADS felt that the creation of the French Jewish school undermined their reason for being. Consequently, L'Ecole Maimonedes was excluded from the ADS for its first seven years. In 1978 L'Ecole Maimonedes received 80 percent of its funding from the provincial Ministry of Education.

There were other sociological indications of Ashkenazi-Sephardi discord in the initial years after the mass immigration of Sephardi Jews to Quebec. Among the first wave of French-speaking Jews, for example, intermarriage was more common with non-Jewish, French Canadians than with Ashkenazi or English-speaking Jews. As Jean-Claude Lasry's study shows,[9] the new immigrants seemed to be more comfortable working and socializing with French Canadians than with Anglo Jews. This may have been due to the situation in North America that allowed Jews from more traditional countries to mix with non-Jews in an unprecedented way, and culturally they may have felt closer to French-speaking Canadians.

Further complicating the new challenge to Jewish identity in Quebec was the provincial government's perception of the newcomers. The arrival of French-speaking Jews was an impressive addition of a French-speaking population to Quebec. In the struggle for cultural and linguistic hegemony, French-speaking Jews were encouraged by the provincial government to preserve their language and distinct culture.

Despite provincial support, however, Elie Benchetrit, coordinator of the Communauté Sepharade du Quebec, himself an immigrant to Quebec, described the situation in the new society as one that presented myriad complications.[10] First-wave Sephardi immigrants in Montreal faced a constant battle against both French and Ashkenazi stereotypes of Jewish identity. Benchetrit remembers constant exposure to Quebecois ignorance about the Jewish people. As a student at one of the French universities he was asked whether he was a Catholic Jew because he spoke French and not English. "Normally," he said, "the perception of the Jewish community by the Quebecois was that it was English-speaking, Chassidic, and wealthy." The general population's ignorance of the Jewish community's diversity, both economically and culturally, was challenged by these new immigrants.

This challenge also confronted the Jewish community itself. Claude Lasry's work on North African Jews characterizes the Canadian Jewish response to the new immigrants as rejection and condescension. Lasry suggests that this response explains the "high degree of social integration that North African Jews established with the Franco-Quebecois society."[11] But if the Ashkenazi community looked down on the new immigrants, why did they oppose the Sephardi community's desire to organize separately? As Lasry explains, the intracommunity tensions are in keeping with a historical tendency among Jews in the Diaspora. Waves of immigration have traditionally caused tension for both the established group and the newly arriving immigrants. Lasry cites another historical problem reflected in this conflict: the problem of European racism toward Arabic culture. Deep feelings—perhaps unacknowledged—of cultural superiority entered into the relationship between Ashkenazi and Sephardi Jews.

As Elie Benchetrit, put it, "in Morocco we were Jews, here we became Sephardim." Sitting among the boxes of Sephardi-style holiday food to be distributed to Sephardi families for Rosh Hashanah, he explained: "If the representatives of the Anglo-Jewish community were distributing boxes of food they would have brought them to the homes of Jews from Morocco or other Mediterranean countries who would have looked at the food and said: what's this? . . . they would throw it out!"[12]

While the issue of cultural distinctiveness is not simply about food, this scenario illustrates the multicultural aspect of the Jewish community and the need on the part of Sephardi Jews to preserve their uniqueness within the community. Sephardi organizations have been constructed in large part, therefore, to instill pride and continuity in their distinct Jewish culture.

This shift in the composition of the community, from mostly unicultural to bicultural, mirrored the larger language dispute in Quebec. While the twenty thousand French-speaking Jews "understood the French fact," English-speaking Jews experienced francophone nationalism as a threat.

> The francophone Jews did not have a history of rejection and isolation from the French-Canadian majority, but they had often felt like second-class citizens in the Jewish community—in Canada, in Israel, and in other places where they lived with Ashkenazi Jews. As such they identified emotionally with the anger of the French Québécois. They spoke the same language and felt closer to French-language culture than they did to the English-language culture of the established Jewish community.[13]

The resentment was mutual. For the Ashkenazis who were facing a possible loss of political power, the French-speaking Jews proved that it was advantageous to speak French in Quebec. At the same time, English-speaking Jews remained skeptical that learning French would allow them to enter fully into francophone society. They also worried that the government was encouraging a division within the Jewish community by supporting the separate aspirations of the French Sephardi Jewish community. And, in fact, aspirations for Quebecois independence from Canada have been received quite differently by the Sephardi community. As Benchetrit says, "politically, the Sephardi community is Canadian first, but if independence happens there will not be a huge exodus of them."[14] In the case of a national vote in favor of independence, the French Jewish and English Jewish positions will reflect this split: one will stay, the other will leave.

However, some hope of a unified response comes from what appears to be a gradual transformation in the anglophone Jewish community. Lasry views this development rather cynically, suggesting that it is a result of resignation rather than change: "After having tried to anglicize the Moroccan Jews and refusing to recognize the specificity of this new group, the Jewish Anglo-community has resigned itself to the partial francization, due to the constraints of Bill 101, of its organizations and institutions."[15]

Easing Tensions between Ashkenazi and Sephardi Jews

Perhaps over the years the Ashkenazi community has recognized how francophone Jews can operate as a liaison between the Jewish community and the provincial government. This link has fostered more opportunity for participation and expression in what were once Ashkenazi-established institutions. The development of an independent relationship between francophone Jews and the provincial government, once a threat to anglophone Jews, has now come to be accepted and perhaps appreciated.

Resentment on the part of Sephardi Jews toward the Ashkenazi community has abated significantly. A combination of increased security in their new home and the complexity of a political situation that necessitates a unified Jewish response have both worked to dissolve earlier tensions. As early as 1975 the ASF changed its name to the Communaute Sepharade du Quebec (CSQ), a signal that the community organization encompasses Sephardi Jews of all languages and not just French. In support of this movement, Benchetrit described his feeling of being a Jew first and a Sephardi Jew second; as such, his current objective is to use his close contacts with French Canadians to enlighten them about the whole community and not just the Sephardi community. In addition, Ghila Benestray Sroka, editor of *The Tribune Juive*,[16] an important Montreal cultural magazine, went further and questioned the need for separate Sephardi community centers and organizations: "[Sephardim] should struggle for power within the already established Jewish organizations; they shouldn't be afraid of that."

Years of bilingualism has erased many of the old barriers between the Sephardi and Ashkenazi communities. In fact, the Jewish community today is more bilingual than almost any other ethnic group in Quebec. So how does this affect Jewish-Quebecois relations? An example may be made of how Sroka's magazine fares in this cultural terrain. Although *La Tribune Juive* offers an important bridge between the Franco-Quebecois society and the Jewish community, she has difficulties securing funds. She, like Benchetrit, spoke about how even Sephardi Jews who speak French and are integrated in French Quebec still do not feel entirely accepted by Francophones. Sroka's funding problems are aggravated by the fact that as a representative of an ethnic minority she is relegated to seeking funds from multicultural granting agencies. Although this is helpful, she finds that she is not as highly considered by mainstream arts councils. Such experiences suggest that these programs keep ethnic groups ghettoized from the main cultures.

> Only the people we call "pure laine" (100 percent French Canadian) have privileges. If tomorrow I ask for subvention (funding) to write a book, I won't get it. If any idiot who is pure laine tries to get subvention, he will get it. This I can say because I have experienced it. I am a victim of the system because, as an immigrant, I don't have the privileges or the same rights as the Quebecois or the Canadians. So I must say, unfortunately, multiculturalism is helping me but only a little. Multiculturalism is here to help us because Canada as a country, or Quebec won't do much for us.[17]

Sroka suggests that multiculturalism programs, provincial or federal, may actually serve as a crutch. They may be temporarily helpful, but in the long run these programs will need to be reevaluated to ensure that the communities and individuals they serve do not become ghettoized. Additionally, everyone I spoke with agreed that while multicultural and intercultural programs are useful and needed, the community must continue to nurture its own self-reliance and foster its own rapprochement with the larger society. David Rome puts the situation in historical context: the Jewish community has always looked after its own needs.[18] The will and commitment on the part of the Quebecois Jewish community are such that even without these multicultural programs (federal and provincial) they will continue to support their own institutions.

In consequence, today it is not at all surprising to hear about inter-cultural and interfaith encounters between the Jewish and French Canadian communities. At the Montreal Jazz Festival in 1993 there was a fantastic performance of Jewish Klezmer Music and Quebecois folk music organized by the Dialogue St. Urbain (an intercultural group). A massive crowd swayed to the sounds of the folksy fiddle and the jazzy, mystical sounds of klezmer.

Conclusion

Since this essay was first written, the PQ was voted back into power, and in 1995 (as they had forewarned) they called a referendum on the question of Quebec separating from Canada. Although the "No" side (those voting against separation) won by a thin margin, ten-sion immediately following the referendum increased, particularly as a result of the negative view offered by Premier Jacques Parizeau. In his concession speech, Parizeau blamed the separatist loss on "money and the ethnic vote." His remarks were received with thunderous applause by his pro-Separatist audience. The very next day an unrepentant Parizeau resigned as the leader of the PQ. The new premier, Lucien Bouchard, has vowed to put the question of Quebec's sovereignty to a referendum in the near future.

What does this all mean? It depends on who you ask. Some seem more determined than ever to leave and forget about a future in Que-bec, while others seem to have become more resolute in their decision to stay put.

Today the Jewish population in Quebec hovers around eighty thousand and continues its struggle to determine its future. Will this new victory result in a similar exodus from Quebec? Even though the Jewish community still thrives, political and economic insecurity could both discourage newcomers from settling in Quebec and drive existing members away. Still, as Morton Weinfeld wrote after the PQ first came to power, "many have cast their lot with Quebec and have begun to accept francization as a new reality."[19] This poses the question of whether it will be possible for the Jewish community to one day define itself as French-Canadian Jews. The answer to that question, however, does not rest solely on the shoulders of the Jewish community; it depends on the openness of the Quebecois people and the ability of the two groups (Francophones and Jews) to see each other as allies.

These issues reflect a complex struggle for identity rights that could benefit from the insight offered in Hillel's famous words: "If I am not for myself who will be? But if I am only for myself who as I? And if not now, when?"

As a people used to adapting to larger heterogeneous societies, Jews in Quebec of all linguistic and cultural origins have a wealth of experience and wisdom to bring to the current political situation. This idea is comically illustrated in the bittersweet anecdote about the minister, priest, and rabbi who have learned that a flood is about to engulf the earth: "Let us pray to God to save us," calls the minister, lifting his eyes to heaven. "Let us pray for a happier life in the hereafter," cries the priest, dropping to his knees. The rabbi just shakes his head gravely. "Gentlemen," he says. "We have got twenty-four hours to learn to breathe underwater."

Notes

1.   To help understand the Jewish position in Montreal's multicultural context, I interviewed five individuals for whom these issues are of passionate and pressing importance. I came away with a greater appreciation for the complexity of the situation in Quebec. The interviewees with whom I spoke come from a wide spectrum of society, but share an involvement and commitment to the Jewish community in Montreal. Each works specifically in the area of Jewish and French Canadian relations. Two interviewees are Sephardi and two interviewees are Ashkenazi.

Ghila Benestry Sroka, editor and founder of *Tribune Juive* (an important French-language Jewish cultural magazine), uses the magazine to educate both the Quebecois and Jewish populations about each other. She has become an important cultural figure, and organizes events that bring the two groups together.

Elie Benchetrit is a coordinator at the Communaute Sephardique du Quebec. Elie talked frankly about the role of the center and expressed his personal concerns about the difficult challenge facing the Jewish community to create a sense of continuity and value within the contemporary Jewish identity.

I also spoke to two different representatives of the Canadian Jewish Congress, Alan Rose, executive vice president, and Michael Crelinstein, regional director of the Quebec chapter. I was offered not only the official position of the congress, but also their personal viewpoints.

It was a great privilege to interview at some length historian and professor David

Rome. A lifetime of accomplishments in the area of Jewish history in Quebec and Jewish-Quebecois relations makes David Rome a particularly interesting person with whom to talk. His vibrant personality and curious mind constantly challenged me with his own questions. The historical framework in which he understands the situation here is extremely important. For example, the decision to settle in Quebec has been a question asked by Jews who came here for centuries. Rome reminded me that the gamble about whether French culture would hinder their economic and cultural needs was and still is an important consideration of the Jewish community.

2. What I also hope this essay will do is provide an alternative to Mordechai Richler's now infamous *New Yorker* article (September 23, 1991). In Richler's article Quebec's controversial language laws and anti-Semitic history became the fodder for the writer's insatiable appetite for satire. In this way Quebecois society was caricatured as backward and antidemocratic. The article lacked objectivity or rigorous reportage and read more like an Evelyn Waugh novel than anything else.

All the same, it must be said, the article stimulated vociferous and enthusiastic debate among Jews and Francophones. Whether one agrees with Richler's opinions or even with his method of "airing dirty laundry in public," he unquestionably provoked dialogue. Unfortunately, however, in the United States—where there is a dearth of information published on Quebec—the picture offered by Richler has gone relatively unchallenged. While Richler aptly expressed some of the frustration with the situation in Quebec, he fails to address a number of issues that are more complex.

3. See Irving Abella's *None Is Too Many: Canada and the Jews of Europe, 1933–48* (Toronto: Lester and Orpen Dennys, 1982), which is about Canada's abandonment of Jewish refugees from Nazi Europe.

4. Ibid., p. 110.

5. David Rome and Jacques Langlois, *Juifs at Quebecois Francais: 200 Ans d'Histoire Commune* (Quebec: Fides, 1986), p. 251.

6. Ibid., p. 108.

7. Ibid., p. 234.

8. Thelma J. Wallen, *Multiculturalism and Quebec: A Province in Crisis* (Ontario: Williams-Wallace, 1991), p. 67.

9. Jean-Claude Lasry and Claude Tapia, *Les Juifs du Maghreb: diasporas Contemporaines* (Paris, Montreal: Editions L'Harmattan et Les Presses de L'Universirte de Montreal, 1989), p. 35.

10. Interview with Elie Benchetrit, Montreal, July 1993.

11. Lasry and Tapia, *Les Juifs du Maghreb*, p. 36.

12. Interview with Elie Benchetrit.

13. Erna Paris, *Jews: An Account of Their Experience in Canada* (Toronto: Macmillan of Canada, 1980), p. 112.

14. Interview with Elie Benchetrit.

15. Lasry and Tapia, *Les Juifs du Maghreb*, p. 98.

16. Interview with Ghila Benestry Sroka, Montreal, July 1993.

17. Ibid.

18. Interview with David Rome, Montreal, July 1993.

19. Morton Weinfeld and W. Shaffir I. Cotler, *The Canadian Jewish Mosaic* (Toronto: John Wiley and Sons, 1981), p. 439.

Pioneers in Dialogue: Working Together with Other Communities

Toward a Multicultural Politics
A Jewish Feminist Perspective

MARTHA ACKELSBERG

The dominant perspective on personhood and identity in the United States is an individualistic one: we "are" who we are, independent of our specific communal associations, and we ought to be evaluated and treated according to our individual merit rather than our communal status.[1] That is not to say that we *live* by these criteria (far from it!), but, rather, that it is this individualist perspective that structures much social policy and informs mainstream debate. Contemporary debates about affirmative action only underscore this wariness about the relevance of communal identity to politics and policies.

Strikingly, this emphasis on individuality goes hand in hand with a rather totalizing understanding of community. Rather than seeing individuals and communities as engaged in dynamic relationships, we have tended to freeze our ideas of community, focusing on the norms or imperatives that define them, and then to marginalize individuals who don't conform to those norms. This is certainly true of the Jewish community, which has often tried to impose within its borders a particular notion of what it means to be a "good Jew" (one who supports the policies of the government of Israel, for example). As a variety of contemporary commentators have noted, the tendency to totalize and repress differences seems greatest in communities subjected to significant levels of oppression from without.[2]

How, then, do we move beyond an understanding of politics that denies the relevance of cultural differences to political behavior toward a politics that effectively confronts the realities of a multicultural world? And if we do transform the prevailing conception of politics to one that can take into account the ways we are fundamentally affected by differing cultural contexts, how do we do so without "freezing" identities in ways that misrepresent their complexities and make coalitions more difficult?

Much contemporary feminist discussion and debate has centered on these and related questions, and can contribute to the development of a truly multicultural politics. Specifically, important strains of feminism in the United States have been wary, if not directly rejecting, of liberal individualism. On the one hand, feminism at its most basic questioned, and continues to question, the ways supposedly neutral individualist criteria effectively excluded, or at least disadvantaged, women. On the other hand, more radical feminist critiques joined with those of the New Left and others to challenge the goals of individual success that so define the mainstream of U.S. culture. At the same time, many contemporary feminists have begun to problematize identity, exploding the notion of a simple and common "women's" identity and insisting on the multiple dimensions along which gender is constructed.

By the late 1970s increasing numbers of Jewish women, women of color, and lesbians were criticizing the invisibility of differences along lines of class, sexuality, and culture in mainstream feminist analyses, and the assumption that there was a common women's experience independent of racial/ethnic/class background. The Combahee River Collective argued, in 1977, that it might be necessary for all women— and particularly women of color—to organize around what were sometimes referred to as particular identities (of race, religion, or ethnicity, for example) as a necessary first step toward broader social change.[3] Nevertheless, this focus on "particularist" identities evoked considerable criticism from both socialist and radical feminists, who insisted that feminist organizing required recognizing supposedly more "basic" forms of oppression, such as class or gender, respectively. Thus, in one of the more striking critiques of early identity politics, a group of prominent Jewish socialist-feminist scholar/activists wrote to *Ms.* in response to an article discussing anti-Semitism in the women's movement that

> The desire to reclaim the positive dimensions of one's cultural heritage is understandable. When our common enemies are so powerful, however, it seems counterproductive to engage in a politics that emphasizes the national and social identities of distinct groups, which too often attack one another rather than allying to seek redress for grievances of common concern. In other words, we are distressed that within the Women's Movement, a politics of *identity* (Jewish, black, lesbian, disabled, fat, and so on) appears to be superseding a politics of

issues. We urge a renewed effort to work across cultural and social lines toward a more egalitarian society for us all.[4]

These sentiments were paralleled by the critiques of some other feminists, whose writings implied that a truly inclusive feminist analysis of the "oppression of women" could and would supersede any focus on particular racial/cultural differences.[5]

The era of such "grand theories" that rooted women's oppression in either class or gender, however, was soon followed by greater attention—among both activists and academics—to the demands of those, in particular, women of color, who insisted on recognizing the diversity of women's experiences. On the activist front, critics argued for addressing sterilization abuse as well as abortion rights; attending to welfare rights and homelessness as feminist issues; and for the need to engage women of all colors, classes, sexual orientations, and physical abilities in determining what a feminist *agenda* ought to include. On the academic front, we witnessed a veritable explosion of writings, particularly by women of color, which explored difference and insisted that there is no such creature as woman, independent of her historical, class, ethnic, and religious location.[6] Politically, this increasing focus on the particularity of identity often meant that many people were engaged in a search of infinite regress for that group in which they could finally feel fully welcomed and "at home."

The Politics of Provisional Identities

Recent years have seen a questioning of these forms of identity politics on a number of fronts: (1) the increasing force and popularity (at least within the academic community) of antiessentialist, deconstructionist critiques of the notion of a stable and unitary identity; (2) an increasing despair and frustration on the Left in the face of an apparent global political retrenchment and the fall of communism in the Soviet Union and Eastern Europe; and (3) the development of multicultural programs and curricula that often seem to privilege certain identities and to make others invisible and, at the same time, make it seem that any search for common ground is doomed to failure. In the remainder of this essay, I look more specifically at issues of identity and the possibilities of collective action in a context that takes seriously not only the problematic and unstable character of identity, but also the need for attention to *politics*. How, that is, can we acknowledge differences among ourselves—and the fluid nature of our identities—while still making space not only for connections among people but for productive alliances as well?

There are, it seems to me, at least two components of an alternative way of thinking about politics and collective action in a world of provisional identities. One has to do with making room for diversity; the other, with the grounds on which we act together.

As numerous contemporary studies have argued, radical-feminist and socialist-feminist women's movements, the lesbian-feminist movement, and many more broad-based leftist movements in the United States foundered on the assumption that there was one true analysis of oppression, with its source in one basic factor (be it gender, sexuality, or class), and that effective resistance to oppression required that everyone accept that analysis as true and be willing to subordinate his or her other personal issues to that more comprehensive analysis and the politics that arose from it.[7] While such global perspectives may have offered a sense of power and possibility at the initial stages of consciousness raising—suggesting that women could unite and overcome their oppression, for example—they soon became oppressive in their own right. As Shane Phelan has aptly noted with respect to the early lesbian-feminist movement, "Most lesbian feminists did not learn the lesson that global theories are dangerous; they learned that other global theories are defective."[8]

Whether they be women, Jewishly identified Jews, or people of color within the New Left; lesbians, Jews, working-class women, or women of color within the "women's movement"; women of color, Jews, or working-class women within the lesbian-feminist movement; or women, gays and lesbians, or working-class people within the Jewish community, those whose own situations were not adequately addressed within prevailing understandings of oppression, and who felt themselves committed to others in ways that did not fit with the prevailing analysis, were once more relegated to a situation of marginality. And, as we all know, they increasingly spoke from that position, turning the new ideologies of resistance back upon themselves and demanding that they not be marginalized again in the name of unified struggles against the oppressor.[9] Significantly, that political/cultural resistance was taking place among activists and theorists[10] at more or less the same time that postmodern, deconstructionist perspectives were making their way into the academy, carrying with them roughly similar messages about the dangers of totalizing theories or unitary notions of identity.

But, at least until recently, the *political* implications of the two approaches (what we might term the "particularist" and the "deconstructionist") have been rather different. While Jews, women of color, and other so-called marginalized groups within the feminist and lesbian-feminist movements—and feminists within the Jewish community—criticized dominant "unitarian" perspectives, for example, they did not rest with critique, and insisted that a movement that would truly speak for all women (or all lesbians, or all Jews) would have to account in a meaningful way—both theoretically and practically—for the diversity among them. While these critics spoke theoretically, they did not speak abstractly; their analyses were rooted in their own and others' day-to-day experiences in organizing. Somehow, they insisted, there had to be a way to resolve what seemed like an impasse—and to resolve it *through politics.*

On the other hand, at least until fairly recently, the political implications of the antiessentialist, deconstructionist turn in the academy were much less clear. While many feminists adopted postmodern perspectives and analyses, others argued that the political implications of deconstructing women as a group were quite devastating. Christine Di Stefano summarized one perspective by stating that "the postmodernist project, if seriously adopted by feminists, would make any semblance of a feminist politics impossible."[11] And Nancy Hartsock, focusing her critique less on the deconstruction of the category of "woman," than on Foucault's (and other postmodernists') critique of power, argued that, in locating power everywhere (and, therefore, nowhere), postmodernism makes any attempt at transformation difficult, if not impossible, to discuss (let alone to engage in!): "postmodernism represents a dangerous approach for any marginalized group to adopt."[12] I have come to believe, however—as many recent critics have argued[13]—that these two positions (particularist and deconstructionist) are not necessarily as far apart as they might originally have seemed, but that neither, by itself, has yet provided much help to us in figuring out how to act politically in the face of this confusion.

What followed from those initial critiques of feminist "globalizing" by those who were marginalized by it? Most simply (in direct

analogy to the claim women and Jews had made vis-à-vis Western culture more generally) they insisted on being treated equally while at the
same time having their distinctiveness recognized and celebrated. As
Paula Hyman put it, "women and Jews are both hated because each
demands the right to be both equal and distinctive . . . we make the
'superior' group angry because we want to maintain our uniqueness
without being penalized for it."[14] In short, they insisted that feminist
movement(s) must account, and allow space, for the diversity of their
members.

But what would/did this mean? How could it be accomplished?
In part, it meant making room for previously submerged voices: making a place and a space for the marginalized to speak of and from their
experience without immediately trying to assimilate it into a larger
framework. In the context of the National Women's Studies Association, where many of these struggles were played out, one result was a
series of plenary sessions (in 1983, 1984, and 1987) in which women
from a variety of different "locations" (including Jews, Christians,
Muslims; poor, working-class, and middle-class; lesbians, heterosexuals, and bisexuals) spoke of their experiences and/or oppression. It
meant sitting with the contradictions and tensions evidenced by those
presentations, and recognizing that, even though we had no theoretical framework within which to fit it all, the speaking and hearing was
an important part of the work. Audre Lorde was, perhaps, the woman
who most clearly and insistently articulated the need to attend to our
diversity, even though she, too, often stopped short of developing a
concrete plan of action around it. As she put it in one oft-quoted essay,

> As women, we have been taught either to ignore our differences, or to
> view them as causes for separation and suspicion rather than as forces
> for change. Without community there is no liberation, only the most
> vulnerable and temporary armistice between an individual and her
> oppression. But community must not mean a shedding of our differ-
> ences, nor the pathetic pretense that these differences do not exist.[15]

More recently, María Lugones has used the term *mestizaje* to connote
the multifaceted, rather than fragmented, character of identity, and the
metaphor of "curdling" to address the complexity of identity and its
formation in a context of resistance to cultural dominance.[16] Her
point, I believe, is similar to that made by Shane Phelan, who has argued that a new feminist politics must be "inclusive" without being

"assimilationist"; that it must try neither to eliminate nor to incorporate otherness, but "'strive to create more institutional space to allow otherness to be.'"[17]

Rethinking Politics

Most of the models of politics on which we acted until now have assumed some common understandings, usually derived from a global theory, either of action or of oppression. But Jewish experience over the centuries, the experience of feminist movements over the past twenty years, and the conclusions of postmodern/poststructuralist analyses lead to the realization that such "common understandings" are neither common nor innocent: they mask and express power. For example, the dominant cultural values in the United States—identified, usually, as "nonsectarian"—are, in reality, Christian, as any Jew is made all too aware of at Christmas. Neither liberal models of pluralist tolerance, in which each interest group gets its moment in the sun, nor Marxist or radical feminist models that root all oppressions in one basic tension or contradiction, provide adequate grounding for political action in a situation where dominant values masquerade as everyone's, and where opposing identities, and the values and practices associated with them, are necessarily multiple, fragmented, and at best provisional. How, then, do we move? Where do we turn for inspiration? Must we give up on politics altogether, because it seems necessarily to entail globalizing and essentialism?

The most fruitful feminist postmodernist theorizing acknowledges this tension while insisting on the possibility—even the necessity—of politics. Donna Haraway poses the question in this way: "What kind of politics could embrace partial, contradictory, permanently unclosed constructions of personal and collective selves and still be faithful [and] effective?"[18] Judith Butler insists that "the deconstruction of identity is not the deconstruction of politics; rather, it establishes as political the very terms through which identity is articulated."[19] Lisa Duggan asks whether we can "avoid the dead end of various nationalisms and separatisms, without producing a bankrupt universalism."[20]

The fact that we cannot necessarily agree on what is "most basically" at stake in the multiple ways power is exercised does not mean that we cannot—and ought not—resist its subjugating effects when and where we can. In part, as Shane Phelan has argued, following Iris Young, "doing justice to people requires attention to the specific voice(s) or language(s) in which they speak and to what they are saying." Drawing on the early work of the Combahee River Collective, Phelan suggests that our situation of fragmented and provisional identities requires that we engage in local actions, developing political agendas that stem from our own experiences and identities, not from those given by others.[21] In short, even though we recognize the partial and provisional nature of our identities, we need not abandon them completely as bases for action: "the realities of institutions and U.S. politics require that we base common action on the provisional stability of categories of identity, even as we challenge them."[22]

But even if we have resolved (however provisionally) the question of the relationship between identities and action, we are still left with the problematic character of *common* action. How, and on what bases, might we engage collectively with others, given, on the one hand, that nondominant groups, by definition, will usually not be able to effect change on their own and, on the other, the fact that their very "groupness" is, itself, problematic, provisional, and often built on its own exclusions? What does it mean, for example, to talk about the possibilities of Black-Jewish alliances, when the existence of a cohesive group called Jews is as problematic as the existence of a cohesive group called Blacks? Who can claim to speak for each? What would we need to achieve, how many people would we need to include, in order to claim that we had constructed such an alliance?

One context in which feminists have started thinking about such questions has been Bernice Johnson Reagon's "Coalition Politics: Turning the Century."[23] In it, Reagon uses the metaphor of "home" to discuss what is entailed in the coalition building she sees as essential to social/political change. "Home" (which we sometimes attempt to construct as a "barred room," so that we can keep out those who challenge us and make us feel uncomfortable) is the "nurturing space where you sift out what people are saying about you and decide who you really are . . . [where] you act out community."[24] But, of course, as Reagon makes clear, the kind of community acted out in that barred room is misleading: it is based on trying to include "only those X's" who are interested in working on subject "X" in the ways in which "we" are interested in working on it. It is necessarily precarious and exclusionary.

Let me illustrate this point from my own experience. Some years ago I helped establish what is now an ongoing Jewish feminist spirituality collective (B'not Esh), whose goal was to develop a "Judaism that takes women's experience seriously."[25] The initial meeting called together women who were knowledgeable both as Jews and as feminists, and experienced the tensions (and conjunctions) of being both Jews and feminists as central to their/our identity. One would think that members of such a group of people would be very similar; and, of course, in the context of the U.S. cultural and political mainstream, we were. We all came to the meeting expecting to find a "home" with others "just like us."Yet, within hours, each of us became acutely aware of our differences; each felt that she, somehow, did not belong— that she was too traditional or too radical, too "straight" or not "straight" enough, too angry or too satisfied. Each experienced the pain of disappointment that she had not, in fact, found that idealized home. While the group has continued to meet, we have all been frequently made aware of the fragility and precariousness of the community we create. It is, for certain, based on exclusions (most basically, of course, of those who are not Jewish, who are not feminists, who do not share our interests in spiritual striving, and, most dramatically, who would increase our numbers beyond the twenty-four that our meeting space holds); but even those exclusions cannot guarantee the feeling of home of which Reagon speaks, and for which we all yearned when we first began.

Further, Reagon argues, any group trying to create such a home will feel compelled (by the logic of its own goals) to let in at least some others—a process that will eventually lead to the disruption of that home as we know it. It no longer feels comfortable; it becomes, instead, the site of coalition—which is very much *un*like home:

> Coalition work is not work done in your home. Coalition work has to be done in the streets. And it is some of the most dangerous work you can do. And you shouldn't look for comfort. . . . You don't get fed a lot in a coalition. In a coalition you have to give, and it is different from your home. You can't stay there all the time. You go to the coalition for a few hours, and then you go back and take your bottle wherever it is, and then you go back and coalesce some more.[26]

But while Reagon's analysis of what is at stake in "coalescing" is compelling, it tends to a binarism that even she seems, at moments, ready to recognize and move beyond. True, some places may seem (or even *be,* occasionally) more comfortable, more safe, than others; but, as we have learned to our great discomfort, and as I noted above, even home is precarious: *each and every home is based on exclusions.* In the Jewish context, our temporary comfort in the Jewish community often depends on a particular definition of what it means to be a Jew, which not only excludes those who are not Jewish, but also enforces a homogeneity and rigidity within the community that is often destructive of some of those who *are* Jews—women, or gays and lesbians, for example, to name just two groups that have felt marginalized.[27] So the model of politics for which we search can no longer depend on a home–coalition dichotomy, either; even *it* is too restrictive and confining.

What, then, does it mean to engage in a multicultural (necessarily coalitional) politics that recognizes not only the temporary and constructed nature of the coalitions, but also of the very cultures themselves? How do we find the energy and strength to engage in the dangerous work of coalition politics when there is no simple home to sustain and nurture us?

While a great deal of attention has been devoted to trying to address this question on a theoretical basis, my own sense is that we can find important clues to an answer by looking at the real political activities in which people have engaged. Because, despite the day-to-day difficulties of negotiating complex identities or attempting to find grounds for coalitions, people have resisted, and continue to resist, what they experience as unfair exercises of power and privilege. Whether we talk of national-level activities such as the Civil Rights or antiwar movements, movements for (or against) abortion rights, coalitions against the nomination of Robert Bork or Clarence Thomas to the Supreme Court, or organizations calling for an end to the ban on gays in the military; local-level activities ranging from resisting forced sterilization to opposing toxic waste dumps, creating community-based support services for people with AIDS, struggling for more adequate welfare benefits, protecting local services, reforming schools, or demanding housing; or feminists within the Jewish community arguing for admission of women to rabbinical schools, for a solution to the problem of *agunot,*[28] or for new definitions of "families" that accurately reflect the diversity of contemporary Jews, people have joined together with others both like and unlike themselves either to pressure those with power and authority to take action or take direct action on their own behalf. Can we learn from such activities anything about the issues we have been struggling with so intensely in the academy?

First, many of these struggles manifest a kind of "localist" politics that would seem to respond to the claim in the Combahee River Collective Statement that "the most profound and potentially the most radical politics come directly out of our own identity, as opposed to working to end somebody else's oppression."[29] But the most successful of these struggles engage people in working *from* one's own identity (with all the caveats about its provisional character) while still maintaining some connection with others committed to similar (if not identical) values. Thus, the power of the Civil Rights Movement of the 1950s and 1960s came both from its mobilization of thousands of Black people to demand their rights *and* from its insistence that its goals were those to which every good American supposedly was committed, that is, "liberty and justice for all." Underlying the movement was an insistence that politics need not be a "zero-sum" game: that a gain for some, rather than being seen as a necessary loss for others, could be understood as a gain for all in making the larger context more inclusive and democratic. Similarly, in a much more limited context, Jewish feminists have argued that opening up Jewish communal and religious practice to full and equal participation by women will transform the community (and religious practice) in ways that should be beneficial to all. Working *from* one's particular identity in this sense challenges the dominant individualist strain of politics in the United States and insists that there are ways to conceptualize (and to engage in) social change that expand the universe of participation, rather than simply displace some for the benefit of others.

That perspective, it seems to me, is the basis of a multicultural politics. In many respects, it is an anarchist-inspired politics—anarchist in the sense of refusing a unidimensional understanding of domination. Where communalist anarchists in the tradition of Bakunin, Kropotkin, Malatesta, Landauer, and Buber, for example, differed from socialists, in fact, was in their insistence on the *multiplicity* of nodes and modes of domination: capital, the state, religious institutions, and gender were among the types of relationships that needed to be attended to and transformed. All were perceived as interconnected, with none taking clear priority over the others. Although the practice of anarchist "politics" has not always conformed to this theoretical

model, this anarchist sensibility on domination and resistance may offer a way of describing what we are looking for in an "alliance-friendly
activism."[30]

Just as many Jewish feminists have refused to choose between
commitments as Jews and as women, the women of the Combahee
River Collective insisted that "we . . . find it difficult to separate race
from class from sex oppression because in our lives they are most often
experienced simultaneously. We know that there is such a thing as
racial-sexual oppression which is neither solely racial nor solely sexual."[31] And a decade of writings by other women of color, working-
class women, and lesbians (and all the combinations and permutations
thereof) have made clear that none of these identity categories—
while they may constitute both the grounds for oppression and for
solidarity—either exists or is experienced in isolation from the others.
Nor can resistance be expressed along one dimension without effectively implicating others.

In short, our theories and models of politics are only just beginning to catch up with the best of our practice. While we may have become increasingly attentive (in scholarly debate) to the complications
of identity, we have not looked as carefully as we might at those places
where people from a variety of identity categories have actually engaged in real-life political struggle and resistance. This is certainly true
in a feminist context, where the activities of diverse groups of women
at the grassroots level to address housing cost and quality, food costs,
battery, welfare reform, school desegregation, toxic wastes, or a variety
of other issues remain to be effectively tapped as resources for
theory.[32] We ought to be looking much more closely at the experience of such organizations as CARASA (Committee for Abortion
Rights and Against Sterilization Abuse), a multiracial, multiethnic
organization of women in New York, which developed in response to
the criticisms of women of color that the abortion rights movement
was racist in its narrow focus; or examining the struggles, successes,
and failures of organizations such as New Jewish Agenda or Jews for
Racial and Economic Justice, two organizations attempting to build
coalitions both with non-Jews and with others in the Jewish community by being "a Jewish voice" in the progressive community and a
"progressive voice" in the Jewish community.

"Multiculturalism" is still hotly contested, both on campuses and
in the wider culture. It has been derided as valueless relativism, and

praised as offering an opportunity to build up weakened identities and to allow neglected cultures to achieve recognition within the larger U.S. context. But neither characterization is completely accurate. On the one hand, there is no neutral, national culture that is free of relations of power and domination. On the other hand, no identity is permanent or fixed. The primary goal of a multicultural politics, then, is to allow people the flexibility to develop and experience the richness of their identities, which will, almost of necessity, change over the course of their lifetimes, as they move in and out of relationships with others both like and unlike themselves. Our politics must recognize that people can (and do) attempt to act and effect change, even while experiencing the contingent and contested nature of their identities. And only a truly multicultural context can be open both to the power of those identities and to their contingency.

Specifically on the issue of identities and alliances: since identities—particularly group identities—are not something we develop independently of politics and then bring fully formed into the political arena, but, rather, are constructed precisely in and through politics, it is not only reasonable but necessary to look to politics as the ground on which our differences might finally be constructively addressed. If we can begin to understand coalition building as a process through which we not only act together with others, but develop and change our own identities at the same time, we may open up new possibilities both for identity and for politics.

Notes

1. This chapter is a revised version of an article that appeared in *Frontiers: A Journal of Women's Studies* 16, no. 1 (1996): 87–100. I am grateful to Marla Brettschneider, Cynthia Daniels, Shane Phelan, Judith Plaskow, Marilyn Schuster, Linda Zerilli, and students in my feminist theory and urban politics seminars at Smith College for conversations in which many of these ideas were developed and refined.

2. See, for example, Diana Fuss, *Essentially Speaking* (New York: Routledge, 1989), esp. chaps. 5–6; Steven Epstein, "Gay Politics, Ethnic Identity: The Limits of Social Constructionism," *Socialist Review* 93–94 (May–August 1987): 48; and Shane Phelan, "(Be)Coming Out: Lesbian Identity and Politics," *Signs* 18, no. 4 (Summer 1993): 773.

3. "The Combahee River Collective Statement," reprinted in *Capitalist Patriarchy and the Case for Socialist Feminism,* ed. Zillah Eisenstein (New York: Monthly Review, 1979), pp. 362–72, esp. p. 365.

4. Letter to the Editor from Deborah Rosenfelt, Judith Stacey, et al., *Ms.* February 1983, p. 13.

5. I have in mind, here, for example, Mary Daly, *Gyn/Ecology: The Metaethics of*

Radical Feminism (Boston: Beacon, 1978); Andrea Dworkin, *Our Blood: Prophecies and Discourses on Sexual Politics* (New York: Harper and Row, 1976); Catharine MacKinnon, *Feminism Unmodified* (Cambridge: Harvard University Press, 1987); Susan Griffin, *Woman and Nature:The Roaring Inside Her* (New York: Harper and Row, 1978).

6.   The titles here are too numerous to cite. Among the early influential ones are Diane K. Lewis, "A Response to Inequality: Black Women, Racism, and Sexism," *Signs* 3, no. 2 (Winter 1977): 339–61; Margaret A. Simons, "Racism and Feminism: A Schism in the Sisterhood," *Feminist Studies* 5, no. 2 (Summer 1979): 389–410; Bonnie Thornton Dill, "Race, Class and Gender: Prospects for an All-Inclusive Sisterhood," *Feminist Studies* 9, no. 1 (Spring 1983): 131–50; María C. Lugones and Elizabeth V. Spelman, "Have We Got a Theory for You! Feminist Theory, Cultural Imperialism, and the Demand for 'The Woman's Voice,'" *Women's Studies International Forum* 6, no. 6 (1983): 573–81; Audre Lorde, *Sister Outsider* (Trumansburg: Crossing Press, 1984); Gloria T. Hull, Patricia Bell Scott, and Barbara Smith, eds., *All the Women Are White, All the Blacks Are Men, But Some of Us Are Brave* (Old Westbury: Feminist Press, 1982); *Conditions: Five. The Black Women's Issue* 2, no. 2 (Autumn 1979); Beverly Smith with Judith Stein and Priscilla Golding, "The Possibility of Life Between Us: A Dialogue Between Black and Jewish Women," *Conditions: Seven* 3, no. 1 (Spring 1981): 25–46; Marilyn Frye, *The Politics of Reality: Essays in Feminist Theory* (Trumansburg, N.Y.: Crossing Press, 1983).

7.   On these movements, see Sara Evans, *Personal Politics* (New York: Vintage, 1980); Alice Echols, *Daring to Be Bad: Radical Feminism in America, 1967–1975* (Minneapolis: University of Minnesota Press, 1989); Shane Phelan, *Identity Politics* (Philadelphia: Temple University Press, 1990); Fuss, *Essentially Speaking*; Harry Boyte and Sara Evans, *Free Spaces* (New York: Harper and Row, 1986).

8.   *Identity Politics,* p. 56.

9.   Among the key texts here were Cherrie Moraga and Gloria Anzaldúa, eds., *This Bridge Called My Back:Writings by Radical Women of Color* (Watertown: Persephone Press, 1981); Hull, Scott, and Smith, eds., *All the Women Are White, All the Blacks Are Men, But Some of Us Are Brave*; bell hooks, *Feminist Theory: From Margin to Center* (Boston: South End Press, 1984); and Elly Bulkin, Minnie Bruce Pratt, and Barbara Smith, *Yours in Struggle:Three Feminist Perspectives on Anti-Semitism and Racism* (Brooklyn: Long Haul Press, 1984). In addition to these written texts, many meetings of the National Women's Studies Association (especially between 1983 and 1989) became the field on which such battles were waged—and where important initial steps were taken toward moving beyond the stalemate.

10.   I realize that these two are not necessarily separate; but, especially since the early years of the women's movement, neither have they always been the same.

11.   "Dilemmas of Difference: Feminism, Modernity, and Postmodernism," in *Feminism/Postmodernism,* ed. Linda Nicholson (New York: Routledge, 1990), p. 76.

12.   Hartsock, "Foucault on Power: A Theory for Women?" in Nicholson, ed., *Feminism/Postmodernism,* p. 160.

13.   Notably, Fuss, *Essentially Speaking*; Phelan, *Identity Politics*; Donna Haraway, "A Manifesto for Cyborgs," in Nicholson, ed., *Feminism/Postmodernism*; Gayatri Spivack, *The Post-Colonial Critic* (New York: Routledge, 1990).

14.   Quoted in Letty Cottin Pogrebin, "Anti-Semitism in the Women's Movement," *Ms.,* June 1982, p. 46.

15.   "The Master's Tools Will Never Dismantle the Master's House," in *Sister Outsider,* p. 112. See also "Age, Race, Class, and Sex: Women Confronting Difference," and

"Eye to Eye: Black Women, Hatred, and Anger," both in ibid. Virtually all of Lorde's work, until her recent death, focused on that theme.

16.   "Purity, Impurity, and Separation," *Signs* 19, no. 2 (Winter 1994): 458–79.

17.   Phelan, *Identity Politics,* p. 167, citing W. Connolly, "Taylor, Foucault, and Otherness," *Political Theory* 13, no. 3 (August 1985): 375.

18.   "A Manifesto for Cyborgs," in Nicholson, ed., *Feminism/Postmodernism,* p. 199.

19.   *Gender Trouble* (New York: Routledge, 1990), p. 148.

20.   "Making It Perfectly Queer," *Socialist Review* 22, no. 1 (January–March 1992): 26.

21.   "(Be)Coming Out," pp. 778, 783–84. See also Iris Young, *Justice and the Politics of Difference* (Princeton: Princeton University Press, 1990), esp. chaps. 4, 6.

22.   "(Be)Coming Out," p. 779. On this point, note also Arlene Stein's assertion that "identities are always simultaneously enabling and constraining" ("Sisters and Queers: The Decentering of Lesbian Feminism," *Socialist Review* 22, no. 1 [January–March 1992]: 52), and Butler's claim that "Construction is not opposed to agency; it is the necessary scene of agency" (*Gender Trouble,* p. 147).

23.   Printed in *Home Girls: A Black Feminist Anthology,* ed. Barbara Smith (New York: Kitchen Table: Women of Color Press, 1983), pp. 356–68.

24.   Ibid., p. 358.

25.   For more information on the founding and practice of B'not Esh, see my "Spirituality, Community, and Politics: B'not Esh and the Feminist Reconstruction of Judaism," *Journal of Feminist Studies in Religion* 2, no. 2 (Fall 1986): 109–20; also Merle Feld, "Brigadoon: A Place for Dreams to Grow," *The Reconstructionist* 60, no. 1 (Spring 1995): 72–80.

26.   "Coalition Politics," p. 359.

27.   For discussions of such marginalization, see, for example, Elizabeth Koltun, ed., *The Jewish Woman: New Perspectives* (New York: Schocken, 1976); Judith Plaskow, *Standing Again at Sinai: Judaism from a Feminist Perspective* (San Francisco: Harper and Row, 1990); and Christie Balka and Andy Rose, eds., *Twice Blessed: On Being Lesbian, Gay and Jewish* (Boston: Beacon, 1989).

28.   An *agunah* is, literally, a "chained" woman. According to Jewish law, a man may divorce his wife (and does so by giving her a *get,* or bill of divorce), but a woman has no power to divorce her husband. The term *agunah* refers to a woman who has not been given a *get* by her husband and who, therefore, is not free to remarry. Considerable numbers of Jewish women are being held in a kind of "limbo" state by their (former) husbands, who use their power to extort money or otherwise make the women's lives miserable. See Judith Plaskow, "The Year of the Agunah," *Tikkun* 8, no. 5 (September–October 1993): 52–53, 86–87.

29.   "Combahee River Collective Statement," in Eisenstein, ed., *Capitalist Patriarchy,* p. 365.

30.   On gender conflicts among Spanish anarchists, see my *Free Women of Spain: Anarchism and the Struggle for the Emancipation of Women* (Bloomington: Indiana University Press, 1991), esp. chaps. 1–2.

31.   "Combahee River Collective Statement," in Eisenstein, ed., *Capitalist Patriarchy,* p. 365.

32.   There are some beginnings in a number of recent anthologies: Ann Bookman and Sandra Morgen, eds., *Women and the Politics of Empowerment* (Philadelphia:

Temple University Press, 1988); Louise Tilly and Patricia Gurin, eds., *Women, Politics and Change* (New York: Russell Sage Foundation, 1990); Guida West and Rhoda Lois Blumberg, eds., *Women and Social Protest* (New York: Oxford University Press, 1990); Linda Gordon, ed., *Women, the State, and Welfare* (Madison: University of Wisconsin Press, 1990). See also Celene Krauss, "Waste and Toxic Waste Protests: Race, Class and Gender as Resources of Resistance," paper presented at "A Celebration of Our Work," Douglass College, May 1993. *Bridges to Power: Women's Multicultural Alliances,* ed. Lisa Albrecht and Rose M. Brewer, published in cooperation with the National Women's Studies Association (Philadelphia: New Society Publishers, 1990), offers essays and reports on coalition building and alliance building among contemporary women's groups. Manuel Castells, *The City and the Grassroots* (Berkeley: University of California, 1983), was an early effort at case studies of a variety of locally based resistance movements.

Stayed on Freedom
Jew in the Civil Rights Movement and After

MELANIE KAYE/KANTROWITZ

For the Harlem Education Project.

Jew for Racial and Economic Justice?

Since early 1992 I've been working as director of a New York-based organization called Jews for Racial and Economic Justice. Several times at conferences or meetings, a typo has rendered my identification tag or program listing thus:

Melanie Kaye/Kantrowitz
Jew for Racial and Economic Justice

When I began to write this essay, the peculiar, slightly mortifying label drifted back to me. That's how it would have been in the Civil Rights Movement, had we identified ourselves: *Jew for Racial and Economic Justice.* Individual. Alone. Even though there were rabbis, Jewish organizations, and thousands of Jews. More than half the white Freedom Riders. Nearly two-thirds of the white Mississippi Freedom Summer volunteers.[1] But we were neither organized nor visible as Jews.

I meet Debra Schultz for lunch. She is writing her dissertation on Jewish women in the Civil Rights Movement and has started to contact some women to interview. She reports that, when she phones, several of them ask, "Why are you focusing on *Jewish* women?" or announce, "My being Jewish had nothing to do with it."

Indeed, given that most of us operated without reference to our Jewishness, why insert this reference now? The answer comes at two levels. Most simply, then we had no language to discuss *identity.* We were Americans, we subdivided into Black and white, and our goal was to disrupt this division. Period. In the radical corner of the Civil

Rights Movement we knew that the right to sit at the lunch counter
meant little without money for lunch; economics was part of our political agenda, but we rarely discussed our own class position or our differences from each other. Sexual orientation was never mentioned
publicly and hardly ever privately. Gender, ethnicity, culture went un-
remarked, except for sexual innuendo, sometimes combined with a
borderline-playful taunting, as when a male co-worker, a teenager like
myself, sang me a Harlem version of the old Wobbly song on the bus
returning from the 1963 March on Washington:

> Jew girls from Brooklyn they go wild over me
> And they hold my hand where everyone can see
> They paint their face like whores
> Have me leave them at their doors
> They go wild, simply wild over me.

What could one do in response to such a song? I dissociated. I vowed
not to be like those others. It seems important to note that while anti-
white sentiment was freely spoken, this song was the extent of anti-
Semitism that I heard or remembered in the Civil Rights Movement.[2]

The Civil Rights Movement called for undivided focus on what
seemed the primary contradiction of our society. Initially *black and
white together* represented, for Jews, one more permutation of the
universalism we had been encountering and articulating for several
generations in communist, socialist, and liberal thought; for Jews, the
emphasis on common humanity, at least in earlier generations, dove-
tailed neatly with the pressures of anti-Semitism, both external and
internalized. Univeralism had quietly promised an escape from anti-
Semitism. I did not hear or need this promise, for I had been raised in
the strongly Jewish neighborhood of Flatbush on its assumption (*all
men are brothers* [sic]).

Now, on the contrary, universalism sallies forth from the armory
of sophisticated racists, while progressives share a discourse of inclusive history, and of politics grounded in identity. These require categories. Now we ask who did what when in which combinations, a
questioning popularized by the Civil Rights project of locating the
history of African Americans. But the questioning could not stop

there, and as other people of color, feminists, queers, and ethnics followed the leadership and inspiration of African Americans—with varying degrees of recognition of intellectual and political debt—we have returned to the site of events and movements to comb them for our past.

So, too, Jews. To bring into focus the often invisible presence and explore its significance. Why were Jews drawn to the Civil Rights Movement in such numbers? What did Jewish participation mean for the movement? (Indeed, what did white participation mean? What about those neither Black nor white?) Did Jewish participation add strength to the movement, or mostly offer important experience to our individual selves? How can we value that experience without being nostalgic? Are there lessons for Jewish progressives today? Finally, what are we doing with the experience gleaned in the Civil Rights Movement of the sixties?

To explore Jewish participation in the Civil Rights Movement assumes that Jewish identity is significant; such significance has not, in progressive movements, been a given. (My being *Jewish* had nothing to do with it.) Most important, this quest is linked to concern about tensions—real and media-hyped—between Jews and African Americans. Progressive Jews seek a positive history and models. Some seek understanding of what went sour, became problematic. Some—I am monitoring my own work for this impulse, but it is cunning—seek credit.

And some work to challenge those Jews who explain with great show of reason and maturity why their earlier radical politics have now shifted. We want to contradict their claim to speak for all of us. To place this history in a context of a responsible present and a vision for the future. We aim to recreate a new mass movement for civil and human rights in which Jews contribute forcefully, and we want to know how to do it right.

Most Jews—need it be said?—were not active in Civil Rights; it's only in comparison with other whites that we look so progressive. In the sixties, the complex swirling of Jewish history, ethics, bigotry, and—for some—a family tradition of antiracist activism created a pressure that some Jews responded to and others ignored.[3] Years after her work in the movement, Civil Rights activist Marilyn Lowen wrote, *we went to Mississippi to spit in Hitler's eye.*[4] Yes—though I think

few of us did so consciously. Many Jews raised in the United States in
the wake of the Holocaust experienced it like a family secret—hover-
ing, controlling, but barely mentioned except in code or casual reference. In the early sixties I doubt even Marilyn fully grasped the Jewish
content of her commitment.

Harlem Education Project, 1963–65

In June 1963 the Harlem Education Project (HEP), a branch of
the Northern Student Movement (NSM), itself the Northern arm of
the Student Non-Violent Coordinating Committee (SNCC), put
out a call for students interested in tutoring Harlem schoolchildren.
I was seventeen.

At that first orientation meeting, I was assigned a block unit and a
student to tutor. Stokeley Carmichael (later Kwame Toure) spoke on
the evils of racism and how together we would fight it, interspersed
with jokes about blue-eyed devils. All the white people, myself included (I have blue eyes), laughed nervously, but I was thrilled to be
hearing the movement's most radical vision. Coordinators for the
various HEP projects described their work. They were Black and
white, including a sprinkling of what was then to me an unknown
quantity: upper-class WASPs. Lew Anthony, African American from
Philadelphia, explained the science project, including a trip to Maine
for kids on "the block" to watch the approaching solar eclipse, using a
protective apparatus the kids were building under his direction. ("The
Block" was 144th between 7th and 8th, where a lot of HEP community activities were centered.) Kathy Rogers, the tutorial project director, was a tall upper-class WASP from Sarah Lawrence. Roger
Siegel, a Jewish college dropout, headed Community Organizing.
Lew's brother Carl, an architecture student, showed plans for the community park he'd designed with block residents. Then Carl and Rufus
(editor of the HEP newsletter) talked about class differences in the
Black community. Finally Carl and Rufus led us in singing "This
Little Light of Mine" and "Woke Up This Morning with My Mind
Stayed on Freedom."

That meeting was the most compelling event so far in my young
life. The diversity of the Black community, the vision of the community park, the energy, the swell of voices as we sang together. . . .

Where were the African American women? Harlem was full of strong activist women, in the neighborhoods and churches, soon in the schools, as parents and HEP worked together to demand Black history, organize school boycotts, and create freedom schools. Miz Addie, who owned (or ran?) the candy store with the back room where I later taught reading was "typical": a grandmother, tough as traffic—the kids obeyed even her whisper. Young African American women came to Harlem to work with HEP, but the young women in the neighborhood stood back. The wildly cross-racial sexual energy of the Civil Rights Movement mostly meant white women paired up with Black men, a dynamic that can't have helped foster much sisterhood.[5] The other direction (Black women, white men) was burdened with a history of rape and sexual exploitation and a present of race-*and*-gender dominance, though, again, we had language for none of this.

That summer I attended every meeting, volunteered for every work shift, borrowed tattered paperbacks—Baldwin, Marx, SDS Manifestos—and brought them back the next day asking for more. I taught math to a fifteen-year-old named Yvonne, who brought at least two friends to each session and quit after a couple of weeks. I did better with the teenage boys (today I can read the sexual politics in that too) and the children. Sammy, with blue eyes and gap teeth, was another teenager, utterly pragmatic. He needed to learn to read and write in order to send letters to businesses to get donations for his baseball team. With that motivation, teaching was easy. Next I began working with preschoolers, with word cards and texts created from their stories, using principles developed in *Teacher* by Sylvia Ashton-Warner, the white New Zealander who had taught Maori children. The Civil Rights Movement was profoundly connected to education.

Weekends I'd show up to haul garbage from the inner-block lot which, under Carl's direction, was becoming a community park. I handed out leaflets for rent strikes, licked envelopes, and helped organize for the 1963 March on Washington. I helped Mrs. Reed, an elderly woman from Barbados, create a block library in her front room; twice a week we drank tea together, along with whatever family had dropped by. My next student was her five-year-old grandson, George.

For me, a teenager entering the world of Harlem in the early sixties, being Jewish *meant* being white, meant being called "blue-eyed devil"—tinged with irony, anger, or even mild affection—by Stokeley or by the Black Muslims hawking *Muhammed Speaks* on 135th and Lenox (now Malcolm X Avenue). It never occurred to me that Muslims and Jews shared a non-Christian status in this country, or that Jews might have a sustaining culture like the Black Baptist Church. In HEP we talked a lot about Marx, a little about Jesus. No one ever mentioned that both were Jews.

Today it's shocking to realize that I, a white girl from Brooklyn, handed out flyers for rent strikes and not one person said, at least not in my presence, *Who the fuck is she to tell us what to do?* Current assumptions about organizing are predominantly separatist. We're accustomed to groups organized by identity rather than by political principles, though recent AIDS organizing is a notable exception, reaching across racial and often class lines to transform issues of health care, immigration, and housing.[6] Still the mixed group is the exception.

But Civil Rights organizations *were* mixed. Ideas of *separatism, privilege, arrogance, trust, rage* were already explosive. Malcolm X held far more appeal than Dr. King for the well-under-thirties who comprised HEP. The prevailing ideology was *black and white together,* but there were a lot of edgy grain-of-truth jokes, and in 1965 I didn't need Stokeley's proclamation of Black Power to know it was time for me to leave Harlem. This was not about fear or anti-white sentiment; I was running a reading workshop and I could not give the children what they needed, because they needed Black teachers. I had come to understand something about separatism, dignity, autonomy. A few years later, when I encountered women's liberation, this grasp of separatism served me well, though it would be yet another few years before I came, again, to see critical play between separatist strategy and a coalition model. First I had to see how dangerously small our focus would shrink: mass movement to smaller movements to support groups.

Jew Girl from Brooklyn

I had been raised on stories of labor struggles, Sacco and Vanzetti, the Spanish Civil War, the voice of Paul Robeson, Eleanor Roosevelt's resignation from the DAR because they refused to let Marian Anderson perform in their hall. When news of the contemporary Negro (we said then) struggle for equality reached me, I had been waiting for it all my life.

I entered the movement as a seventeen-year-old, naively full of all I had to offer poor oppressed Black people. Like a lot of young whites, Jewish and not, I brought an unexamined empathy with oppression. Some of this was parental teaching: the Holocaust; the picket line. And some of what attracted me was my own sense of powerlessness; my parents meant to raise us by the Spock-bible, but in practice they were often abusive. The Civil Rights Movement allowed me to export my rage and misery onto African Americans, so I could feel privileged (accurately and inaccurately) and could (generously, not selfishly) fight for justice—not for myself, but *for them*.

That was the initial impulse; but the people I encountered were far too vital and complex, the energy swirling in Harlem far too dynamic. I learned, first and fast, my own ignorance; that what I had to offer was a willingness to work hard. I learned to divest myself of the superiority that always girds pity. And I learned what Harlem had to offer me: a vision of collective possibility and the transforming opportunity to participate.

This impulse was complex—partly about vision and values, and partly about snobbery and class mobility.[7] In the Civil Rights Movement, I could escape Flatbush, my parents' clothing store, the world of working- and lower-middle-class Jews, a world I thought of as *materialistic*. Despite my intimate knowledge of class range in the Jewish community, including in my own extended family, my measuring sticks quickly became the poorest neighborhoods in Harlem. Against *materialistic* stood the world of struggle and change—I didn't say *revolution* yet—along with beatniks, sex, poetry, art, folk music, soul, and funk. Every day I watched my parents leave our Brooklyn apartment to take the subway to work and return home drained, and I, with my seventeen-year-old energy, vowed to live differently. I believed I was confronting my parents' hypocrisy; in truth, I was also punishing them. These were their values? Then I would live these values, scorn their inability or unwillingness to do the same. Evidence of their racism filled me with contempt: *they were fakes and I was real.*

It took twenty years before I understood that my rebellion had been enacted simultaneously by thousands of young Jews; that it was in fact a collective Jewish rebellion, articulated in a classically Jewish fashion. As Trotsky's master biographer Isaac Deutscher explained "the non-Jewish Jew" to the World Jewish Congress in 1958: "The Jewish heretic who transcends Jewry belongs to a Jewish tradition."[8]

What did I know of Jewish? Only that it was the norm. I knew nothing about Jewish culture, religion, or history that could sustain or inspire me. Nothing that taught me my yearnings came partly *from* it. My parents' most admirable friends, Communists and fellow travelers, virtually all Jewish, seemed to me "non-Jewish." My family were not synagogue-goers, and when I, at thirteen, in quest of meaning attended shul on Rosh Hashanah, I saw people flaunting their new clothes. What I knew of religion seemed formulaic, empty, and much too connected with material well-being: the cost of synagogue membership, tickets for services, Hebrew school, the ostentatious plaques and seats reserved for the *makhers*. I found no ethical content. It seemed as if those who spoke as Jews were often politically conservative and religious; *politically conservative* and *religious* were yoked in my mind—I knew nothing of Stephen Wise, Abraham Heschel, or other progressive rabbis.[9]

Recently I was speaking to a Jewish group on Jewish-African American relations, and a man raised the issue of gratitude. Why weren't *they* grateful for *our* help in the Civil Rights Movement? I resisted asking him if he himself had actually worked for Civil Rights, and answered more kindly than I felt (I've learned how effective kindness can be) that you'd expect gratitude only if you thought of yourself as having done a favor. And I went on to say what is perfectly true, that I myself felt grateful for the opportunity to work in the Civil Rights Movement.

Later, I relayed this exchange to a friend, also a long-time activist, who cracked, "Yeah, and I feel grateful to the Vietnamese for . . . ," illuminating the absurdity and the danger. My opportunity came from extreme suffering: it is possible to colonize even a liberation movement if its main use seems to be the growth—even the political growth—of supporters protected by the same privilege that allowed us to choose whether and how we might participate in the struggle. So while I know I was also fighting for my freedom, the legacy I responsibly derive from my work in Harlem must honor the specificity of that movement, as well as its far-ranging implications; that is, to maintain also an unswerving commitment to the liberation of African Americans.

Post–Civil Rights: Berkeley in the Late 1960s

In a post–free speech, burgeoning, antiwar-movement Berkeley, bereft of the movement that had been my life, I turned from a committed organizer into one among the masses. I showed up, I marched, I raged against our government, and I saw what I had learned in Harlem about racism and capitalism confront New Left/hippie culture. But I had little sense of community, and my energy and skills were never tapped.

The Civil Rights Movement, especially in its emphasis on education and community building, had drawn on the less public skills—ability to communicate, build trust, encourage, and persist. In contrast, the antiwar movement operated in a top-decibel way I now understand as quintessentially masculinist. To mobilize young American males against the war meant depicting antiwar resistance as more macho than doing battle. White male radicals tried to emulate the tough, militarist stance of African American radicals like H. Rap Brown and Huey Newton. In Oakland, Black Panthers fought the domestic version of anti-imperial struggle waged by the Vietnamese abroad. The antiwar movement mirrored male heterosexual fantasy liberation. There were certainly pacifists in the antiwar movement, but in Berkeley they were mostly outshouted. There were even a few women leaders, but they were either "exceptions" (women who sounded/postured like men) or they were fucking important men. Lesbians—and gay men—were severely closeted.

I had no important male lover. I was not confident or articulate. Not until Women's Liberation did I find myself as a leader (and as a lesbian). I accepted instruction from Black militants that we were not needed in Black communities; we were needed in white communities to struggle with white people, our own people, about racism. But the thought never crossed my mind that, for me, this might mean struggling with Jews.

Why not? Partly it was the times, the New/White Left's rigid polarization of young against old: Who in their early twenties wanted to engage politically with the community they grew up in—their parents, aunts, uncles, neighbors? It was the exact opposite of sexy.

But in addition, I barely thought of myself as a Jew. In June 1967 the Six-Day War broke out, and an occupying army marched inexorably through the lives of Palestinians and Israelis, shaping those lives

to this day. For many, Jewish consciousness soared as a result of perceived Israeli vulnerability/strength. African American activists,
invoking African unity and third world alliance against Europe, identified with Palestinians. I may as well have been in a coma for all I remember. I barely noticed the '67 War.[10]

Today I'm ashamed: What kind of a Jew was I?

The answer is instructive: *That's the kind of Jew I was.* The kind who
didn't identify with other Jews. Who didn't feel afraid, ashamed,
joyful, grieving, according to the fate and/or behavior of Jews. Who
didn't see Jews as "my people." I was oblivious to the way others responded to me as a Jew. I didn't understand that however I thought
about or related to my identity and my history, I could no more walk
free of these than I could be genderless. Nor did I notice that those
who spoke as white radicals were also often Jewish. Not until I became
conscious of myself as a Jew. Not until I understood at some gut level
that there was no escape.

On the other hand, in that preidentity era, I almost didn't think of
myself as a woman—at least not politically. The first time I heard a
woman claim that women were oppressed, I was outraged—not, as
you might think, at the oppression, but at the claim. *I had worked in
Harlem. Didn't I know* real *oppression? What were these middle-class white
women trying to claim?* (Did I know their class? As it turned out, I was
dead wrong about some of them. Could I assume they were all white?
I was wrong about that, too.)

And I remember a woman in a Shakespeare seminar I attended
briefly (we were almost always on strike in those days, so class attendance, at least on campus, was a sporadic affair). She was offering what
I now would call a feminist critique of Christopher Marlowe, and
though there is no Elizabethan more ripe for a feminist critique, I was
mortified. She was talking about her *feelings.* Her voice was loud. And,
though I didn't register this consciously at the time, her accent was
New York Jew.

Loud Pushy Jewish Women

In women's liberation, in Portland, Oregon, in the early seventies, I began to learn about anti-Semitism and to claim my Jewish identity, though these were two disparate acts. I was teaching, and the
experience of reading Hannah Arendt's *Eichmann in Jerusalem*—

selected initially because of its discussion of language—with a class of goyish first-year students caught me up short. After that, I made a point of including at least one Jewish text each semester. Yet at the first Socialist Feminist Conference in Yellow Springs, Ohio, in 1975, when I overheard women on the lunch line mention the Jewish caucus, I tuned out. I didn't even eavesdrop.

I was absorbed in the fabulousness of being a woman and, as I wrote, *when I became a lesbian and no longer cared what men thought, I came into my power.*[11] Strength and pushiness were suddenly desirable in women. Amy Kesselman, a founder of Chicago Women's Liberation, has suggested that the very character traits that women's liberation had validated and freed were, well, Jewish—at least a certain kind of Jewish.[12] For a woman to be urban, sharp-tongued, intellectual, tough, and pushy was suddenly a hit—in New York, Philadelphia, Chicago, Los Angeles. . . .

The greater Diaspora was more problematic for Jewish women. And as feminists translated our practice from a gender-mixed environment to a female space in which we were supposed to be genetically supportive, cooperative, and gentle—entirely different from men— there was an assumption that, among women, we wouldn't need our strength. The evolving feminist ethic—noninterruptive, nonconfrontational, nonargumentative—made some of us feel like we were on the wrong planet, subjected to unfamiliar forces of gravity.

As feminists of color challenged white hegemony, they created a model and articulated a rationale that also helped Jews understand exclusion. Collectivizing our experiences of "wrongness," we began to grasp that the "normal" feminist was not only white and middle-class: she was determinedly Christian. Sometimes what was said about whites fit us and sometimes it didn't;[13] yet often when Jews voiced our differences (for example, Were *we* afraid of anger? Could *we* expect to see *our* culture taught in the public schools?) white Christian women responded as though we were trying to wiggle out of something. But the "religious" category into which we—if mentioned at all—were usually crammed, was an uneasy fit for what we often perceived as vast cultural, historical, and sometimes physical differences. Everything split into white/color, European/third world dichotomies (the Israeli/ Palestinian conflict only underscored this polarization), while feminist radicals inhaled and exhaled assumptions of Jewish wealth and privilege, just like everyone else in North America.

Today there are still progressives, Jewish and not, who respond to the work of Jews for Racial and Economic Justice with a, usually un-voiced, attitude: *What are you trying to get away with? Why are you harping on an insignificant category? It's one thing if you're religious (although how could you be, all that patriarchy), but aren't you just evading your white skin and (assumed) class privilege? Aren't you avoiding the implications of white-ness?*[14]

Holy Songs

Today as I'm writing, the psalm-based song pops into my head:

By the waters of Babylon where we lay down and wept
when we remembered Zion . . .
The wicked carried us into captivity, required of us a song.
How can I sing a holy song in a strange land?

Holy and whole stem from the same root: *halig*. By the waters of Baby-lon—the Willamette, the Columbia River Gorge, the Rio Grande, the Chama, the Ogunquit, Penobscot Bay, the Winooski—where Jews were scarce, I began to comprehend my estrangement. How I monitored my accent, curbed my gestures. I was not whole. Women had problems with "my style"; I certainly had trouble with theirs. But I barely knew what Babylon meant to the Jews, or Zion either. I could articulate almost nothing about Jewish history, culture, or tradition. I knew no Jewish songs. "My" holy songs came from the Civil Rights Movement.

In 1980, living in Santa Fe, I began to gather with other Jewish women. Began to learn, to teach one another. To write the essay that became part of *Nice Jewish Girls: A Lesbian Anthology*, a collection that made Jews visible in the lesbian and feminist movement, to non-Jews and, most significantly, to each other.[15] I joined New Jewish Agenda, founded in 1981 to voice Jewish perspectives on the Left and Left con-cerns among Jews.[16]

Today a number of groups are building on the principle of explic-itly Jewish progressive activism. In Seattle, the African American-Jewish Coalition for Justice offers one model; Jews for Racial and Economic Justice in New York, another; Jewish participation in coali-tions against homophobic and anti-immigrant ballot measures, a third. In Los Angeles, Minneapolis, Portland, and Detroit, Jews have begun to organize explicitly Jewish antiracist groups.[17]

Why now, and not then? When progressive Jews are silent as Jews, we permit the more conservative voices in the Jewish community to speak for all of us, thereby strengthening conservatism and alienating progressive Jews from Jewish community, culture, continuity, and history.

I'm reminded of a harsh Jewish joke.

> Two Jews walk down the street chatting.
> "Don't look now," says the first Jew, "We're being followed." And indeed, two anti-Semites—Nazis, Klan, skinheads, take your pick—follow close behind. They begin to call names, make threats.
> "I'm going to confront them," says the second Jew, "I'm going to tell them to shut up."
> "Shhh," says the first Jew. "They're together and we're alone."

I tell this joke to make a point not about anti-Semites, but about Jewish conservatives—either the minority of ultraorthodox Jews who are, unfortunately, also ultraorganized, or those Jews, mostly male and wealthy, who claim to speak on behalf of the Jewish community but represent only the interests of the privileged—for whom economic survival, the struggle to obtain decent health care, schooling, the safety of women and children (*their* women and children always excepted) are of no concern, or do not resonate with sufficient urgency to place these issues where they belong, at the top of the Jewish and every other agenda.

This is the *they* in my application of the bitter Jewish joke. Powerful conservative Jews act together and we—progressive Jews—feel and act alone. *Jew for Racial and Economic Justice*?

I know there are some—even many—progressive Jews, who feel uncomfortable or disconnected around this sort of discussion, which assumes the desirability of reclaiming Jewish identity. *I don't feel like that at all. It wasn't about being Jewish.* I'm often stunned by this lack of connection, until I remember who I was in 1967 and why.

I've learned that I can often bond with these Jews in practice, as we work together in various coalitions. They usually turn out to be appreciative of an outspokenly progressive Jewish presence, and happy to identify with the tradition of Jewish progressive activism. Especially hungry for this history are young Jews, confronted by campus anti-Semitism and surrounded by identity politics; for them the double identity of Jewish/progressive is critical.

I know there are also Jews with whom I disagree vehemently on such issues as racism in the Jewish community, strategies to combat anti-Semitism, solutions to the Israeli-Palestinian conflict. I see the fear that dogs them, the perception of any anti-Semitism as potential extermination; often they are convinced that no one will look out for our interests, and they refuse to be suckered again by looking out for others. *"They" hate us; why should we care about "them"? We made it, why can't "they"?* Here, *they* are, usually, African Americans. Or, as in *"they" want to drive us into the sea*—Palestinians, Arabs. The controlling world-view: bleak, survivalist.

Yet we can often bond over our concern for Jewish survival, our love of Jewish culture. Our common ground often provides a bridge of—at least—mutual respect. We encounter each other at an exhibit on Ethiopian Jewish culture, at a klezmer performance, in shul. Allies in the mainstream Jewish community invite us in to address and discuss our differences, and we find these differences are not always as vast as we'd imagined: the Jews who stayed home have not necessarily stood still.

I Have a Dream

Not like Dr. King's long-range dream of a free nation, but a short-term vision of how to move toward that dream.

In my dream, to meet the palpable nightmare of a growing Christian fundamentalist right wing, a new Civil Rights/human rights movement emerges from the separate movements into which the sixties and seventies dwindled. The smaller movements still function as community or issue-bases, as channels between each community and the larger movement, but the larger movement can *MOVE* like a mighty wave. Maybe there's an African American wing of the movement, a Latino wing, a First Nation wing, an Asian wing, and all the other people of color, but more, crisscrossing there's a labor wing, and a wing of the movement for nonunionized workers, queers, feminists, youth, a health care wing, AIDS activists and women's health activists, teachers, environmental groups, homeless people, immigrant rights:

all the ways that people are organized for freedom and justice come together. In this movement, rape, environmental racism, and poverty are deemed crimes against humanity. Housing and food, health care, and education are considered basic human rights.

As this movement pushes and bumbles toward the world we want, Jews form one wing. We are not segregated; like others, we participate also in all the appropriate places where our multiple identities and concerns lead us. But Jews in this new movement know and are proud of our history. We continually reach out to other Jews, to hear their concerns and share our perspectives. We argue, very Jewishly, with our families, our friends, our co-workers, Jewish and non-Jewish. Our leaders are not all Ashkenazi men in suits who belong to a synagogue. We recognize and embrace our diversity of race, culture, sexual orientation, observance, and secularism. Ladino and Yiddish are valued with Hebrew, and Ladino is valued also as a bridge with other Spanish-speaking cultures. Women are key figures, lesbians and gay men and bisexuals, mothers, young Jews, old Jews, workers and poor Jews, artists and writers. Jews of color lead toward alliances with the communities they span. The coalition work between Israeli and Palestinian women, and the pressure it continues (in my dream) to exert toward completion of the project of Palestinian liberation, is an honored model of feminist leadership and of radical boundary crossing. We bond with Japanese and other Asians against the use of the term "Jap," and against any *model-minority-we-made-it-why-can't-they* cooptation; we bond with Muslims and other non-Christians against Christian hegemony. We recognize the leadership of African Americans in progressive struggle, but we do not imagine that the issues of other communities of color, and of all working or impoverished people, are magically included under the category of African American. We are not obsessed with being liked by African Americans, but rather with contributing our part to create the world where untainted human relations will be possible. We form a human chain of commitment between those able or willing to give money or time, those who risk their careers or freedom, and those who risk their lives. We comprehend the process whereby activists edge and are edged toward greater commitment, greater and greater risk.

In this movement Jews understand white skin privilege. We understand that some of us have it and some don't, that some of us have it sometimes in some places. We know what it is and what it is not. We know it is not liberation. We oppose absolutely assimilation, cultural loss, and devaluing. We know that passing can confer safety, but also signifies loss. We are not willing to settle for being white in America. We want more. We want to abolish racism, to abolish the political significance of the categories *white* and *color*.

In this movement, Jews are visible. Non-Jews know that Jews are not whites/Europeans who go to Jewish church, but a people whose history, culture/religion, and sometimes complexion situate us shiftingly between the categories of white and color. Non-Jews know and respect the history of Jewish oppression and resistance, of Jewish allies. Through our crisscrossing identities, friend- and loverships, families, and concerns, and most of all through the political change that we accomplish together, we come to trust the power and the transfiguring joy of solidarity.

Finally, this movement is a singing movement, like the one that first taught me to keep my mind stayed on freedom. In my dream we sing and teach one another to sing our holy songs in this strange land, transforming it from strangeness.

Acknowledgments

I am indebted to Marla Brettschneider for the initial sparking interest and for extraordinary patience; and to Nancy Ordover and Debra Schultz for incisive and generous critical response, which strengthened this work immeasurably. I am of course responsible for whatever weaknesses remain.

Notes

1. Jonathan Kaufman, *Broken Alliance: The Turbulent Times between Blacks and Jews in America* (New York: Simon and Schuster, 1988), p. 93. According to Debra Schultz, doctoral student at the Union Institute for Graduate Studies, historical research on Jews in the Civil Rights Movement is in such a nascent state that reliable statistics for broader Civil Rights activity—in the North, for example—are hard to come by.

2. I may have missed something—I was young and had virtually no experience with anti-Semitism—but clearly it was not a dominant theme.

3. Nancy Ordover, doctoral student in Ethnic Studies at University of California–Berkeley, has drawn my attention to Mark Naison's term "cultural reflex." In his distinguished study *Communists in Harlem during the Depression* (New York: Grove Press, 1985), in an appendix ("Black-Jewish Relations in the Harlem Communist Party"), Naison offers the following intriguing remark: "Though their Jewish ancestry may have endowed them with cultural reflexes that dictated a strong emotional response to black oppression, and though as individuals they may have been aware of this, the assimila-

tionist atmosphere in the Party, as well as their own political ambitions, probably discouraged them from calling attention to it in any systematic way" (p. 322; notes, p. 327). Considering that many Jewish Civil Rights activists *were* these Jewish Communists (by then, often, ex-Communists) or their children, the concept of "cultural reflex" seems worth exploring.

4.   Marilyn, a Jew from Detroit, was, with Bob Fletcher (an African American, also from Detroit), my block leader during my first summer in Harlem.

5.   In the mid-seventies, a white feminist talking with Alice Walker explained, with practically criminal innocence, how she had trouble with Black women though never with Black men. "That's because you didn't have trouble with the men," Walker responded. "If you'd had more trouble with the men, you would have had less trouble with the women." Interview published in the Eugene, Oregon *Women's Press*, paraphrased here from memory.

6.   I am indebted to Nancy Ordover for this observation. As this book goes to press, California organizing for immigrant rights and affirmative action also exemplifies multicultural, issue-based politics.

7.   Jewish students who participated in the Civil Rights Movement are usually assumed to have been economically privileged. This may have been true of many who went south, for obvious reasons: there were expenses—at the very least, a summer not spent working and saving for the school year. My memory of most whites/Jews in HEP was that they attended private colleges, had spent time in Europe, had access to cars, luxury apartments, and so on. But of course I was envious; I probably missed noticing others like myself. A class analysis of Civil Rights (and New Left) activists might challenge some stereotypes.

8.   "Spinoza, Heine, Marx, Rosa Luxemburg, Trotsky, and Freud . . . all went beyond the boundaries of Jewry. They all found Jewry too narrow, too archaic, and too constricting. . . . Yet I think that in some ways they were very Jewish indeed. . . . As Jews they dwelt on the borderlines of various civilizations, religions, and national cultures" (Isaac Deutscher, *The Non-Jewish Jew and Other Essays* [London: Oxford University Press, 1968], pp. 26–27). Typically the non-Jewish Jew fails to see herself or himself as acting within the Jewish tradition. Deutscher's essay is a must-read, though distressingly blithe in its analysis of anti-Semitism.

9.   There were no women rabbis yet. Today I wonder what might have been the impact on me of contemporary feminist rabbis such as Susan Talve, whose St. Louis congregation is engaged in a range of inventive grassroots antiracist work.

10.   Yet fifteen years later, when Israel invaded Lebanon, the Israeli occupation of the West Bank and Gaza—a direct result of the war I hadn't noticed—was already a central preoccupation. See "The Next Step" and "I've Been to Israel and to Palestine" in *The Issue Is Power: Essays on Women, Jews, Violence and Resistance*, ed. Melanie Kaye/Kantrowitz (San Francisco: Aunt Lute, 1992).

11.   "Some Notes on Jewish Lesbian Identity," reprinted in ibid., p. 83.

12.   Remarks on "Organizing in the Post-Holocaust Era" Panel at *In Gerangl* / In Struggle: 100 Years of Progressive Jewish History, Teach-In and Cultural Festival, Cooper Union, New York City, December 12, 1993; this event was organized by Jews for Racial and Economic Justice and cosponsored by the *Village Voice*.

13.   The experience of Jewish women varied widely, in accordance with our sense of identity, vulnerability, history, and so on.

14.   For example, in 1990 an essay of mine was rejected from a feminist anthology

on fighting racism because, according to one source, "I didn't deal enough with whiteness." (Never mind that I analyzed and advocated deeply Jewish imperatives for struggling against racism.)

15.   Evelyn Beck's editorship and the soliciting of the anthology from her by Persephone's Gloria Greenfield deserve historical credit. The reading given in Boston when *Nice Jewish Girls* came out (pun intentional) was an astonishing event. Hundreds of Jewish women shrieked, clapped, and stomped when I suggested we reclaim the terms "loud and pushy." And some picketing Orthodox Jewish men leafleted the crowd, claiming that we, the lesbians, were excommunicated.

16.   New Jewish Agenda's impact, especially on Middle East peace work, was significant and undercredited. NJA also organized explicitly Jewish political work on Central America, feminism, homophobia, racism, and economic justice.

17.   Women's leadership in all of these is noteworthy.

Black, White, and Red
Jewish and African Americans in the Communist Party

GERALD HORNE

It should come as no surprise that both Jewish and African Americans would be attracted to radical movements generally and to the Communist Party in particular. Those who feel the most pain scream the loudest; and those in search of an echo chamber to magnify the sound of their screams historically have veered toward movements for socialism that have put forward the theory that it is the "god of profit" that undergirded the evil of discrimination. Interestingly enough, radicals of varying stripes have argued for years that, ultimately, it was discrimination itself that helped split the working class and kept erstwhile natural allies in mortal combat.[1]

In this essay I put forward the idea that the U.S. Left and the Communist Party pioneered in the fight against racism and anti-Semitism and in building an alliance between Jewish and African Americans. I argue further that this Black-Jewish alliance reached a zenith in 1943 when Ben Davis, an African American Communist, was elected to the New York City Council with substantial Jewish support. I argue also that such electoral successes helped inspire a massive Red Scare that followed the conclusion of World War II, and that this effort to discredit and destroy the Left created favorable conditions for the rise of narrow nationalism and xenophobia in both the Black and Jewish communities; it is this dual narrow nationalism that has led directly to the present crisis in racial relations generally and in Black-Jewish relations particularly.[2]

The triumphalism of the West that has marked the end of the Cold War has not been able to obscure the fact that its proponents often heavily relied on narrow nationalism in order to subdue class-based alliances.[3] In Guyana, the English-speaking nation on the northern coast of South America, conflict was stoked deliberately between the African and Indian populations; this U.S.-inspired maneuver not only prevented the ascension to the presidency of Cheddi Jagan—who was considered "pro-Castro"—but has poisoned the well of ethnic relations in the country to this very day. In South Africa, conservative circles of the United States have given maximum support for the longest time to the Inkatha Freedom Party and its leader M. G. Buthelezi, despite the fact that its "Zulu nationalism" threatens to tear the nation apart and despite this party's chauvinism, which has led directly to murders of thousands of political opponents. If one seeks to understand the unravelling of Black-Jewish relationships in the United States, it is necessary to keep this point firmly in mind: religious, racial, and ethnic comity over the past decades has fallen victim to larger geopolitical aims dictated by the Cold War.

In the aftermath of World War I, when the Communist Party was being organized, the Democratic Party was the party of the Jim Crow South and the Ku Klux Klan. It was the major political party at the time that stood in the way of full exercise of voting rights for African Americans. It was anti-Catholic as well as being the party of anti-Semitism.[4] Pitchfork Ben Tillman, Hoke Smith, the Talmadge dynasty in Georgia, and the Byrd dynasty in Virginia were not only opponents of full voting rights for racial minorities; they bore the stain of anti-Semitism as well.[5]

This point was illustrated most dramatically when Leo Frank, the son of a wealthy Jewish merchant, was lynched in Georgia. Frank managed an Atlanta pencil factory. When one of the workers, Mary Phagan, was found murdered on the premises, unsubstantiated rumors of sexual perversion helped fix suspicion on Frank. This suspicion quickly degenerated into an anti-Jewish fervor driven by allegations concerning wealthy Jews who were supposedly exploiting Southern womanhood. Strikingly, Tom Watson, who theretofore had been notorious for his vicious attacks on African Americans, led the charge against Frank. With undue haste Frank was convicted, but a furor ensued when the governor commuted the sentence to life imprisonment. A boycott of Jewish merchants began; mass meetings throughout the state cried out for vengeance. The inevitable happened: a group of white Christian men seized Frank from prison and murdered him.

It was the case of Leo Frank, as much as anything else, that convinced Jewish Americans of a simple fact: to the extent that bias, lynchings, and terror were aimed at one minority, like African Americans, ineluctably such horrors eventually would be aimed at another, like Jewish Americans. The subsequent discovery that Frank was innocent did not lessen the pain or diminish the revelation that the fate of these two disparate minorities might be linked in North America. This recognition led to substantial Jewish support for the National Association for the Advancement of Colored People, which had been formed in 1909.[6]

Even in comparison to the Democratic Party, the Republican Party was little better. Its constant embarrassment at having to rely upon a few Black leaders and voters in the Deep South was to be assuaged, beginning in the 1920s, with a systematic effort to root out Blacks and create a so-called lily-white (white and Protestant) party in the South. Ironically, one of the African American leaders removed in this purge was Ben Davis Sr., one of the more affluent African Americans in the nation at the time and the publisher of the Black weekly, the *Atlanta Independent*.[7]

Ben Davis Sr. was not just a rank-and-file Republican. From 1908 until his death in 1945 he attended all the conventions. In 1916 he was on the platform committee that tried to force a plank on lynching—in obvious reaction to the Frank episode—and advocated that southern representation in Congress be decreased in proportion as Black citizens were disfranchised. He served six years as GOP committeeman, was secretary of the GOP State Executive Committee for eighteen years, and served as president of the Young Men's Republican Club of Georgia as late as 1943. As head of the party in Georgia he had a substantial role in handing out patronage during the intermittent GOP administrations in Washington. The sight of White men coming to the home of an African American man like Davis, seeking favors and patronage, was a gross violation of prevailing racial etiquette. This led directly to the purging of Davis Sr. from the leadership of the GOP.

Ben Davis Sr.'s wealth allowed him, however, to send his son, Ben Davis Jr., to Harvard Law School. In Cambridge Davis Jr. struck up a friendship with another African American who was to leave his mark on progressive and Left politics in New York City—Ewart Guinier. Guinier wound up marrying a Jewish woman and their daughter, Lani Guinier, went on to become a contemporary symbol of the two-party system's betrayal of voting rights.[8]

In Cambridge Davis Jr. encountered a bigotry that was not

focused exclusively on African Americans. A dormitory at Harvard was called disparagingly "Little Jerusalem" because of the large number of Jewish students that had been placed there. President Abbott Lawrence Lowell proclaimed that the school had a "Jewish problem" and spearheaded efforts to limit the enrollment of Jews. The curbing of their enrollment, he concluded, would lessen anti-Semitism![9] Sadly, such thinking was not unique to Davis's alma mater but was the consensus nationally. From this experience, Davis came to see the links between anti-Black racism and anti-Semitism.

At the time Ben Davis Jr. graduated from Harvard Law School he could see the GOP pushing his father and other African Americans out of the party. Furthermore, he was loathe to align with the Democrats, whose reputation as being the party of the Jim Crow South was all too fresh. So Ben Davis Jr. joined the Communist Party.

The party Davis joined had a substantial Jewish membership, particularly in New York City, the site of its largest district. The heavy Jewish membership in the Communist Party of New York was a reflection of the Jewish membership in such trade unions as the Teachers Union, the needle trades (particularly the International Ladies Garment Workers Union), the nascent Hospital and Drugstore workers' union (which was to serve as the foundation of today's Local 1199), and a number of other unions that are now defunct.[10]

Together these Jewish and African American comrades in the 1930s helped make places such as Scottsboro a symbol of the racist terror that was Jim Crow. In that case, the allegation that nine Black youth had sexually assaulted two white women in rural Alabama energized millions globally but it seemed to have a special and dramatic effect on a Jewish community still reeling from the outrage of Leo Frank's lynching. Ben Davis Jr. was also the attorney for another symbol of the Jim Crow South: Angelo Herndon. Herndon's attempt to organize against hunger and the ravages of the Great Depression in Georgia resulted in a long prison sentence. The Scottsboro and Herndon cases both led to major victories in the United States Supreme Court, which eroded the foundations for the Ku Klux Klan-dominated system of criminal justice.[11] Such court cases, by creating more rights for those accused of crimes, not only helped the particular defendants involved but also aided others similarly situated—the Leo Franks of the future. Due to the notoriety he gained in the Herndon case, Ben Davis Jr. was obligated to move from Georgia to the relatively safer climes of

New York City. There he quickly rose to the top levels of the Communist Party.

In 1943 the party was in the process of naming Carl Brodsky as its nominee for city council. When it became obvious, however, that Adam Clayton Powell was going to leave the council, run for Congress, and thus leave the council bereft of any Black members, the Jewish Brodsky stepped down and Davis took his place. In words that ring awkwardly in our modernist cynical ears, Brodsky in relinquishing the communist nomination said, "As a member of the Jewish people I can appreciate what it means not to have the great Negro minority represented." The Party paper, the *Daily Worker,* was similarly portentous: "Marking the first example of its kind on record, a white candidate for City Council last night withdrew from the Councilmanic race in order to give place to a Negro nominee."[12]

This idea of unity between Jewish and African Americans became a major theme of the campaign for city council, which was taking place against the backdrop of the Holocaust in Europe; Davis and other Black communist leaders like William Patterson and Claudia Jones (a native of Trinidad) frequently drew comparisons between the slave trade and the Holocaust, linking directly the fate of these two significant minorities: Jews and Blacks.

Davis won this election and attributed his victory in no small part to support from the Jewish community. He said:

> The tremendous vote that I received from the Jewish working class community was one of the highlights of my election. . . . I was told by experienced election campaigners that my name had become as familiar in Jewish workers' families as one of their own and that never before had a Negro candidate received such a high percentage of votes in a white neighborhood. . . . There were many Jewish candidates among the white aspirants for the Council posts but in certain Jewish districts I topped them all. . . . On each of the occasions that I spoke in the Jewish community at the other end of [Manhattan], I received ovations and huge crowds that rivalled those in Harlem.[13]

Davis won in 1943 and was reelected by a huge margin in 1945. On the council he became a frequent defender of the rights of the Jewish people, along with his Italian American communist comrade, Pete Cacchione. Indeed, throughout his career Davis was remarkable in his fierce support of the rights of the Jewish people, most notably their threatened existence in Europe, where the rise of fascism jeopardized the future of this community. In the spring of 1938 Davis assailed the "plight of the Jewish people in Germany, Austria, Poland"; this, he intoned, "makes all mankind shudder." Again, seeking to link the destiny of his people with the Jewish people, he concluded, "show me an anti-Semite and I will show you a Negro-hater."[14]

This latter theme was repeated continuously during the war years. Like most African American intellectuals of that era (W. E. B. Du Bois, Paul Robeson, and others), Davis was a staunch supporter of the founding of the state of Israel. As the war wound down, Davis in particular became a vocal supporter of the plan to repatriate Jewish refugees in Palestine. A bilingual (Hebrew and English) campaign leaflet issued during his 1945 election campaign was blunt: "As regards Palestine, I have demanded the immediate abrogation of the British White Paper and the opening of the door of Palestine to those victims of Nazi terror who wish to live there. I support the building of a Jewish National Home in a free and democratic Palestine on the basis of Arab-Jewish collaboration."[15]

He did not yield on this, even as the political climate in the United States moved sharply to the right. In the spring of 1947 Davis called for a United Nations mandate over Palestine and an open-door policy in the United States and Palestine for displaced European Jews. He admonished the United Kingdom for their obstinance on this question and demanded that the United States "guarantee the national rights" of both Arabs and Jews in order to "bring about a transfer of the mandate over Palestine from the British government to the end that it may establish in Palestine a free, democratic and sovereign state." Months later he backed a city council resolution in favor of partition and criticized his fellow Black Harvard alumnus Ralph Bunche—who was a negotiator for the United Nations—for his "Machiavellian role" and his "hostile and callous attitude toward Israel."[16]

The Black-Jewish relationship was not just a one-way street. The development of race relations in the Hollywood film industry provides an example of the way in which during this era Jews led the fight against the oppression of African Americans. A major controversy erupted in New York City earlier this decade when a prominent African American professor claimed that the negative image of Blacks in the movies could be laid at the feet of, among others, Jewish movie moguls. This was, however, only a partial truth. It is true that Warner and Laemmle and Zukor and Cohn and Mayer and Schulberg and other movie moguls were disproportionately Jewish, as Neal Gabler has noted.[17] However, the omission in Gabler's work—which this professor relied upon heavily for his thesis—is the virtual absence of a discussion of where these moguls received their financing.

Consider the "ethnic origins" of those banks that bankrolled the film industry, which had seats on the boards of the major studios, and, frequently, had veto power over scripts and film content. The Bank of America in San Francisco was controlled during the time of the moguls by a prominent Italian American family.[18] Leading banks in New York City, like Chase Manhattan, were controlled by Protestant families like the Rockefellers.[19] Today Japanese conglomerates such as Sony and Matsushita control major studios like Columbia and Universal. Unfortunately there is substantial ethnoreligious blame to spread when indicting Hollywood for what it has done to African Americans.

The point is, however, that in the period before the Red Scare, some of the most effective antiracist work in the movies was done primarily by Jewish communist screenwriters, like John Howard Lawson, Party leader in Hollywood. This diminutive man, who walked with a distinct limp and, appropriately, wrote with his left hand, was just one of many Jewish men and women of the Left who toiled tirelessly not only to improve the on-screen image of African Americans but to provide them with employment in this booming industry as well.

Indeed, when Dixiecrats such as Congressman John Rankin of the House Un-American Activities Committee launched their devastating attack on Hollywood after World War II, one of the major things that motivated them was this kind of antiracist labor. Rankin, for example, may have had in mind the scene from *Sahara* starring Humphrey Bogart. Here a Nazi prisoner of war is being guarded by a Black soldier. The Nazi objects and the Black soldier's comrade—who is of the same "race" as the Nazi—comments that the ancestors of this Black man were building great civilizations while the ancestor of the Nazi was still in caves. This premature Africentrism was written by Jewish communist screenwriter John Howard Lawson.[20]

Lawson was a prime organizer of the Screen Writers' Guild,

which constantly pressured the industry about the promotion of anti-Black stereotypes. Unfortunately, the Red Scare intervened after World War II and killed these promising initiatives. It was during this period that the former New Dealer and leader of the Screen Actors' Guild, Ronald Wilson Reagan, was catapulted into prominence. This move occurred in the wake of a massive strike in the film industry in 1945 and a tumultuous, violence-prone lockout in 1946. Many of the leaders of the unions during this hectic time were Jewish—and many of those were Communists. As was the pattern in France, Italy, Japan, and elsewhere at the time, the ruling elite here called upon the muscle and mayhem of the mob—organized crime—to break the strike and the unions.[21]

Lawson became a member of the so-called Hollywood Ten, writers and directors who were "blacklisted." Six of the ten were Jewish and many had been or were Communists. The leader of the Party in Los Angeles was Pettis Perry, an African American who had come to the Party in the 1930s because of the Scottsboro case. When the Party was assaulted during the Red Scare, so too was a central institution in the fight against racism: the Communist Party.

The result of the assault of the Red Scare on Hollywood can be viewed most graphically in Los Angeles, the home of the film industry and of a Black community in Watts that grew dramatically after the war. Here a so-called communist front, the Civil Rights Congress, pioneered in the struggle against racial bias. The CRC in LA included a panel of attorneys, led by the prominent Jewish litigator Ben Margolis, which specialized in cases of police brutality. In 1950 their record was enviable: ninety-eight cases tried, thirty-three won, three lost, and the rest in process. The largest categories were twenty-five cases involving Mexican Americans and fourteen involving African Americans.

Antiracist films, like the War Department's World War II classic *Don't Be a Sucker,* were often shown at CRC functions. In 1952 the East Hollywood unit of CRC held an extraordinary conference to "examine and study the problems of white chauvinism, to exchange ideas and experiences." Note that this was during the height of the Cold War and Red Scare, the era of the supposedly "quiet 1950s," before Martin Luther King Jr. was a household name. The CRC in the Los Angeles focused particularly on "ending the practice of Negroes being the last hired and the first fired." They vowed to escalate the cru-

sade to end discrimination in housing in East Hollywood and to encourage the hiring of African American teachers and librarians in local institutions.

Their antiracist efforts did not go unchallenged. That same year,
1952, Los Angeles was rocked by a series of anti-Black and anti-Jewish
bombings, as a protest against efforts to pierce the "iron curtain" that
mandated that these minorities only reside in certain neighborhoods.
The CRC joined hands with the NAACP and the Emma Lazarus
Federation of Jewish Women in a ringing protest.[22] By 1956 the CRC
also had passed from the scene, driven out of business by government
harassment aimed not only at Communists but at so-called communist fronts as well.

Meanwhile, back in New York City, Ben Davis was defeated for
reelection in 1949 as the GOP and Democrats supported one candidate against him. Ironically, to break this Black Communist's hold on
his constituency, both parties—but particularly the Democrats—
began to open their doors wider to African Americans, a process that
was to culminate with the Voting Rights Act of 1965, a bill passed days
before Watts erupted. Though not recognized widely at the time, passage of this pathbreaking legislation came at a heavy price: the isolation of forces on the Left that traditionally acted as a glue holding
together disparate racial and religious forces in these diverse United
States.

In the fateful year of 1949 Davis was also on trial for violating the
Smith Act, thought-control legislation designed to outlaw the propa-
gation of Marxism and the ideas of socialism. Davis was convicted and
spent five years in the federal prison in Terre Haute, Indiana.

In 1949 the top leaders of the Black community—Davis, Du Bois,
Robeson, Patterson—were of the Left. By 1956, due to the devastating effects of the Red Scare and McCarthyism, they were
marginalized and isolated, while the Nation of Islam began to rise.
The year 1956 was not only the year of the revelations about Josef
Stalin at the 20th Party Congress in Moscow and the Soviet intervention in Hungary. This year also marked a major rift between Black and
Jewish comrades in the wake of the Suez war involving the joint Israeli, British, and French attack on Nasser's Egypt. This rift—which
could just as easily be deemed an ideological split involving people of
various ethnic and religious backgrounds—sparked by interference of
the Federal Bureau of Investigation's disruptive COINTELPRO

agenda of dirty tricks, was converted into an inflamed Black-Jewish confrontation that was to set the stage for further conflicts involving Mid East wars and crises in 1967, 1973, 1979, and beyond.[23]

By 1965 CRC was a dim, distant memory; few recalled John Howard Lawson and the effort to improve the Black image on the Silver Screen. Fewer still recalled the fruitful collaboration between Jewish and African Americans that, for a while, had put a dent in the ongoing rampage against police brutality. In August 1965 Los Angeles erupted in one of the bloodiest "riots" of this century as African Americans took to the streets in droves to protest against police brutality. A special target of their wrath were Jewish merchants in their neighborhoods, as a new era of Black-Jewish relations commenced. Akin to the pattern in Guyana, South Africa, and other areas across the globe, as the Left was besieged and class consciousness waned, narrow nationalism rushed to fill the vacuum. The Nation of Islam, which had originated in the 1930s when massive union organizing drives were unfolding, had a tiny membership until the 1950s when organizations like the CRC were eclipsed. If there was a "vanguard" organization in August 1965 in Los Angeles, it was the Nation of Islam, whose approach to the Jewish community could easily be characterized as anti-Semitic.[24] Likewise, the Red Scare served to undermine Jewish support for African American causes and helped spawn a "neoconservatism" that was viewed widely in Watts and Harlem as insensitive at best, racist at worst. In the wake of Watts 1965, the civil rights movement was placed on the defensive, as images of meek and pious civil rights demonstrators were replaced by images of angry Blacks with Molotov cocktails in hand. Ronald Reagan, a key participant in the violent labor turmoil in Hollywood of the 1940s, was able to parlay revulsion toward what had happened in Watts into a successful race for the governorship of California in 1966—a platform that led him directly to the White House in 1980, inaugurating a new reign of conservative ascendancy.[25]

As has been the case all over the world, when the Left was weakened, favorable conditions were created for the rise of various forms of narrow nationalism in both the Black and Jewish communities. Just as gangsters were used to subdue Left-led unions in Hollywood during the Red Scare, Left influence among Black Angelenos was supplanted by the growth of gangs that by the 1990s had thousands of members.[26]

The Cold War, which gave birth to a narrow and right-wing nationalism, may have ended, but like a beard that continues to grow on
the face of a dead man, narrow nationalism continues to complicate
relations between Jewish and African American communities. The
blinkered perspective that narrow nationalism brings is reflected in
those who praise unequivocally what the Cold War has wrought but
wring their hands about the state of Black-Jewish relations; it is reflected in books like the wildly popular *The Crisis of the Negro Intellectual,* which argues that the main problem with the Black movement
over the past few decades is not ruling elite oppression, or Dixiecrat
racism, but the influence of Jewish Communists like John Howard
Lawson.[27]

However, it is my considered opinion that if relations between
Jewish and African Americans are to improve, a condition precedent is
a resurgence of a strong and renewed Left that does not stint on racial,
ethnic, religious, or gender identity, but also recognizes the class
question. In building this movement we must note the necessity of
forming class-based organizations in the tradition of Ben Davis, John
Howard Lawson, and others who have excelled in building alliances
across borders.

Notes

1.   William Z. Foster, *American Trade Unionism: Principles and Organization, Strategy and Tactics* (New York: International Publishers, 1947); Gerald Horne, *Black Libera-
tion/Red Scare: Ben Davis and the Communist Party* (London: Associated University
Presses, 1994; much of what follows concerns Davis and New York City and can be
found in these pages); W. E. B. Du Bois, *Black Reconstruction: An Essay toward a History of
the Part which Black Folk Played in the Attempt to Reconstruct Democracy in America,
1860–1880* (New York: Harcourt, Brace, 1935).

2.   Gerald Horne, "Myth and the Making of 'Malcolm X,'" *American Historical
Review* 98 (April 1993): 440–50.

3.   Cheddi Jagan, *The West on Trial: My Fight for Guyana's Freedom* (New York: International Publishers, 1967); Benny Morris, *Israel's Border Wars, 1949–1956: Arab Infil-
tration, Israeli Retaliation and the Countdown to the Suez War* (New York: Oxford
University Press, 1993); Nelson Mandela, *No Easy Walk to Freedom: Articles, Speeches and
Trial Addresses* (New York: Basic Books, 1965); Mzala, *Gatsha Buthelezi: Chief with a Double Agenda* (London: Zed, 1988).

4.   David Mark Chalmers, *Hooded Americanism: The History of the Ku Klux Klan*
(Durham, N.C.: Duke University Press, 1987); Kenneth T. Jackson, *The Ku Klux Klan in
the City, 1915–1930* (New York: Oxford University Press, 1967); Kathleen Blee, *Women
of the Klan: Racism and Gender in the 1920s* (Berkeley: University of California Press,

1991); Larry R. Gerlach, *Blazing Crosses in Zion:The Ku Klux Klan in Utah* (Logan: Utah State University Press, 1982).

5.   C. Vann Woodward, *Origins of the New South, 1877–1913* (Baton Rouge: Louisiana State University Press, 1951); Francis Butler Simkins, *The Tillman Movement in South Carolina* (Baton Rouge: Louisiana State University Press, 1944); Raymond Arsenault, *The Wild Ass of the Ozarks: Jeff Davis and the Social Bases of Southern Politics* (Philadelphia: Temple University Press, 1984); William Anderson, *The Wild Man from Sugar Creek:The Political Career of Eugene Talmadge* (Baton Route: Louisiana State University Press, 1975); Ronald L. Heinemann, *Depression and New Deal in Virginia: The Enduring Dominion* (Charlottesville: University Press of Virginia, 1983); Dewey Grantham, *Hoke Smith and the Politics of the New South* (Baton Rouge: Louisiana State University Press, 1967).

6.   John Higham, *Strangers in the Land: Patterns of American Nativism, 1860–1925* (New Brunswick, N.J.: Rutgers University Press, 1992), pp. 185–86; David L. Lewis, *W. E. B. Du Bois: Biography of a Race, 1868–1919* (New York: Henry Holt, 1993).

7.   Hanes Walton, *Black Republicans:The Politics of the Black and Tans* (Metuchen, N.J.: Scarecrow, 1975), p. 176; Donald Lisio, *Hoover, Blacks and Lily-Whites: A Study of Southern Strategies* (Chapel Hill: University of North Carolina Press, 1985), pp. 42, 53; see also Allan Lichtman, *Prejudice and the Old Politics:The Presidential Election of 1928* (Chapel Hill: University of North Carolina Press, 1979), p. 159: "In their quest for equal rights, black people were confronted on the one hand by a Republican Party whose friendship for their people was a tarnished memory and, on the other hand, by a Democratic Party wedded to southern racism."

8.   Lani Guinier, *The Tyranny of the Majority* (New York: Simon and Schuster, 1994).

9.   Ronald Takaki, *A Different Mirror: A History of Multicultural America* (Boston: Little, Brown, 1993), pp. 305–6; Marcia Synnott, *The Half-Opened Door: Discrimination and Admissions at Harvard,Yale and Princeton, 1900–1970* (Westport, Conn.: Greenwood, 1979).

10.   Celia Lewis, *The NewYork CityTeachers Union, 1916–1964:A Story of Educational and Social Commitment* (New York: Humanities Press, 1968); Leon Fink, *Upheaval in the Quiet Zone: A History of Hospital Workers' Union, Local 1199* (Urbana: University of Illinois Press, 1989); Benjamin Stolberg, *Tailor's Progress:The Story of a Famous Union and the MenWho Made It* (Garden City: Doubleday, 1944).

11.   Charles H. Martin, *The Angelo Herndon Case and Southern Justice* (Baton Rouge: Louisiana State University Press, 1976); Dan T. Carter, *Scottsboro:A Tragedy of the American South* (Baton Rouge: Louisiana State University Press, 1969); James Goodman, *Stories of Scottsboro* (New York: Pantheon, 1994).

12.   Horne, *Ben Davis,* p. 104.

13.   Ibid., p. 117.

14.   *Daily Worker,* April 3, 1938.

15.   Flyer, circa 1945, Box 5, *Robert Minor Papers* (Columbia University Library).

16.   *Daily Worker,* May 26, 1947; *Daily Worker,* March 9, 1948; *Daily Worker,* November 28, 1948.

17.   Neal Gabler, *An Empire ofTheir Own: How the Jews Invented Hollywood* (New York: Crown, 1988).

18.   Julian Dana, *A. P. Giannini, Giant in theWest:A Biography* (New York: Prentice-

Hall, 1947); Gerald D. Nash, *A. P. Giannini and the Bank of America* (Norman: University of Oklahoma Press, 1992).

19.   Michael Kramer, *"I Never Wanted to Be Vice-President of Anything!": An Investigative Biography of Nelson Rockefeller* (New York: Basic Books, 1976); James E. Underwood, *Governor Rockefeller in New York: The Apex of Pragmatic Liberalism in the United States* (Westport, Conn.: Greenwood, 1982); David Horowitz and Peter Collier, *The Rockefellers: An American Dynasty* (New York: Holt, Rinehart and Winston, 1976).

20.   Any Black nationalist or leftist would gladly relinquish their weight in "X-caps" to be able to claim authorship of such a line. See also Gary Carr, *The Left Side of Paradise: The Screenwriting of John Howard Lawson* (Ann Arbor: UMI Research Press, 1984); John Howard Lawson, *Film in the Battle of Ideas* (New York: Masses and Mainstream, 1953); idem, *Theory and Practice of Playwriting* (New York: Hill and Wang, 1960).

21.   As has been noted, this alliance among the entertainment industry, politicians, and the mob has come to play a pivotal role in both domestic U.S. politics and international affairs generally. See also Dan Moldea, *Dark Victory: Reagan, MCA and the Mob* (New York: Dutton, 1986); Charles Rappleye, *All American Mafioso: The Johnny Roselli Story* (New York: Doubleday, 1991); William Knoedelseder, *Stiffed: A True Story of MCA, the Music Business and the Mafia* (New York: HarperCollins, 1993).

22.   See Gerald Horne, *Communist Front? The Civil Rights Congress, 1946–1956* (London: Associated University Presses, 1988), p. 331 and passim.

23.   Ward Churchill, *The COINTELPRO Papers: Documents from the FBI's Secret Wars Against Domestic Dissent* (Boston: South End Press, 1990).

24.   For a fuller elaboration of issues presented here, see Gerald Horne, *Fire This Time: The Watts Uprising and the 1960s* (Charlottesville: University Press of Virginia, 1995. (*Note*: This book was published in August 1995, the thirtieth anniversary of the uprising.)

25.   Stephen Vaughn, *Ronald Reagan in Hollywood: Movies and Politics* (New York: Cambridge University Press, 1994).

26.   Leon Bing, *Do or Die* (New York: HarperCollins, 1991); Sanika Shakur, *Monster: The Autobiography of an L.A. Gang Member* (New York: Atlantic Monthly, 1993).

27.   Harold Cruse, *The Crisis of the Negro Intellectual* (New York: Morrow, 1967).

Pioneers in Dialogue
Jews Building Bridges

REENA BERNARDS

*A*t every family seder when I was young, along with my grand-mother who made the gefilte fish and horseradish with her own hands, and my father at the head of the table in a big chair fluffed with pillows, there were always some Gentiles. I remember being surprised that a Lutheran minister could sing along in Hebrew, which he was required to learn in seminary. And I remember the five-year-old daughter of one minister who enthusiastically took a big bite out of a fresh piece of horseradish, only to turn beet red and gag when she learned what this bitter herb was all about. These were not ordinary Christians. They were ministers, priests, nuns, educators, and theologians who had dedicated themselves to understanding Jews. They came to our seder year after year because my father was one of the pioneers in Christian-Jewish dialogue.

In the 1960s dialogue meant Jews and Christians studying together to understand the differences and similarities of their beliefs. It meant explaining to Christians that, in the eyes of Jews, Christianity did not supersede Judaism and that the religion of the Jews remains a unique and philosophically distinct monotheistic faith. It meant exploring with Christians the religious roots of anti-Semitism, helping them re-examine their contemporary texts to remove references to Jews as killers of Jesus or doomed souls because of a lack of belief in Christ. For Jews such as my father dialogue was a natural response to living as a minority in a Christian-dominated society. It was a way to make one-self understood, and to help create a safer environment for other Jews.

The historic course of Jewish involvement in cross-cultural dialogue changed dramatically after the Six-Day War in 1967. The day after the war began my father frantically tried to gather signatures from his Gentile friends for a newspaper ad in support of Israel, to no avail. He was particularly pained by the lack of support from Black leaders. Along with other rabbis he had marched in Selma, Alabama, during the civil rights battles and assumed that the Black-Jewish alliance was strong and in the interest of both communities.

By the late 1960s that alliance could no longer be taken for granted. The painful rift brought yet another phase of dialogue into Jewish life during the 1970s and 1980s, this time between Blacks and Jews seeking to establish an alliance based on a more in-depth understanding of each other. No longer could issues such as Israel, the Palestinians, South Africa, and, most important, the economic disparity between Jews and Blacks be avoided. Many Black-Jewish groups also moved to the personal level, as participants told and compared their stories of growing up as members of a minority community.

My own work in dialogue began well into this stage in the history of Jewish engagement in cross-cultural communication. I founded the Dialogue Project between American Jewish and Palestinian Women in 1989, after the outbreak of the Palestinian intifada. My goal was to build an understanding between mainstream women leaders from both communities. Although it now seems obvious, it wasn't until years later that I realized the connection between my work and my father's. Both come from a commitment to breaking Jews' historic isolation from other peoples. This isolation is certainly a result of anti-Semitism, and it serves to reinforce it.[1]

My father and I came to the process of dialogue from very different directions. He was a leader in the Jewish community (as National Director of Inter-religious Cooperation for the Anti-Defamation League); I was a community organizer active in grassroots efforts to bring together low-income Whites and Blacks on issues of housing, neighborhood development, and community empowerment. I left community organizing to work for Middle East peace because it was an issue that deeply affected me personally. Before I knew it I was promoting dialogue as a means of bridging the tremendous ideological and political gaps between American Jews and Arabs, as earlier Jewish leaders in the United States had used dialogue to bridge gaps between American Jews and Christians.

The Role of Dialogue

This work in Arab-Jewish relations led me to consider the role of dialogue in our increasingly multiethnic society, and I began to teach the practice of cross-cultural dialogue to diverse groups of community leaders in the United States. Other communities, such as African Americans and Asian Americans, are using dialogue as a method of bridging understanding between communities that are often pitted against one another. One such group, the Afro-Asian Relations Counsel, was founded in Washington, D.C., after Korean grocery store owners came in conflict with their Black customers. They discovered that through intensive discussions they were able to separate the cultural issues from the political ones. Whereas they had previously seen the other community as committed to their downfall and in collusion with the racism they faced in the broader society, through the process of dialogue they were able to stop seeing the other as their enemy. Blacks came to understand that immigrant Koreans were able to succeed in opening businesses because they pool capital and help one another overcome economic obstacles. Koreans came to understand that their ways of showing respect to a stranger are seen as distancing and actually disrespectful in the more outwardly expressive African American community.

Such lessons are important, but they do not go far enough in their impact. In order for dialogue to affect significantly the nature of race relations in our country, it must lead to deeper alliances and actions. For example, one potential project that came out of an African-Asian dialogue suggested that Black and Korean college students do internships in the businesses in each other's community, leading to an exchange of skills and knowledge as well as a sense of joint purpose. A Black-Jewish dialogue group in Washington, D.C., decided to focus on the issue of gun control, holding weekly vigils outside the headquarters of the National Rifle Association as well as lobbying for local legislation.

The ultimate purpose of dialogue is to create new relationships that work to change society. While the process may seem slow to many activists, the underlying thrust is radical. By forging alliances among minority groups where differences have kept them apart, the dialogue process breaks down the ability of the ruling establishment to divide and conquer. If members of minority communities do not allow themselves to be polarized, stronger movements for change can emerge. The point is not to recreate the civil rights alliance as it was, but to come together with a new understanding and create new movements that are stronger and have a heightened awareness of the richness of diversity.

Dialogue can also be used to bridge groups that are ideologically opposed to each other. Over the past few years there have been attempts to bring together members of the pro-choice and the pro-life communities.[2] Some of these groups have found common ground on issues such as the need to improve adoption practices, the need for better access to sex education, and the need to better support economically vulnerable families.

The purpose of dialogue is not to obliterate legitimate conflict between groups. Dialogue participants are often aware that the people to whom they are talking are their opponents in a political battle. Each side maintains its right to continue to wage the political fight at every level; participation in a dialogue is not a truce. Yet dialogue enables groups to search for new options and possibilities and to create win-win solutions that were not considered before.

Jewish Participation in Dialogue

In many ways dialogue comes naturally to Jews. Several years ago I attended a workshop for Jews, Christians, and Muslims in Louisiana, led by the renowned Rev. Scott Peck. The purpose was ambitious: to build community with each other. Each group responded differently to the task. The Christians spoke in soft, conciliatory tones. The Muslims were guarded as they rationally explained Islam to the group. The Jews jumped in and bared our chests. We spoke about our own personal dilemmas, argued with fellow Jews, revealed our psychological pain, and challenged the other groups on basic assumptions—all without stopping to catch our breath.

We were at home in that process: this is the water we swim in. Dialogue fits Jewish notions of how you make change in the world: you talk, you study, you discuss, you argue. The Talmud itself is the record of an internal dialogue between rabbis as they tried to figure out the controversial issues of their day. Perhaps, it is no surprise that Sigmond Freud, the father of psychotherapy, was a Jew. What could be more Jewish than having a dialogue with the different parts of yourself?

As members of a minority cultural and religious group in an increasingly multicultural society, Jews have important talents to bring to the table. Jewish community efforts at dialogue with Christians,

Blacks, and Arabs give us a body of experience that provides lessons to others embarking on this road. We are not afraid to talk to our adversaries and venture into areas that others fear, believing in the healing power of building relationships.[3]

Yet I have also noticed that the comfort Jews have with dialogue can lead to some serious problems between ourselves and the other groups we wish to engage. First, we sometimes have a need to control the agenda and are often fearful of giving up this control to the will of the group. Perhaps this comes from our fear of being used, which we have in common with other oppressed groups. Our history makes us mistrustful of those who have not already shown their allegiances to us. But because we Jews are often the initiators of dialogue, we need to remember that for the effort to be successful we have to overcome our fears and allow the power and control to be shared.

Second, Jews are often more willing to talk than to take concrete political action. To many Jews sitting and talking until agreements are hammered out is a natural part of the dialogue process. We believe that our very survival depends on being understood. Our yardstick of success is often whether we think learning is taking place on both sides. In addition, while early Christian-Jewish dialogue was often motivated by Jewish concerns for our own safety, dialogue with African American or American Arab partners requires a commitment to their security needs as well. At this point in history they often feel more urgent about their political and economic situation than we do as Jews. We therefore need to note that, to others, "just talking" is often seen as useless and a dialogue is successful only if it leads to concrete political action.

Because of these different expectations and tendencies, it is important to carefully craft the dialogue experience. Every group should pay attention to the steps involved in creating a dialogue, and should build the experience according to the particular needs of their group. What follows are some suggestions.

Setting Up a Dialogue

One important principle applies to all successful dialogues: *all sides must feel empowered by the process.* This means that they should feel that their needs are being considered in the development of the dialogue group. This principle needs to be followed in making decisions on such issues as sponsorship, leadership, place, participant list, development of the agenda, and funding.

There are many other issues to consider over the life of a dialogue group that relate to this sense of empowerment. Should the group be public or confidential, short-term or long-term, discussion-only or action-oriented? Answers to these questions often reveal the important differences between participating communities. Resolving them collectively could be the most important test of the success of a dialogue experience.

I like to talk of a "leadership partnership" as an important ingredient in dialogue. When I started the dialogue between American Jewish and Palestinian women, I put a great deal of energy into building a relationship with my counterpart in the Palestinian community, Najat Arafat Khelil, president of the Arab Women's Council. Najat and I have spent many hours together, building both our friendship and our work relationship. We have lived through political crises together, including the intifada and the Gulf War, working to understand each other's perspective. It hasn't always been easy, and there were times when we shouted at each other or went for days without talking. We always knew, however, that we would work through it because we have a deep commitment to each other and to the success of our group. I believe that this was the glue that held our project together. Najat and I modeled that it is possible to work through issues and to bridge the ideological, religious, and political gaps.

Due to the sensitive nature of the dialogue experience, it is important to use a consultatory leadership style in order to involve other people in the decision-making process. I recommend that early on leaders set up a steering committee with an equal number of members from the different communities.[4] This committee can help decide all structural issues for the group, setting up the agenda for meetings and deciding on joint projects.

Raising funds can be particularly challenging for Jews engaged in dialogue with other minority groups. Jews in the United States often have more access to funding sources and more experience in philanthropy than people of other constituencies. In addition, the Jewish members may themselves be wealthier. It is therefore important to establish early on that the act of giving is valued over the amount that a person gives. All parties in the dialogue need to be involved in the fundraising efforts, even if the dollar amounts they are able to raise are different. Some groups make the mistake of allowing one community to raise the funds, with the understanding that the other community will take on other pieces of the work. This can lead to a power imbalance and a difference in the sense of ownership of the project. A more equitable solution is to engage each community in raising what it can in the manner that it is most accustomed. In addition, the two communities can meet together with foundation boards or donors, helping expand and share access to funding sources.

Agreeing on Goals and Expectations

There are five potential goals for a dialogue group:

1. *Building community and celebrating differences*: Members of an organization or community come together to learn about each other's culture. The sharing of music, dance, food, and life stories is used as a means of building a sense of camaraderie.
2. *Healing pain and building understanding*: Participants are given an opportunity to voice their unique feelings and perspectives on a given problem or experience. This kind of open dialogue can be used after a traumatic event occurs in a community, or as a means of hearing from diverse people within a common institution.
3. *Problem solving about areas of conflict*: A more in-depth discussion occurs to find new solutions to intercommunal conflicts. Participants move from seeing the problem as a conflict between them, to seeing it as a common dilemma, engaging in joint problem solving.
4. *Modeling a different relationship*: Community leaders make a conscious commitment to demonstrate to the broader community that a more positive type of relationship is possible between members of their groups. They show by example that a relationship of mutual respect can lead to alternative ways of interacting.
5. *Action toward political change*: Dialogue participants embark on a joint political campaign, organizing their communities to change the conditions that lead to separation between groups.

> Groups sign a joint statement, hold press conferences, organize rallies, support candidates, and engage in other visible activities designed to build coalitions on issues where there is common ground.

The most important criterion for a successful dialogue is that the goals and expectations be clear from the beginning. It is legitimate to say that you just want to celebrate differences, and to accomplish those goals you organize a potluck dinner or a cultural event. It is also alright to build a dialogue around problem solving without going to the next stage of action, *as long as this is clear from the beginning.* But most leaders and community activists will want to be engaged in dialogue for the purpose of ultimately taking action. Be aware of differences in expectations that need to be acknowledged and managed along the way.

In addition, dialogue organizers need to be persistent and at the same time pay close attention to timing. Does your group want to attract publicity or remain confidential? Sometimes agreeing on stages of public exposure is helpful. For example, members may choose to first write or speak about a dialogue only within their own communities. As the project proceeds, the group can then decide to go more fully public.

Exploring Areas of Agreement and Disagreement

No issue is too hot for a group to handle, as long as it is managed well. Whether members of a project are high-profile leaders or grassroots community members, the group can address highly charged and emotional issues without falling apart. By setting some guidelines and ground rules a group can create a more open and safe environment that allows difficult topics to be discussed. For example, a group may decide early on to engage in dialogue with the assumption that the two communities will not be able to reach agreement on everything that divides them. Two groups with differing interpretations of the historical developments leading to their current tensions may never come to agreement on the precise "facts" (or the significance of certain "facts") of that history. However, the joint group can make a commitment to trying to understand how each party sees the past. One concrete suggestion is to have two presentations on the history of the conflict from each community's perspective; then make a commitment to each other to put the disagreement over history aside, and direct the group's energy toward building agreement on a common future.

Dealing with difficult issues means allowing for the expression of emotion. For example, on many occasions a woman has cried in our group and we understand that this is an important part of the process. No one tries to quiet her down or insist that she stop the tears in order to participate as an "adult." We understand that the pain being expressed will be healed only when it is acknowledged, and that is something people can do for each other. This is one of the particularly important skills that women bring to the dialogue process. Sensitivity and kind words to someone who is in pain can make a great deal of difference and enable the person to continue to participate. Allowing for emotional expression can help people see each other as human beings, and can break through deep political divisions to arrive at a new level of understanding.

Using an experienced facilitation team will often enable a group to handle difficult conflicts more successfully. This special team can include members of each community (such as the organizers), who can understand what the participants are going through and detect any unexpressed emotions. You may also want to add a third member of the team from outside both communities who is able to provide support to both groups.[5] In addition, the facilitation team can help the group reexamine its guidelines for dialogue. These guidelines should be periodically reviewed by the group, so that any necessary changes can be made. For example, a group may decide to add to its original guidelines that certain words not be used if they are found to be inflammatory to one of the parties. These suggestions help ensure safety even when the issues feel scary.

Another important ingredient for safety is to allow for separate caucuses. Caucusing means that there are times when the members of each community will go into separate meetings to check in with members of their own group. For example, if you as a Jewish participant have a strong reaction to what a member of the other group has said, before getting angry you can discuss your feelings with your fellow Jews, ask for their advice, and hear their perspectives. Then, if you decide to confront the issue in the dialogue, you will feel on stronger footing and will have had a chance to work out some of your own emotions first.

Sometimes the caucuses can be given a task. Specific tasks will, of course, differ depending on the nature of the relationship between the groups. However, readers may find the following exercise helpful: ask each caucus to come up with potential solutions to a problem. When the caucuses return from their private space, write the solutions on flip-charts for the joint group to see. Take some time to explain, question, and analyze these visions. Often, this session generates points of agreement that can serve as a basis for future discussions. Another task for each caucus may be to come up with a list of questions for the other side. This allows both groups to summarize what they do not yet understand, and helps turn confusions or nagging doubts into questions that the other side can deal with in a straightforward manner.

Political action engaged in by dialogue groups can take many forms. A dialogue group can decide to issue a joint statement on principles, hold a press conference, lobby political leaders together, or lead their communities in organizing on a specific political issue. The Dialogue Project found that effective action was to take on joint speaking ventures before organizations from both the Jewish and the Arab American communities. When you go out into the community as a joint team you are modeling a different kind of relationship between the two groups, and you have the opportunity to change hearts and minds.

Furthermore, the example of good relationships between members of two groups experiencing serious conflict provides hope to people who feel despair and becomes, in and of itself, an important political act. Our group ultimately took a joint trip to Israel, the West Bank, and Gaza in 1993. We came at a time of particular difficulty, just after the expulsion by the Israeli government of four hundred Palestinians into southern Lebanon. Although there was much despair about peace in both communities, we found that our presence communicated hope. Even those who were more hard-line in their position told us to continue our activities.

Expecting Crisis

Every dialogue group can expect to go through at least one major crisis. In fact, every dialogue meeting will have its own minicrisis; that is the time when the group is experiencing some chaos as it faces unresolved issues. This is the nature of group interaction, but it is also endemic to the dialogue process. If you expect a crisis then you will not be overwhelmed when it happens, nor will you experience the crisis as a failure. Instead, the crisis becomes an opportunity for each group to go deeper and to further understand the nature of their relationship to each other.

When the Dialogue Project was on its joint trip to the Middle East, our major crisis involved visiting Yad Vashem, the Holocaust memorial museum. We had agreed ahead of time that each community could show the other community its homeland in any way they chose. The Jewish women decided a visit to the museum should be on the agenda. Palestinians, however, were reluctant to go. They already knew about the Holocaust and felt that its memory had been used politically against their community despite the fact that they were not responsible for its occurrence. The tensions this caused the group were resolved only after a visit to a refugee camp in Gaza. The Palestinian women could see that the Jews were deeply affected by the visit, and they were moved by the Jewish women's recognition of their pain. They then told the Jewish women that they would go to Yad Vashem, because they understood the need to witness each community's pain together. In this case, the group came through this crisis stronger and more assured of each other's commitment to peace.

The Limits of Dialogue

The process of dialogue has its critics. Jonathan Kuttab, a West Bank human rights lawyer who was one of the first Palestinians to meet with Israeli Jews after the 1967 war, speaks of the pitfalls of a "false dialogue."[6] A false dialogue is one where participants are more interested in getting along than in delving into the depths of the conflict. Kuttab warns that dialogue groups may abandon moral positions in the name of compromise. Because of the desire to succeed there may be a tendency to underplay political differences and to focus on more comfortable issues such as mutual stereotypes, which downplay the nature of the oppressive situation. Dialogue participants can be tempted to ignore the realities in their own societies as they attempt to build a bridge to the other side.

Kuttab claims that a key pitfall in dialogue is the assumption of a false symmetry between groups where there is actually a large power imbalance. The basic condition of oppressor and oppressed is ignored, and members of the group are subtly pressured into an acceptance of the status quo. In this sense participants in dialogue can be coopted or misused. Finally, Kuttab charges that dialogue should never be a substitute for action.

Yet Kuttab himself speaks of a dialogue in service of "peace, justice, and reconciliation." By setting up a process that empowers both sides an honest and open exchange can occur. Potentially through the process of exploring the dynamics of conflict, each community and individual will find new sources of power to effect political change.

Conclusion

When Israeli Prime Minister Rabin and Palestine Liberation Organization (PLO) Chairman Arafat shook hands on an initial agreement, it was perhaps the most powerful example yet of the value and special contribution of dialogue. The agreement would not have been signed if it were not for the Norwegians who brought Israeli academics together with members of the PLO for nonstop meetings in mansions and apartments throughout their country. Their walks together in the woods, meals together, and late-night laughs were crucial to the process. These encounters followed hundreds of dialogue meetings, conferences, and informal living room discussions between thousands of Jews and Palestinians over the course of the past twenty-five years. What official diplomats could not accomplish in suits and ties in formal negotiations, others made happen away from the camera's eye. The lessons they learned "filtered up" to the governmental level and saw their way into a historic agreement. This type of citizen dialogue known as "track two diplomacy"[7] augments governmental efforts and can keep the reconciliation process moving forward when "track one diplomacy"—official diplomacy—stagnates.

In a world where interethnic, interreligious, and intercommunal conflicts threaten global security, conflict resolution methods are needed more than ever. Here in the United States, as our country becomes more multicultural, building an understanding among groups is essential for our cohesion as a nation. The experience that Jews bring is a vital resource. The more we as Jews can hone our skills, improve in problem areas, and become conscious about what makes dialogue work, the more we will be able to make a valuable contribution to a multicultural society. Dialogue is the wave of the future.

Notes

1.   The connection between breaking down Jewish isolation and safety for Jews may not have been fully understood at the time, but Eva Fogelman in her study of Christian rescuers of Jews during the Holocaust found that 28 percent were people who had a close connection to Jews or a strong, positive feeling about the Jewish people. See Eva Fogelman, *Conscience and Courage* (New York: Anchor Books/Doubleday, 1994).

2.   Carol Becker, Laura Chasin, Richard Chasin, Margaret Herzing, and Sallyann Roth, "The Public Conversation Project Focuses Dialogue on Abortion," *Family Therapy News,* June 1992.

3.   There is even a dialogue taking place between children of survivors of the Holocaust and children of the Third Reich. These brave souls, led by two Boston women, one Jewish and one German, have traveled with their group "People Helping People: Face to Face," to Germany to bring their message of reconciliation to high school students. The students were so moved by their joint presentation that some of them insisted on going with the American group to Buchenwald, where they prayed together.

4.   Contrary to common belief, a dialogue does not necessarily imply a discussion between only two groups. The word "dialogue" can be traced from the Greek words *dia,* which means "through," and *logos,* which means "words or reason" (William Morris, *The American Heritage Dictionary of the English Language* [Boston: Houghton Mifflin, 1969]). In our multicultural society we may need to engage with a variety of groups at any one time, further enriching but also complicating the process.

5.   The facilitation team for the Dialogue Project comprised myself, Najat Arafat Khelil, and Donna Jenson.

6.   Jonathan Kuttab and Edy Kaufman, "An Exchange on Dialogue," *Journal of Palestine Studies* 17, no. 2 (Winter 1988).

7.   The phrase "track two diplomacy" was coined by former U.S. ambassador Joseph V. Montville. See Joseph V. Montville, "The Arrow and the Olive Branch: A Case for Track Two Diplomacy," in *The Psychodynamics of International Relationships,* vol. 2, *Unofficial Diplomacy at Work,* ed. V. Volkan, J. Montville, and D. Julius (Lexington, Mass.: Lexington Books, 1990).

Of Haiti and Horseradish

TOBA SPITZER

When I arrived in Philadelphia for my first semester at the Reconstructionist Rabbinical College, I had no idea I'd be traveling to Haiti in a few months. I had decided to become a rabbi after wrestling with how to fulfill two desires: to work for justice in the larger society and to work for the survival of Judaism and the Jewish people. As I began my studies at RRC, becoming increasingly immersed in Jewish study and Jewish community, I started looking for what Judaism has to teach about how and why we should make commitments beyond our own ethnic/religious group. In a world in which—until very recently—Jews made up a distinct and semi-autonomous community, Jewish imperatives to care for the poor and needy, to strive for a godly measure of justice, were generally concerned with other Jews. Where in Judaism, I wondered, is there a model for building coalitions for social justice? Is it possible to articulate, in the particular language of Jewish texts and tradition, a commitment to a broad-based struggle against oppression?

It was in Haiti that I began to find answers to some of my questions. On February 14, 1993, I stepped off a plane in Port-au-Prince— the culminating moment of months of organizing a rabbinic mission to protest the abuses of the military regime and to support Haiti's prodemocracy movement. Seven rabbis and three rabbinical students, we were the only white faces in the crowd descending onto the tarmac. The warm breeze was a welcome contrast to the wintry New York air we had left behind; the mountains ringing the airport provided a beautiful backdrop. Later we would find out that these hills had been almost completely denuded of trees, logged by corporations to make turpentine or cut down by poor people desperate to get a few dollars for wood and charcoal. But in those first few minutes we simply enjoyed the gorgeous sunset, pink and orange bands settling behind the hills.

In spite of our trepidation we made it through customs and past the soldiers without incident. As we climbed into a dilapidated truck and began the ride to our motel, Haiti's notorious poverty became immediately apparent. The road was in complete disrepair; the pigs and cows rummaging in the garbage that lined the streets were unbelievably thin. It was the beginning of an almost surreal five days in a country of contrasts: staggering poverty amid incredible beauty; seemingly endless oppression matched by steadfast determination and hope; the pride of the world's first independent Black republic clashing with the degradation of the hemisphere's poorest country.

I had begun planning this trip the previous September, during the High Holidays, in the course of a conversation with a good friend who has for many years been involved in Haitian solidarity work. It had been one year since Jean-Bertrand Aristide was ousted by a coalition of Haiti's military and economic elite. President Aristide had gone into exile, but many of his supporters remained in Haiti. This prodemocracy movement had sent out a call for delegations of international observers to help document violations of human rights by the military regime and to build international support for Aristide's return. As my friend told me about the various groups that had already sent delegations, I realized that the majority had an affiliation with a Christian church or identified themselves as Christian. An explicit Jewish presence in the solidarity movement for Haitian democracy was seemingly nonexistent.

This came as something of a surprise, for a number of prominent Jewish organizations had been the first to speak out on behalf of the Haitian boat people fleeing the violence of the military regime. Scenes of Haitian refugees being denied entry to the United States, sent back to persecution and possible death, evoked memories of Jews fleeing Nazi terror and being denied safe haven on these shores. The organized Jewish community was vocal in its opposition to the Bush administration's policy of turning the refugees back or detaining them in camps. A staff member of the Jewish Federation in Miami told me that those turning out to protest the treatment of the boat people in that locale were "the Haitians and the Jews." Yet the Jewish community's leadership on behalf of the Haitian boat people had not translated into active support of the prodemocracy movement in Haiti. The plight of the refugees was symptomatic of a much larger problem—the ongoing attempt by the military and the economic elite in Haiti to abort any effort to establish real democracy. If one truly wanted to address the suffering of the Haitian people, it was necessary to confront this deeper issue.

The call for international observers provided an opportunity to help promote democracy, and so I decided to try to organize a rabbinic delegation to Haiti. I had a number of reasons for bringing a group of rabbis and not a broader Jewish delegation. One reason was purely tactical: since much of the purpose of the trip was to raise awareness about the Haitian situation in the United States, a rabbinic delegation seemed sufficiently out of the ordinary to garner some attention from the press. Another reason was the central role played by clergy in the Haitian struggle for democracy (Father Aristide being the most powerful example), and the importance of bringing other clergy to stand in solidarity with the Haitian priests, nuns, and ministers.

Most important was my own motivation in wanting to organize such a delegation. I was still in the process of digesting my decision to leave the secular world of progressive organizing and to work for social justice within the context of the organized Jewish community. The Christian clergy in Haiti—vocal opponents of social and economic injustice, speaking a distinctly religious language of love and hope—offered me inspiration and a model for my own vision of the rabbinate. I wanted to see the workings of liberation theology up close, to meet and to learn from the Haitian clergy, and to bring other rabbis to learn from them as well.

I was overwhelmed by the positive response to the letter I sent out describing the project. After what seemed an endless series of phone calls and letters to and from rabbis from the four major branches of American Judaism, trying to find a handful who could actually get away for the same five days, the group ended up consisting of seven rabbis from the Conservative, Reconstructionist, and Reform movements, two students from the Hebrew Union College in New York, and myself. Three months after the first letters went out, we were on a plane to Haiti.

Why Have You Come?

We arrived in Port-au-Prince a year and a half after President Aristide had been deposed. Many priests and activists who had returned from exile in 1986, when the regime of Jean-Claude "Baby

Doc" Duvalier ended, were again in hiding. The coup had destroyed
the tentative gains of Aristide's seven months in office. Thousands of
civilians had been killed in the weeks immediately following the coup,
and tens of thousands were in internal exile. The priest who served as
our host in Port-au-Prince was unable to return to his hometown,
which he had fled six months earlier. An ineffective international em-
bargo was depriving poor Haitians in the countryside of medicine and
food, while a few rich families and the military hoarded goods and
quadrupled prices.

Our group came to Haiti to witness firsthand the effects of the
military regime and to help create, simply through our presence, a
"safe space" for prodemocracy organizing. For five days we met with
clergy, educators, and human rights activists; visited upper-class
neighborhoods and the slums of Port-au-Prince; and learned as much
as we could about Haiti's history and culture. We were told repeatedly
about Haiti's successful slave revolt two hundred years earlier, and the
Haitian people's subsequent success in maintaining their own form of
African culture and religion. Haiti is a deeply religious society; at one
point we were told that "Everyone is Catholic, and everyone is
Voodoo." As Jews, we appreciated how the strength of their cultural
traditions had sustained the Haitian people through centuries of economic and political oppression.

We also learned about recent history—life in Haiti since the 1991
coup. We heard stories of people being arrested and tortured merely
for mentioning Aristide's name; we met a young woman whose
mother had been imprisoned and beaten by the army for the daughter's crime of organizing a memorial Mass for an Aristide supporter
killed in prison. In all of our meetings we were received with an abundance of warmth, respect, and appreciation. Yet we were repeatedly
asked, "Why are you here?"—by which they meant, "Why has a group
of Jews come to Haiti?"

We had a few immediate answers. As Americans, our government
was implicated in the current situation in Haiti. As Jews, our community had been horrified to see, once again, refugees denied entry to the
United States and sent back to oppression and even death. But over the
course of many conversations, another, perhaps deeper, answer began
to emerge. Somewhat to our own surprise, we found ourselves referring most often to the Israelite exodus from Egypt and our tradition's
imperative to remember that experience. Perhaps not coincidentally

our trip fell, in the yearly cycle of reading the Torah, in the middle of the book of Exodus. There in Haiti the Biblical tale of slavery and halting steps toward a promised land, of prophetic leadership and the difficulties of creating a free nation, took on an immediate and forceful reality in a way none of us in the delegation had expected.

In Christian liberation theology, the story of the exodus provides the paradigmatic Biblical example of God as Liberator, as champion of the oppressed. For the Haitian clergy with whom we met, the Exodus story was not only a powerful religious metaphor; it reflected the underlying reality of their experience. Like the Israelite slaves, the Haitians were struggling to throw off the bonds of hundreds of years of oppression, and were marching slowly through the desert with Aristide, their prophet, at the head. For those of us in the rabbinic delegation, the Exodus was mythic history, a narrative of movement from slavery to freedom that continues to define our understanding of ourselves as Jews and to shape our relation to the world. The Haitians spoke about the immediacy of their current enslavement and the hope that our—Jewish—history holds for their future. We told the Haitians that because we once were "strangers" in the land of Egypt, we were compelled to stand by others in their struggles. Our presence in Haiti made real for the Haitians the triumph of the exodus from Egypt, the possibility of making it to the promised land. The Haitians' gift to us was a lived experience of Torah, glowing with intensity—our own text and history, refracted back to us through a new lens.

Seders and Solidarity

The Haitian activists charged us to bring a message back to the United States: to tell our communities about the reality of suffering under the military regime and the urgent need for action. Once back in the States, we did our best to add our voices to those in the press and on Capitol Hill calling for sanctions against the de facto government. We also decided to continue sharing our people's stories, our work of mutual learning and empowerment, by organizing Passover seders focused on the situation in Haiti.

Passover is the Jewish holiday of liberation, when Jews are called upon to remember and recount the redemption from slavery in Egypt. Since the late 1960s the format and themes of the traditional Passover

seder have been used by progressive Jews to speak out on contemporary issues. With its commemoration of struggle and celebration of renewal, the Passover seder has provided a wonderful vehicle to bring
together Jews and non-Jews to protest racism and economic injustice,
to express a commitment to Jewish feminism, to welcome into sanc-
tuary Central American refugees and criticize U.S. foreign policy, and
to speak out for peace between Israelis and Palestinians (see the selected bibliography of issue-oriented modern *haggadot*).

Two months after the rabbinic delegation returned from Haiti,
twenty-five Haitians and twenty-five Jews in Philadelphia sat down
together for an Haiti Solidarity Seder. The four of us from the delegation who had planned the event were careful to ensure that it would
balance the experience of a Passover seder with a telling of the Haitian
story of bondage and freedom. We limited the number of those who
could attend, and pledged that no more than half would be Jews. We
then worked with a few members of the city's Haitian community to
solicit input and participants. Using the structure of a traditional seder,
we wove together themes of Jewish liberation with Haitian history
and culture. For each of the four cups of wine, we spoke of a moment
of liberation in Jewish history and a moment of liberation in Haitian
history. For the first cup, we recounted the Haitian slave revolt and national independence, and the Israelite liberation from slavery in Egypt;
for the second, the adoption of the 1987 Haitian Constitution and the
establishment of the state of Israel; for the third, the election of President Aristide and the liberation of Jewish women; and for the fourth,
final cup, two hopes for the future—the return of democracy to Haiti
and Jewish liberation from anti-Semitism and self-hate. Alongside the
telling of the exodus from Egypt, a member of the Haitian community spoke of Haiti's long struggle for freedom, beginning with
the historic slave revolt in 1791. We sang songs in Hebrew, Yiddish,
and Creole, and ate matzah and horseradish along with Haitian deli-
cacies. For all of us, Jews and Haitians, it was a new and powerful
experience.

In organizing the rabbinic delegation and the solidarity seder, I
did more than just learn about Haiti and its struggle for democracy: I
grew as a Jew. I had taken a significant step in bringing together the religious and political aspects of my Jewish identity and in discovering
a Jewish paradigm for cross-cultural solidarity and commitment to
social justice. This paradigm speaks out of the Passover tradition itself.

The Passover seder is the ritualized fulfillment of the Torah's injunction to the Israelites to tell of the redemption from slavery to their children, and to keep telling this story through the generations. The question for American Jews has become: Why, after thousands of years, do we keep telling this story? Why does the tradition command to us to say, "I was a slave," when the majority of us live lives of relative privilege and freedom?

During the Passover seder we sing this sentence: "avadim hayinu, ata b'nei chorin" ("we were slaves, now we are free people"). The Passover tradition emphasizes the necessity of remembering both our oppression and our liberation, and of giving those memories power in our lives. "Avadim hayinu" (we were slaves): the experience of being oppressed is both past and ever-present, for no matter how distant it might feel to many of us, we must never forget that experience. The seder reminds us of the long history of Jewish oppression, from ancient Egypt to medieval Spain to twentieth-century Europe. In telling the story, each of us is forced to acknowledge the deep effects of anti-Semitism, whether one is a survivor of the Holocaust or has never experienced overt anti-Jewish discrimination. The legacies of hurt and shame live on within each of us, and so each person must tell of being a slave in Egypt as if it is her or his own personal story—because it is each of our stories.

"Ata b'nei chorin" (now we are free people): yet even as we acknowledge oppression in the past and in our lives today, we also recognize and celebrate our liberation as a people and our own individual roles in the struggle for continuing liberation. Redemption is real; we experienced it. As we discovered in Haiti, this legacy of hope is our Jewish gift. The memory of being freed once has propelled us to work for the redemption of the entire world. If slavery is both past and present, then freedom is past, present, and future.

Thus the Passover imperative is, first, to acknowledge how as a people and as individuals we have been hurt, and to celebrate how we have struggled to be free. But what do we then do with this knowledge, this memory? The book of Exodus commands us: "do not oppress the stranger among you, because you know the heart of the stranger, for you were strangers in the land of Egypt." Our particular Jewish experience demands from us that we stand in solidarity with others struggling to escape bondage. The message of this tradition is that we stand in solidarity not simply because we are charitable people and want to help; we do it not because good deeds will get us into heaven. We do not even do it so that evil won't befall the Jews again. We struggle alongside others because deep in our hearts we know what it is not to have freedom. That knowledge drives us to fight for freedom and justice for others who suffer, because we feel it as if it were ourselves.

Illuminations

In the course of organizing the rabbinic delegation, I happened to see this sign hanging on the wall of the Washington Office on Haiti: "If you have come here to help me, you are wasting your time. But if you have come because your liberation is bound up with mine, then let us work together." This is the core of the hard lesson of working with others to achieve peace and justice. But since "liberation" is not necessarily congruent with what I might understand as my self-interest, first I need to understand what liberation means for me, and then to discover in what ways it is "bound up with" the liberation of others.

What I learned in Haiti and at the seder is that in working with another people, we can open up windows that let new light shine in on our experience and our tradition, a light by which we can see more clearly where we are and where we are heading. The following are three distinct moments when we, Jews and Haitians, helped illuminate each other's path to freedom.

  1. Before going to Haiti, I often had difficulty relating to the psalms in the morning prayers that speak of God's justice in terms of a vengeful, violent uprooting of evil from this world: "Let praise of God be on their lips, and a double-edged sword in their hands; to execute judgment on the godless, to bring punishment upon the nations, to bind their kings in chains and put their princes in irons" (from Psalm 149). Yet as I stood outside my motel room each morning in Haiti, praying quietly out of a traditional prayerbook, I found myself caught up in the power of these ancient words. In a country where evil was embodied in the ruling junta, where the effects of that evil were rampantly evident in torture, rape, and endless murders, I urgently wished for the fierce hand of God to sweep the evil

away. I now understood how people had been sustained for millennia by these words, Jews and non-Jews for whom the effects of human evil were neither abstract nor benign. I felt the tradition's wisdom in giving daily voice to this longing for just retribution—not so much a call to violence as an outlet for deep cries of pain and frustration.

2. At the end of our trip, our delegation had the privilege of attending a meeting of the Conference of Haitian Religious, an organization of priests and nuns that had been consistently outspoken in its protest against the coup leaders. Over this issue the Conference was in direct conflict both with the Haitian bishops and with the Vatican, the only government in the world to recognize the Haitian military regime. As he spoke to the Catholic clergy about the message of the Torah portion that week, one of the rabbis emphasized the obligation for Jews to treat the "stranger" with justice, for once we were strangers in the land of Egypt. He spoke of how the Haitians had become strangers in their own land, and, more pointedly, how these clergy had become strangers in their own church. After the presentation, a few of the nuns came up to him and quietly pointed out that the papal nuncio had been sitting in the room when he made that last comment. The rabbi started to apologize, but the nuns shook their heads and thanked him for giving voice to what they could not, repeating his words to themselves with satisfaction.

3. At the Haiti Solidarity Seder, when it came time to eat the maror (the bitter herbs), some of the Haitians seemed a bit puzzled as we offered them a taste of horseradish. But one woman paused and looked at the bowl filled with ground white root, and asked the Jewish woman sitting across from her: "I'm supposed to eat this because of the tears, so that when I eat it I remember Haiti and cry?" Her tablemate nodded, and the Haitian woman stuffed a large spoonful of horseradish in her mouth, tears streaming down her cheeks. A year later, the Jewish woman told me this story, its impact still resonating in her voice.

How is my liberation bound up with yours? When in facing your experience, my own spiritual tradition becomes clarified; when in learning about my history, you can give voice to your anger and your pain. These are the lights we shine for each other.

Community and Partnership

According to Rabbinic midrash, there are only two moments in Jewish history when each and every Israelite encounters the divine in a direct, personal way. These are the moment of revelation—the giving of the Torah at Mount Sinai—and the moment of redemption—the parting of the Red Sea as the Israelites crossed to freedom. As the walls of the sea parted and the people walked through on dry land, each of the freed slaves—from the nursing mothers to the patriarchs of the tribes—gazed upon the God who had saved them. In mythic terms the midrash teaches that the Exodus was a moment of personal, spiritual redemption as well as of national, political liberation—that, in fact, each is necessary for the other. The midrash further teaches that these individual experiences of historical and spiritual liberation are made possible in the context of communal liberation. And so my own crossing of the sea, my own liberation—as a Jew, as a human being—is always "bound up with" the liberation of others.

What I also learn from this midrash is that I will do my work in this world much better if I stand grounded in Jewish community. To the extent that my own tradition and my own history shine in and through me, to that extent I am able to shed light on the struggles of others. And in return, as I learned in Haiti, the experience of working in coalition with others strengthens me and my tradition. But working in coalition is by no means simple, especially when the struggle is closer to home. The American Jewish community has a long way to go in understanding how our physical and cultural survival is intimately bound up with achieving justice for everyone in our society. Sitting on the veranda of our motel in Port-au-Prince, I and others in the rabbinic delegation were struck by how much simpler it was to work on an issue such as democracy in Haiti than on problems affecting African American communities in our own cities. Haitians did not identify us with the oppressor class in their country, and we risked nothing in calling for a radical change in the structure of Haitian society. The violent effects of racism and the complexities of class make it far more complicated for me and for many other Jews to stand in solidarity with

African Americans and with other oppressed people here in the United States than with the Haitian people, hundreds of miles distant.

But despite the gulf that separates me—with my white skin and economic privilege—from so many of the oppressed communities in this country, I do think that we can find ways to work in coalition. In fact, I believe that our survival—as human beings and as Jews—depends on it. The redemption of our own people is no longer sufficient; the entire world and all the peoples in it are in need of redeeming. To work for this redemption as Jews means acting out of a strong sense of identity and pride in being who we are, not out of guilt or shame. It means connecting to those aspects of our tradition that give us strength and provide us with models for struggle, and remembering those times in our history and in our own lives when we have been hurt for being Jews. It means working to really know the heart of the "stranger," being ready to learn from and to follow the lead of others. In this way I believe we can get away from a paternalistic paradigm of "giving" to create instead a model of partnership—partnership for liberation, for survival, for the sake of Judaism, for the sake of the world.

Selected Bibliography

The *haggadah*—literally, "the telling"—is the text used at the Passover seder. In order to tell the full story of the liberation from slavery, the traditional *haggadah* includes material from ancient Rabbinic sources, Biblical passages, songs, and blessings associated with the eating of ritual foods. Today there exist a variety of *haggadot* that include references to more recent Jewish history, along with readings, songs, and poems from many cultures related to the themes of freedom and renewal.

The first published radical *haggadah,* addressing contemporary issues of racial, economic, and social justice and including material from non-Jewish sources, was Arthur Waskow's *Freedom Seder.* The first Freedom Seder was held in Washington, D.C., on April 4, 1969, the one-year anniversary of the assassination of Dr. Martin Luther King Jr. Eight hundred people—Jews, African Americans, white civil rights activists, and others—gathered to commemorate that event and to continue the struggle for justice in America. Since that date, both the Freedom Seder and new *haggadot* have been used in many different communities across the country, addressing a wide variety of social issues, from nuclear disarmament to feminism to homelessness. The following is a brief sample of some feminist and issue-oriented *haggadot* that have been written and compiled over the past twenty-five years. It is not intended to be an exhaustive listing.

Broner, Esther, and Naomi Nimrod. "The Women's Haggadah." In *The Telling*. Ed. Esther Broner. San Francisco: Harper, 1993. A feminist seder as told through the voices of Jewish women of the Biblical and Rabbinic periods.

Cantor, Aviva. "A Jewish Women's Haggadah." In *Womanspirit Rising: A Feminist Reader in Religion*. Ed. Carol P. Christ and Judith Plaskow. San Francisco: Harper and Row, 1979. This *haggadah* supplements a traditional seder with readings on Jewish women's history and experience, from the Bible to modern times.

Homeless beneath the Pyramids: A Haggadah Honoring the Struggle for Housing and Economic Justice. Compiled by Congregation Mishkan Shalom and Philadelphia New Jewish Agenda. Philadelphia, 1990.

Kalechofsky, Roberta. *Haggadah for the Liberated Lamb.* Marblehead, Mass.: Micah Press, 1990. A guide to a vegetarian Passover, motivated by a concern for animal rights.

The Shalom Seders. New York: Adama Books, 1984. This is a compilation of three *haggadot*: the Rainbow Seder, focusing on broad issues of peace and world survival; Children of Abraham, focusing on Israeli-Palestinian reconciliation; and Seder of Liberation, a Jewish feminist *haggadah*.

Sprague, Jane, ed. *San Diego Women's Haggadah*. San Diego: Women's Institute for Continuing Jewish Education, 1980.

Waskow, Arthur. *The Freedom Seder*. New York: Holt, Rinehart and Winston, 1970. Includes songs from the civil rights movement and poetry by Allen Ginsburg, among others.

The Educational Potential

Jews and the Multicultural University Curriculum

EVELYN TORTON BECK

It is a well known principle of dialectical thinking that all attempts to correct errors of the past themselves contain the seeds
of new errors and the likelihood of different distortions. It is in this
light that I interpret the exclusion of Jewish material from the multicultural curriculum as it is currently conceived in North American institutions of learning. This exclusion is especially disturbing in light of
the fact that numerically Jews are indisputably a "minority," totaling
less than 3 percent of the U.S. population. One can only conjecture
that the "myth of the Powerful Jew"[1] makes us appear to be more numerous and far more powerful than we in fact are.

A brief history of the function and purpose of multicultural education in the university may help us tease out possible explanations for
this deliberate exclusion of Jews.

1. *Multicultural education developed in the United States as a strategy to
help society fulfill its promise to those groups that were underrepresented in the
professions and whose history had been previously omitted from the curriculum.*

The underrepresentation of minorities of color in the professions
was perceived to be the fault of our educational system, which did not
offer an inclusive curriculum that would provide the necessary "mir-
roring face" to these populations. The belief was strong that if people
of color (and women in all their diversity) do not see themselves reflected in the curriculum, they would not be able to imagine themselves in the professions or in other positions of power. The Civil
Rights Act of 1964 was meant to ameliorate that exclusion, and it was
hoped that a transformed curriculum would help people of color enter the professions in larger numbers. While Jews could not appropriately be included under that rubric—we have been well represented
in the professions once they were open to us—we nonetheless still

belong under the category of "historically oppressed minority" whose history and contributions to culture have been systematically excluded from the traditional curriculum.

In fact, the institutionalized anti-Semitism of the pre–World War II days that took the form of open discrimination against Jews in housing, jobs, public accommodations, educational opportunities, and social life, and which marked American life prior to World War II has never been addressed publicly, least of all in our educational system.[2] Once the horrors of the concentration camps and the annihilation of the Jews in Europe became public, open anti-Semitism went underground, and now, fifty years after those memories have faded, it is reemerging once again the world over, even in countries like Japan and Poland that have virtually no Jewish populations at all.[3] What is true today in the United States is that Jews in business and professional life (like women of all ethnicities and men of color) face a glass ceiling that prevents them from moving beyond a certain level.

2. *A second foundation for the multicultural curriculum was the growing sense that, in a rapidly shrinking world, it is becoming increasingly necessary to expand students' understandings of other cultures and to recognize that what had been defined as the totality of knowledge was, in fact, only partial.*[4] At the same time, the "melting pot ideology" that promoted cultural homogeneity was being challenged, especially as the post–World War II promise of economic parity was not fulfilled equally for all groups in the United States. In this respect, Jews as a group fared better than most other racial/ethnic minorities, especially when compared to the majority of African Americans. However, this should not lead us to ignore the fact that there are still Jews living well below the poverty line (there are actually many more poor Jews than most people realize). But because all Jews are assumed to be rich, many of these really poor Jews (especially the elderly) living in inner cities are ignored and are never reached by social services.[5]

It is beyond the scope of this essay to address the larger issue of how best to implement multicultural education in institutions, but it is important to note that the existence of special-focus programs (such as Jewish Studies, Women's Studies, African American Studies, Gay/Lesbian Studies) have not assured the inclusion of materials about these populations in the rest of the curriculum. However, I must note that these area studies are themselves in serious need of transformation

with respect to inclusivity. Each of these has its limits: some omit a focus on gender; others omit Jews and people of color; others omit gays
and lesbians. Since the focus of this essay is on Jews, let me note that
Jewish Studies Programs in the university most often define themselves solely in terms of Biblical Studies and do not include either Jewish secular perspectives of Jewish history and culture or materials in
Yiddish or Ladino, or Sephardi culture, or gay men and lesbians, or
women in general.[6]

And while I am certain that we cannot introduce students to all
cultures, I am equally certain that by expanding students' understanding of the world and teaching new ways of seeing, we can break open
the ethnocentrism that is so rampant on college campuses. If we can
teach our students to look more deeply and widely, to see the world's
complexity and to recognize that their own experience is extremely
limited, we will have done a great deal to break the hold of that ethnocentrism. We can do more in this way than if we simply ask students to
immerse themselves in a culture other than their own—a strategy that
is widely used in colleges and universities across the country. And
while I have no objection to such a requirement, I find it does not necessarily result in a transformation of perspective, nor does it provide an
analysis that recognizes that "differences are organized into systems of
inequality, and that groups and individual members of groups have
differential access to power and privilege associated with these differences."[7] To this end I suggest that it is not sufficient to introduce students to cultures other than their own; we must also introduce them to
the complexity of the dynamics of power as they play themselves out
in the field of "differences." This entails an understanding that culture
does not stand outside, but is deeply embedded in, the social structures—having been shaped by, and at the same time, shaping them.[8]

If we begin with the premise that "the personal is political," it
quickly follows that the academic is political too. In entering the debate on multicultural education, we must first acknowledge that we
are currently engaged in a contemporary "Battle of the Books" not
unlike the seventeenth-century debate in which the classicists viru-
lently attacked the modernists. When I studied this quarrel in graduate school, I could not understand the venom these earlier critics of
culture brought to the study of literature and language. I now understand the deeply political nature of this apparently "only" intellectual

quarrel. If we want to enter this debate as Jews, we had better know what larger political issues are at stake, so we at least have a chance for our voices to be heard.

3. *In the 1990s we are still living with the legacy of the ferment of the late 1960s and the many liberation movements that were active at that time,* including the Civil Rights Movement, the antiwar movement (Vietnam), the second wave of the women's movement, the students' rights movement, the lesbian and gay rights movement. While Jews participated in these movements in proportions larger than our numbers in the population, our presence was either not noted or was often negatively marked as "interference" or "taking over." In the 1980s Jews increasingly began to organize as Jews (in New Jewish Agenda, or Women in Black protesting the Israeli mistreatment of Palestinians, or as Jewish lesbians who felt excluded from other Jewish institutions).

Out of this ferment grew the disciplines of Women's Studies, Black (African American) Studies, and programs of "Ethnic Studies." In these projects, especially in Ethnic Studies where race played a major role in conceptualizing the field, Jews were equated with European "whites" and ethnicity was defined to include only the major North American "peoples of color." Of course, these categories are more complex than such a dichotomy allows. For some, however, fear of diluting the antiracist project created resistance to the inclusion of Jews and other minorities, such as gays and lesbians (to a degree, both homophobia and anti-Semitism were at work in these exclusions).

While it cannot be said that Jews were underrepresented in the professions (as were peoples of color), *Jewish contributions to culture have never been included in the Eurocentric curriculum that has perpetuated the most blatant Jew-hating stereotypes. So we are about to be excluded when we were never included in the first place.* Moreover, the stereotypes and distortions of the traditional curriculum have largely gone unchecked. One has only to think of Shylock in *The Merchant of Venice* and Fagin in *Oliver Twist*, the poetry of T. S. Eliot and Ezra Pound to grasp the degree of blatant anti-Semitism that remains unquestioned except by a few fringe groups of Jewish activists whose protests are usually ignored. It is not clear to what extent the anti-Semitism in these works is ever problematized when they are taught.[9]

4. *In the past decade, as a result of powerful political upheavals, we have witnessed major population shifts (which are still in progress), as a result of which the United States is experiencing the influx of people from all parts of the*

globe. Paired with the economic depression set in motion during the Reagan–Bush years, increasingly jobs have become scarce and competition harsh. The anger engendered by economic forces is often aimed at Jews, who have historically been scapegoated as a byproduct of class antagonism. When looked at in terms of the group as a whole, it cannot be denied that Jews have moved upward on the economic scale and have achieved some positions of influence in the relatively open society of the United States.[10] But it is extremely revealing of American Jews' sense of vulnerability that this economic success makes most Jews extremely anxious rather than pleased. Cornel West writes that

> The Jewish case in this country is also quite revealing. On the one hand they are a people whose very physical survival often depended on education and literacy. They are a highly literate people who have put a tremendous premium on interpretive skill and intellectual endeavor. When anti-Semitic barriers began to fall—at special elite institutions only within the last 20 or 30 years—highly talented Jewish men and later Jewish women began to make astonishing entree into institutions they had only recently been excluded from.
>
> However, one does not see the logical movement by Jews from elite educational institutions into the highest levels of corporate America. There are still certain anti-Semitic barriers at the highest corporate levels, even for a group that has a history not only of suffering oppression and exploitation but of intellectual excellence.[11]

The splash made when the first "Jew" was appointed president of Yale University attests to this largely unacknowledged barrier. The "Jewish" seat on the Supreme Court long stood empty (without any visible protest), and was only recently filled by Ruth Bader Ginsburg, whose Jewish identity was the subject of much comment. Ironically, the better Jews do economically, the more anti-Semitism rises and the less seriously it is taken.

5. *In the past decade there has been a sharp rise in hate crimes of all kinds, and on college campuses anti-Semitism has risen more dramatically than any other hate crime—with gay bashing a close second.*[12] On February 8, 1991, and again on January 27, 1994, the *Washington Post* reported that anti-Semitic incidents had doubled in the Washington, D.C. area in the previous years. Such a rise in hate crimes against Jews must be

linked to the economic crisis, with the result that there is a kind of class warfare going on in this country (as evidenced by the looting of Jewish, Korean, and Latino-owned stores in the 1993 LA riots). Issues of social and economic class are also played out on college campuses and have resulted, among other effects, in the baiting of the Jewish woman as "J.A.P" or "Jewish American Princess." This insulting epithet combines sexism with anti-Semitism and forces the Jewish woman to bear the brunt of the class antagonism that historically has fallen on Jewish men.[13]

6. *There is still widespread ignorance of the long history of anti-Semitism (which neither began nor ended with Hitler), which can be viewed as a paradigm of hatred for a people based only on what they supposedly are, not on what they do.* At the same time there has been a rise in revisionist histories that either trivialize the murder of Jews in the Holocaust or deny that it took place at all.[14] A recent poll reveals that one in five Americans find it reasonable to doubt the reality of the Holocaust or believe that the documentation of deaths are exaggerated if not falsified.[15] While this poll remains controversial, its results are nonetheless suggestive in that they mirror the widespread ignorance of the Holocaust found on most college campuses. Yet the Holocaust marks the psyche of all Jews, even those who only minimally identify as Jews and do not participate in Jewish religious practices. This fact is not grasped or appreciated by many non-Jews, even those who do not believe they are in any way anti-Semitic. The result is a failure of empathy that can have serious repercussions in Jewish lives. What is often referred to inappropriately as "Jewish paranoia" may in fact correspond to felt and experienced reality.

7. *Although the Israeli government has considerably softened its position, the militarism of the government under Prime Minister Shamir, coupled with its hardened policies toward the Palestinians (which often resulted in a curtailing of their Civil Rights) led to a conflation of anti-Israeli sentiment with anti-Semitism, especially among some people of color in the United States who identify with the Palestinians.* As a result, the inclusion of Jewish material, or even raising the issue of anti-Semitism, is itself often (mis)interpreted as support for militaristic Israeli policies. The current prospects for a negotiated peace have not altered this stance. While Israel carries a special symbolic significance to Jews the world over, there has been serious political disagreement among Jews and a good deal of protest of Israel's treatment of the Palestinians (both in the United States and in Israel).

8. The debates surrounding the definitions of multiculturalism inevitably lead to the issue of power:Who will have the power to decide and to institution-alize such decisions?

Keeping these multiple contexts in mind, it is important to recognize that we are positioned differently, though we are all sitting in the same boat. Factors of race, ethnicity, gender, age, sexual orientation, religion, social and economic class, disability, and geography mark all of us in different ways.

It is equally important to understand that we are not located *singly* (in only one category), or *simply*, or *statically*; our differences intersect, overlap, crisscross, and shift over time and circumstances. While it may be difficult to "speak" the intersections, we nonetheless experience them in our lives on a daily basis.

We also occupy shifting positions of power (over the course of a lifetime or even within a single day). For example, men who have less access to power because of their racial locations can use male privilege against women of their own group and across lines of difference. Gay men, disempowered by their sexual minority status, may still have access to a variety of class, race, and gender privileges. Women can oppress one another across lines of difference. In what is essentially a Christian country, people of color have access to Christian privilege no matter what their social class.[16] Similarly, in a location where white is dominant, Ashkenazi Jews have the possibility of using white privilege, and this is enhanced if they are able and willing to give up community in order to "pass." Such passing is also available to very light-skinned African Americans and Latina/os.

If I say I am a "white" woman, and a professor with relatively secure socioeconomic status, I have a certain power. If I then say I am also a Jew and a lesbian, anti-Semitism and/or homophobia may come into play and I can immediately lose that power and be open to attack even by other oppressed groups, even by other Jews, or by any people who are in considerably lower socioeconomic positions. Let these examples suffice to make the point of shifting power positionalities.

It is also crucial to remember that, although I am here speaking in terms of "groups," no group—no matter how small in number—is monolithic (except to those who view it from the outside). As an example, I may use a group of Jewish lesbians who met over an extended period of time, only to discover that although they shared much, in fact, they were as diverse as any other group of Jews in terms of differences in Jewish education, degrees of observance, political opinions, social class, and the like.

Especially salient in thinking about group oppression is the fact that while many different groups may be the object of oppression, *not all oppressions are the same.* The consequences of the different positionalities in "the web of domination"[17] change over time and place. Each oppression plays upon a different set of fears; although, historically, there is a remarkable overlap in the projections onto people who are made "Other" by the dominant culture and who have unequal access to power. Yet there is also a specificity for each group that has a history and a material reality. *For this reason, being a member of an oppressed minority does not keep anyone from being oppressive to others.*[18] Jews are anomalously allowed some access within the social structure while, at the same time, we continue to be the target of anti-Semitism. For this reason alone it is essential that Jews be included in any form of multicultural education.

At the heart of this project is the concept of Ethnic Studies. I find this term extremely problematic because it preserves the notion of a "center" against which some are defined as "ethnic" as in "stranger," "exotic," "Other," "different"—from *whom?* Such usage equates "ethnicity" with a kind of permanent outsiderhood, equivalent to the Hebrew *goy.* It lumps together all those "funny folk" who are not part of the dominant culture no matter how numerically small those who dominate may be.

I insist that everyone has an ethnicity—as Isaac Bashevis Singer used to say, "everyone has an address." In response to the discomfort voiced by those of my students who resent any challenge to the status quo and to their own presumed centrality, I say: "No one is *nothing!*" I alert them to the concept of "white racial identity" (which Jews do and do not share, because "white" often assumes Christian identity).[19] However, in spite of my objections to the concept of "Ethnic" Studies as currently defined, so long as such programs continue to exist, I will insist that Jews are properly part of them. A redefinition that might free us from this linguistic trap is the use of the term "ethnic minority studies"[20] which implies "ethnic majority studies" and which would keep us from perpetuating the idea of a single center against which all others are measured.

Although Jewish Studies Programs were in existence in one form or another from the turn of the century, their growth in the 1970s was fueled by the ferment of the late 1960s. Out of this, Ethnic Studies (and other studies that challenged the traditional curriculum) developed and were also spurred by events such as the Six-Day War.[21] It is painful to realize that because Ethnic Studies were, from their inception, linked with the "special interests" of disenfranchised groups, many Jews did not wish Jewish Studies to be linked to Ethnic Studies. But there was also marked resistance to the inclusion of Jews in Ethnic Studies, already in its inception, on the grounds that Jews have been associated with European hegemony, a fallacy I addressed earlier in this essay.

Women's Studies presents a somewhat different problem. One of the major themes of feminist thinking is the necessity of speaking up for oneself, in the knowledge that "the unspoken soon becomes the unspeakable[22]." Mitsuye Yamada makes a similar point in her essay, "Invisibility Is Not a Natural Disaster."[23] It is my contention that in multicultural studies "Jew" remains the unspoken. Refusing to remain invisible takes acts of courage; breaking the silence about our invisibility is a political act that some Jews fear will bring anti-Semitism to the surface. One recent example from my own professional experience should make this point clear.

I recently encountered this kind of anti-Semitism while participating in multicultural workshop in psychology. My calling attention to the parallels between war refugees from South America and Holocaust survivors (both groups resist talking about the trauma and shame surrounding their war experiences and its effects on their children) triggered a negative labeling of a Jewish professional who had not been cooperative on a case (previously none of the professionals had been ethnically marked in any way). In response to my comment, the presenter repeated several times, in a very loud voice, and looking directly at me, " . . . and it was the *Jewish* psychiatrist who did not respond to my calls." When I brought this to her attention, her response was, "But so many Jews are psychiatrists." This led her to make a supposedly humorous remark: "I should have protected myself by changing my name to Fongowitz or Fongstein or Fongberg." In response to my protests (and those of other colleagues who entered the discussion), I received the classic clichéd response, made quite unselfconsciously, "But some of my best friends are Jews. I couldn't be anti-Semitic." This incident was all the more disturbing because the presenter was the head of a multicultural counseling center.

To make the problem even more clear, let me cite some further examples. There are currently upwards of three hundred curriculum transformation projects in existence around the country, and most of them exclude Jewish material. When a few Jews like Franz Kafka, Tillie Olsen, or Sigmund Freud are included, they are rarely taught as if their Jewish identity mattered to the meaning of their texts, creating a different kind of erasure.

In Women's Studies classes, Jewish themes (if included at all) are frequently limited to a negative focus featuring the prayer said every morning by Orthodox men who "Thank God [they were] not born a woman." One of the most extensive studies of women in U.S. history that remains a widely used text in Women's History and Women's Studies includes no discussion of Jewish women's history.[24] As yet, only a handful of Women's Studies texts include Jewish women. Johnetta Coles' *All American Women* and Andersen and Hill's *Race, Class and Gender* are notable exceptions. Ron Takaki's most recent contribution also includes Jews.[25] Pleased as I am to discover these inclusive texts, they also serve to highlight the omissions and I find myself angry to discover how grateful and relieved I feel to be included. From the experiences students share with me, I know the negative impact of such omissions on the identity development of younger people who are at a more vulnerable stage of development.

I find it especially ironic that despite homophobia, there are universities that are willing to include gay and lesbian themes but remain unwilling to include Jews in the multicultural curriculum. Cultures of disability, especially the deaf, have had less difficulty in being included than Jews. And despite resistance to including "white" ethnic groups in Ethnic Studies, Irish Americans and German Americans are often listed while Jews are excluded.

The complexity involved in making decisions of inclusion/exclusion is well demonstrated by one of the few texts that tries to bring together issues of race and gender, Butler and Walter's *Transforming the Curriculum: Ethnic Studies/Gender Studies*,[26] which includes two essays about Jewish Studies. However, such inclusion is undermined in Butler's introduction, in which she argues against the inclusion of Jews in Ethnic Studies in the United States. Instead, the author offers that "within a European context, the study of Semitics and of the European Jew may be viewed as Ethnic Studies. In the American context, it may be argued that because of white-skin privilege, Jewish Americans have been able to assimilate. Their distinguishing feature is their religion." A footnote reminds us that anti-Semitism in this country cannot be equated with that in Nazi Germany or the Soviet Union. But Butler's clarification only confuses the meaning of ethnic identity and does not clarify how it differs from racial identity. "Here [in the United States] it [anti-Semitism] refers to a religious and ethnic prejudice, existing in an entirely different context, altered largely by Jewish white skin privilege, class, and at times, ethnic privilege." Butler here fails to understand the complexity of Jewish identity, in which religion, history, and culture are so intertwined that even a purely secular Jew is likely to celebrate and mark the Jewish festivals. Moreover, she fails to understand the degree to which Jewish history marks every consciously Jewish Jew. Finally, it seems galling that the burden of "passing," which is viewed as a terrible affront to people of color, is here viewed as such an "opportunity" for Jews that it overrides what Wistrich pointedly calls "the longest hatred"[27] under whose shadow even the most "assimilated" U.S. Jews live.

Another illuminating example is offered by the resistance of one specialist in multicultural psychology to including "Jews and anti-Semitism" in her newly formed curriculum. She confessed that she agonized over the decision when I pressed her for a favorable response (which eventually was forthcoming). But the question that continues to haunt me: Why would a person of good will have to *agonize* about the inclusion of Jews? What keeps us out of the public discourse of minorities and issues of oppression and exclusion?[28]

Jews have imbibed this sense of exclusion, and the resulting discomfort about being an open Jew (either secular or religious) has taken its toll in Jewish communities. It is my contention that most Jews walk around with a subliminal fear of anti-Semitism the way most women walk around with a subliminal fear of rape. This may explain why so many academicians with Jewish names do not come out as Jews in the university setting. We may, in fact, have been allowed entry into the academy with the implicit agreement that we not be too visible as Jews. Though they may not know its source, many contemporary Jews seem to follow the admonition given by the (Russian) Hebrew poet Judah Leib Gordon (1831–92), "Be a Jew in your home and a man in the street," as a result of which they do not bring their consciousness of being a Jew to their disciplines. In recent years, scholars located in departments throughout universities have become more vocal about the exclusion of Jews from multicultural education. Nonetheless, many Jews who continue to be actively involved in developing multicultural projects most often "forget themselves."

The case of Women's Studies is instructive, for inclusivity is part of the "platform" of the newly emerging discipline, which is dedicated to fighting against the many "isms" that oppress us. I was part of the creation of that field and am thus familiar with the political dimensions of its curriculum. In fact, I served on the committee that drafted the constitution of the National Women's Studies Association (NWSA) and wrote into the preamble that as educators we accept the responsibility to help create a world that would be safe for women in all their diversities. In the early 1970s most Jews in the association, myself included, were not yet conscious of the need to name anti-Semitism as a separate issue. By the time we came to consciousness in the early 1980s, the Jewish Caucus had formed in response to the absence of Jewish material from conferences and curricula. When we approached the NWSA steering committee to change the constitution, we were stunned to discover that not everyone in the association thought it necessary to give anti-Semitism its specificity, while the "women of color" caucus did not wish to include it under issues of "racism." After heated and difficult discussion, the constitution was amended to include opposition against "anti-Semitism against Arabs and Jews," a solution that seems disingenuous at best, since, in common usage, anti-Semitism undisputedly refers to Jew-hating. Anti-Arab racism no doubt has its own specificity and could also be included as a separate item. At the time, however, it was clear that the association refused to go on record as being against anti-Semitism for fear it would be viewed as taking a pro-Israel stance.

With the rise in Ethnic Studies Programs, students in some courses report being discouraged from focusing on Jewish themes. If the student feels strong enough to insist, this experience of nonvalidation creates a Jewish identity that is fraught. The assumption that Jews are "only a religion" serves to contain Jewish issues and contributes to Jewish invisibility. As a result, some Jewish students become uncomfortable about being Jews and non-Jewish students learn that Jewish identity is neither speakable nor important enough to be taken seriously.

The larger the silence surrounding the many forms of anti-Semitism, and the more anti-Jewish incidents on campuses are silenced, the greater room there is for the perpetuation of old myths and the creation of new ones (as in the "J.A.P.," where ignorance of both Jewish history and the history of sexism are contributing factors). Negative myths not only affect Jews; they also infect the psyches of those whose minds they inhabit. If non-Jews do not know Jewish history, they also do not know their own, particularly if they are Christian.[29] I am beginning to believe that we need to develop a kind of Jew-affirmative teaching, parallel to the "gay-affirmative" teaching suggested by some psychologists as an antidote to homophobia. It would be my hope that such Jew-affirmative teaching would also include woman-affirmative and gay-/lesbian-/bisexual-affirmative perspectives, with awareness of color and class differences, or it cannot be fully effective for all Jews. We need to encourage Jewish students to feel good about being Jews. While some believe that Jewish invisibility served to ward off anti-Semitism in the early years of this century, the strategy worked only up to a point. In spite of the fact that Alan Dershowitz writes as if Jewish women did not exist, his perspective on American Jews is useful. He finds that we have accepted citizenship at the price of limiting our expectations, as, for example, his discovery of the widespread belief among Jews and non-Jews (which I have replicated among my peers) that the United States will never elect a Jewish president. He concludes that Jews would do well to have more, rather than less, *chutzpah*.[30] Perhaps this is the time to stop letting invisibility serve us. Perhaps it is time to teach our students that it is possible to be alive and Jewish and doing well—all at the same time—without fear of reprisal or retribution. And as teachers, we must begin with ourselves.

Notes

1.   E. Willis, "The Myth of the Powerful Jew," in *Beginning to See the Light: Pieces of a Decade* (New York: Alfred A. Knopf, 1982), pp. 228–44.

2.   M. Seltzer, *Kike*, Ethnic Prejudice in America series (New York: World, 1972). L. Dinnerstein, *Anti-Semitism in America* (New York and Oxford: Oxford University Press, 1994). For contemporary documentation focusing especially on the changes that have occurred in New York City, see C. Horowitz, "The New Anti-Semitism," *New York Magazine*, January 11, 1993, pp. 20–27.

3.   J. Isaacs, "Waking Up to the Specter of Japan's New Anti-Semitism," *Wall Street Journal*, October 5, 1987, p. 23; and D. G. Goodman and M. Miyazawa, *Jews in the Japanese Mind: The History and Uses of a Cultural Stereotype* (New York: Free Press, 1995).

4. E. Minnich, *Transforming Knowledge* (Philadelphia: Temple University Press, 1990).

5. N. Levine and M. Hochbaum, *Poor Jews: An American Awakening* (New Brunswick, N.J.: Transaction Books, 1974); T. J. Cottle, *Hidden Survivors: Portraits of Poor Jews in America* (Englewood Cliffs, N.J.: Prentice-Hall, 1988).

6. See, e.g., S. Henry and E. Taitz, *Written out of History: Our Jewish Foremothers* (Fresh Meadows, N.Y.: Biblio, 1983); I. Klepfisz, "Secular Jewish Identity: *Yiddishkayt* in America," in *Dreams of an Insomniac: Jewish Feminist Essays, Speeches and Diatribes* (Portland, Oreg.: The Eighth Mountain Press, 1990); C. Dahan, "Spheres of Identity: Feminism and Difference—Notes from a Sephardi Jewess," *Fireweed: A Feminist Quarterly:* Special Issue on Jewish Women, no. 35 (Spring 1992):46–50; M. Kaye/Kantrowitz and I. Klepfisz, *Tribe of Dina: A Jewish Women's Anthology* (Boston: Beacon, 1989); E. T. Beck, *Nice Jewish Girls: A Lesbian Anthology* (Boston: Beacon, 1989); C. Balka and A. Rose, *Twice Blessed: On Being Lesbian, Gay and Jewish* (Boston: Beacon, 1989).

7. B. T. Dill, "Teaching Students to Learn through Difference," paper presented at the annual convention of the American Association of Colleges, Washington, D.C., 1994.

8. Ibid.

9. N. Rosen, "On T. S. Eliot: Geniuses and Anti-Semites?" in *Accidents of Influence: Writing as a Woman and a Jew in America* (Albany: State University of New York Press, 1992) pp. 55–65; J. Hannaham, "Wrestling with Shylock: A Quartet of 'Merchants' for the '90s," *American Theater* (July–August 1995):25–29.

10. H. Feingold, ed., *The Jewish People in America,* 5 vols. (Baltimore: Johns Hopkins University Press, 1992).

11. C. West, "Charlie Parker Didn't Give a Damn," *NPQ: New Perspectives Quarterly:* Issue on Racism 8, no. 3 (Summer 1991):60–63.

12. "Combatting Bigotry on Campus: The Problem, Strategies for Counteraction" (New York: The Anti-Defamation League of B'nai Brith, 1990).

13. E. T. Beck, "From Kike to 'J.A.P.': How Anti-Semitism, Misogyny and Racism Construct the 'Jewish American Princess,'" *Sojourner: The Women's Forum* 14, no. 1 (September 1988): 18–20; also anthologized in *Race, Class, and Gender,* ed. M. Anderson and P. H. Collins (Belmont, Calif.: Wadsworth, 1992), pp. 85–90 and in H. Ehrlich and F. Pincus, *Conflicting Views of Race and Ethnic Relations* (Boulder, Colo.: Westview, 1995), pp. 162–68. An expanded version geared to counseling Jewish women can be found as "Therapy's Double Dilemma: Misogyny and Anti-Semitism," in *Jewish Women and Therapy: Seen but Not Heard*, ed. R. J. Siegel and E. Cole (New York: Haworth, 1992), pp. 19–30.

14. D. Lipstadt, *Denying the Holocaust: The Growing Assault on Truth and Memory* (New York: Free Press, 1993).

15. *Washington Post*, 1993.

16. C. West, "On Black-Jewish Relations," in *Race Matters* (Boston: Beacon, 1993), pp. 69–80.

17. Dill, 1994.

18. E. T. Beck, *Nice Jewish Girls: A Lesbian Anthology* (Boston: Beacon, 1982, 1989); idem, "The Politics of Jewish Invisibility in Women's Studies," in *Ethnic Studies: Women's Studies*, ed. J. Butler and J. Walter (Albany: State University of New York Press, 1992).

19. J. A. Banks, *Multi-Ethnic Education: Theory and Practice* (Boston: Allyn and

Bacon, 1988); R. Frankenberg, *White Women, Race Matters: The Social Construction of Whiteness* (Minneapolis: University of Minnesota Press, 1993).

20. Suggested by Banks, 1988.

21. H. Adelman, "Is Jewish Studies Ethnic Studies?" in *Transforming the Curriculum*, ed. J. Butler and J. Walter (Albany: State University of New York Press), pp. 169–86; S. Horowitz, "Jewish Studies as Oppositional? Or Getting Mighty Lonely Out Here," in *Styles of Opposition*, ed. P. Goldstein (Wilmington: University of Delaware Press, forthcoming).

22. A. Lorde, "The Transformation of Silence into Language and Action," in *Sister Outsider: Essays and Speeches* (Trumansburg, Calif.: Crossing Press, 1984), pp. 40–44; A. Rich, "It Is the Lesbian in Us," in *On Lies, Secrets and Silence: Selected Prose, 1966–78* (New York: W. W. Norton, 1979), pp. 199–202.

23. M. Yamada, "Invisibility Is Not a Natural Disaster," in *This Bridge Called My Back*, ed. Anzaldua and Moraga (Watertown, Mass.: Persephone, 1982).

24. E. C. Dubois and V. Ruiz, *Unequal Sisters: A Multicultural Reader in U.S. Women's History*, 2nd ed. (New York: Routledge, 1994). Jews are cited only twice in the index to a book of almost 500 pages and then only to identify them as Jews.

25. J. Cole, *All American Women: Lines That Divide, Ties That Bind* (New York: Free Press, 1989); M. L. Andersen and P. H. Collins, *Race, Class and Gender* (Belmont, Calif.: Wadsworth, 1992); R. Takaki, *A Different Mirror: A History of Multicultural America* (Boston: Little, Brown, 1993).

26. J. Butler and J. Walter, eds., *Transforming the Curriculum: Ethnic Studies: Women's Studies* (Albany: State University of New York Press, 1991).

27. R. Wistrich, *Anti-Semitism: The Longest Hatred* (New York: Pantheon, 1992).

28. In this, D. W. Sue and D. Sue, *Counseling the Culturally Different: Theory and Practice* (New York: John Wiley and Sons, 1990) is typical of numerous recent texts that focus only on minorities of color. The family therapy literature in psychology is one of the few exceptions to include Jews. See Also E. T. Beck, "Judaism, Feminism and Psychology: Making the Links Visible," in *Jewish Women Speak Out: Expanding the Boundaries of Psychology*, ed. K. Weiner and A. Moon (Seattle, Wash.: Canopy, 1995), pp. 11–26.

29. W. Nicholls, *Christian Anti-Semitism: A History of Hate* (Northvale, N.J.: Jason Aronson, 1993).

30. A. Dershowitz, *Chutzpah* (Boston: Little, Brown, 1992).

Jews and African Americans as Cotrainers in Antiracism and Antioppression Education

NAOMI NIM

This essay examines the unique dynamics I have encountered in antiracism and antioppression training sessions when one trainer is an American Jew of European heritage and the other is an African American. It is out of a commitment to the educational potential inherent in these cross-cultural partnerships that I offer my candid observations and suggestions.[1] In this essay I also propose a multicultural educational model informed by critical pedagogy and explicitly geared toward social transformation.[2]

The goal of multicultural education, at the most superficial level, is building mutual respect across cultures through celebrations of customs, holidays, heroes, and heroines. A slightly more substantive approach attempts to make adjustments in how we talk about the world and builds sensitivity to people who are called "different"; in schools and universities normative texts are supplemented by the study of African Americans, Latino/a Americans, Native Americans, and women.[3]

A more far-reaching model of multicultural education teaches a social justice perspective of history, that racism is learned and perpetuated through our institutions, and that "the social ordering of people and groups is one of the major sources of racist ideas."[4] Students learn to critique their world and to become active agents for a just society.

British and Canadian educators have dispensed with the term "multicultural education" in favor of "antiracist education." "Its aim is the eradication of racism in all its forms. . . . Anti-racist education attempts to equip us . . . with the analytic tools to critically examine the origins of racist ideas and practices, and to understand the implications of our race and our own actions in the promotion of, or struggle against racism."[5]

There is a further distinction in models of multicultural education that is pertinent, and that is the difference between prejudice reduction and antiracist education. While some practitioners of prejudice reduction may broadly concur with the social justice objectives of the antiracist educator, their understanding of the means to achieve that goal leads them to follow very different pedagogical practices. A prejudice reduction model proposes that the reduction of prejudice within individuals leads eventually to the reduction of widely held myths about race, gender, ethnicity, and other forms of oppression within a given group and within society as a whole. In practice, prejudice reduction works to achieve cross-cultural understanding through an examination of the content of racism and oppression that individuals have learned, and through sensitivity training that delves into emotional and experiential sources of individual attitudes that undergird prejudice.

Whereas prejudice reduction seeks solutions to prejudice and discrimination within the psyche of the individual and within intercultural relations inside a group, antiracist education contends that interior changes are to be valued, but they are not ends in themselves or the means to social transformation. Rather, antiracist education proposes that the eradication of racism and oppression is only possible through long-term struggle, and that pedagogy has a responsibility to direct learners toward critical analysis and action.

A Training Scenario

It is the first day of a two-day training for a nonprofit women's organization in a large, multiracial Eastern city where many African Americans and Jews live. All but two of the twenty-five participants in the training session are of European, non-Jewish origin. One of the two is an Ashkenazi American Jew and one is African American. Some participants are from rural and working-class backgrounds; all are currently professionals with middle-class lifestyles.

After much internal discussion on the need for antiracism and antioppression training, a two-day weekend workshop has been arranged by a committee of the organization, with the approval of the membership as a whole. The majority of the membership hopes that training will help them diversify membership and learn more about racism and oppression.

Most of the women have come to the training session with the intention of addressing these goals. However, it is clear from talking with the planning committee and from our observations on the first day that some women are reluctant participants. They attend to appease their friends, but do not really want to address race and oppression in this artistic and social organization that has no explicit political agenda.

It is also clear from the written suggestions of several women submitted to me and my training partner prior to the training that this group of women is primarily interested in learning more about racism. The organization has a goal to increase the membership of people of color and to improve outreach to communities of color. Historically, people of color have come and gone; similarly, Jews have not stayed in the organization.

I am an American Jew of European heritage, and I am cotraining with an African American woman I will call June, whom I have never worked with before. We belong to a trainers' network and share the same theoretical and practical base for our work.

We have spent several hours together in preparation at each other's homes, analyzing the problems that the women's organization is confronting, breaking down the weekend into content areas, and thinking of several approaches to engage participants actively with the material. The planning goes well, and we begin to know more about each other. We enjoy sharing our training repertoires, but there is still a distance between us as the weekend begins.

We are two strong individuals, different in regional background, class, and race, who share some of the experiences of motherhood, teaching, activism, and artistic work. I'm a New Englander from a first-generation family that steadily rose into the upper middle class during my childhood. June grew up poor in a midwestern city.

We also differ in terms of leadership style. I facilitate by placing myself in the background, keeping the focus on the issues the group is considering. I remain reserved about myself, choosing carefully what I will and will not reveal. It is a style that I have assumed over years of group facilitation and is akin to the stance of many counselors and teachers.

June, on the other hand, is far more open and directive. She wants to be known. It is her way of teaching and connecting with participants. She, too, is carefully choosing what to reveal about herself. Her open style that purposefully uses her life story offers participants key insights into the life of an African American woman.

The training begins with introductions in which June and I each speak briefly about ourselves. I identify myself as a Jew and talk about my work in African American, Latino/a, Jewish, and Arab American communities. June talks about her concerns as an African American woman, teacher, artist, activist, and parent of a teenage son.

During the course of the first morning of training, a few polite questions are raised about racism, which are addressed to June. At break and again at lunch, many participants want to confer with June. However, the group as a whole is quiet, polite, and passive.

Because the group is so quiet, and because those participants who have spoken have primarily related to June, I am beginning to think that I am not holding my own. I also distrust the silence, wondering what lies beneath it. Since I am used to being in charge, and find quiet unnerving, I am quite ill at ease.

I bring up the problem privately with June over lunch, not fully revealing how much I am beginning to blame myself for not eliciting more overt participation. Does she notice the silence too? What does she make of it? What should we do to get beyond it? I am feeling very unappealing next to June, whom by now I am beginning to idealize as overwhelmingly dynamic and exciting.

June and I are faced with a dilemma regarding the group's focus on June. Should we structure more leadership time for me than is already planned? Should I jump in and answer questions directed at June? What message are we conveying as teammates if we do allot more time for me to lead, or if I answer for her? But what happens if we do nothing?

We are very conscious of our role as models of interracial cooperation. On the other hand, we're still working on our training relationship. We decide on a much clearer definition of leadership time for the afternoon.

In the second part of the day, the group responds to me and the activities I lead, but June and I end the day realizing that there is a problem. We are both uncomfortable with the passivity of the group. The one Jewish participant and the one African American participant are remarkably subdued. We realize that creating the right conditions for them to speak freely in this group may take more time than the two days allotted for the training.

While I am pleased with my work in the afternoon, on some level I still think that I am not "holding my own"—not "weighing in" on an equal basis. I am even beginning to question my role and usefulness in the training. Is it possible that trainers who are not African American should take a background role when training with an African American partner, especially when the primary subject is racism? But isn't it important for a European American Jew to demonstrate knowledge and clarity on racism, and to teach other European Americans and Jews?

The next day, with leadership responsibilities more tightly structured, June encourages me to jump in whenever I want. We expect that a planned presentation on anti-Semitism will be very important for the group. A few participants discuss their failure to attract and keep Jewish women in the organization. They begin to talk about why this has happened.

During the rest of the day I interject when June is presenting and participate more fully in leading the training. Still, at break and during lunch the participants gather around June, and during the training they turn to her for authoritative information on most issues of oppression.

At the end of the two-day training, the participants are very pleased with what they have experienced and learned. They thank us sincerely. On the evaluation form, one woman remarks that she would have liked to have heard more from me.

June is only moderately satisfied with the training, and somewhat critical of the group for its passivity. To her it is a sign of lack of commitment, and an indication of the possibility that nothing will change in this organization. I, too, am not satisfied with the work we have completed. We leave the training puzzled, not fully able to explain what happened.

Analysis of the Training Scenario

I concluded the training considering what it would mean for me to try June's more open and directive approach. Upon reflection I realized there were many reasons I avoided self-disclosure and authoritative direction. As a Jewish child among primarily white Christian classmates and teachers, I had learned to remain hidden and to cooperate with my surroundings, a practice I later continued as I worked in Latino/a and African American communities.

Just as Jewish anthropologists working in Spain and Latin America may quickly become conversos,[6] I had developed a way of working that deflected attention from me and relied on a rather ambiguous persona of my own creation.[7] I didn't want to face the anti-Semitism I feared I would find if I were to be myself: expressive, warm, outspoken, provocative—and *Jewish*.

Reviewing the training, I realized that my operating principle of self-protection held true: because you can expect anti-Semitism, do everything to contradict its message. Don't be too pushy, too loud, too comfortable, too certain, too much!

A middle-class New England girlhood in the 1950s had cued me to be nice above all, quiet, and self-effacing. This early gender and class conditioning worked hand in hand with the strategies I used to avoid and contradict anti-Semitism. Given my way of negotiating as an American Jewish woman, it is understandable that I chose a facilitative and distant training style that required little self-disclosure.

During the training I was caught between my usual strategy—staying in the background, deferring to June, not disclosing much about myself—and the alternative—daring to be more directive and forthright, explicitly addressing key issues I've confronted as an American Jewish woman. Watching June certainly gave me a stunning example of how the antithesis of the facilitative approach worked both for her and for the group. As the workshop progressed and I began to try the alternative strategy, I felt more powerful and more authentically myself.

I wanted help from June, but I didn't want to burden her. Since I saw her as a strong but somewhat burdened person, I thought that she couldn't give anything to our relationship. I also saw her, in relation to myself, as far more appealing. In fact, I had a skewed understanding of June: idealizing her while seeing her as a victim. In this respect, I had much in common with many participants in this workshop; we were anxious to know June, but we saw her through the lens of our various beliefs about African American women.

June may have felt that, as usual, everything rested on her shoulders, that she couldn't count on me, her Jewish partner, who, for some unexplained reason, was leaving too much to her. Or perhaps she didn't trust me yet, and she was more comfortable being in charge so she could be sure of what was said and what was not said. But she may not have been content with having more responsibility than she had bargained for. Finally, she probably didn't want to take care of me. It was enough to be on guard against whatever racism the participants might present, let alone give me advice and moral support.

How much of these issues in our work together was simply a matter of differences in style? Certainly, if I were truly comfortable remaining in the background there may have been no problem, and June and I would seem perfectly matched. But my style was the outcome of an acquired strategy that ultimately constrained me and diminished my power.

The Group and the Trainers

June was very clear in advance that she would not work with a primarily European American group alone. I was unaware of how I might feel until the training was under way. I had overlooked the fact that there was only one Jewish member, and that this was not an organization where Jews felt welcome. June and I had focused on the African American—European American dichotomy, not taking into account the important historic and cultural differences between me and this group of women.

In this scenario, as in other training sessions where one trainer is European American and the other a person of color, several individuals in the group sought out the African American woman and were markedly less interested in a similar relationship with me, a Jewish trainer of European American heritage. In addition to a training style that made June very approachable, there are several possible explanations for this based in attitudes and beliefs about racism and African Americans, and Jews and anti-Semitism.

The following are my hunches about what participants may have been thinking and feeling. They are based on my observations of views that are often expressed directly or implicitly during antiracism and antioppression training. Regarding African Americans in general and June in particular, some likely beliefs and needs can be stated as follows:

- Racism is the oppression that counts. Racism is my main concern. It sometimes seems like nothing else is nearly as important as working to end racism once and for all. Who can better teach me about racism than an African American woman? It is her daily life and her history, and she is an authority.

- I want a heart-to-heart talk. This is the first time I've ever been able to talk about these issues with an African American woman. She seems approachable and open and friendly. I'm not afraid of her. It feels great to finally talk. Maybe she can explain the behavior of other African Americans.
- I want approval. I like this woman and she likes me. She thinks I'm okay. She doesn't hate me. Maybe I can separate myself from the racism in my history and in my family, and feel better.
- African American culture is cool. I've always loved African American people and all people of color. This woman is really dynamic. I want her to know I've always been an ally.

What about attitudes toward me, the Jewish trainer? I would venture some of the following thoughts and feelings were present:

- Anti-Semitism is no longer a problem. Jews can't claim to be oppressed, and Jews born after World War II have known only opportunity. They are so incredibly and disproportionately successful and powerful. In fact, now in Israel and here, they abuse their power. I don't want to condone any of that and I certainly have no patience for this overly nice Jewish woman.
- Being Jewish is only a matter of religion. Anti-Semitism doesn't affect freedom of religion. Jews are Americans who go to synagogue, some of them. This woman is basically like me, especially if she is secular. What can she possibly teach me about oppression or racism?
- I'm tired of hearing about the Holocaust. Jews have gotten so much mileage out of the Holocaust, and when you look at them, you can hardly see them as any different than other European Americans—only more successful.
- Jews on the Left always support people of color. I'm used to seeing a Jew and an African American work together. (Though they usually don't talk about Jews or about anti-Semitism.) I'm not sure I agree that anti-Semitism should even be mentioned in a workshop on racism and oppression.
- I wonder if we haven't been inhospitable to Jews. The Jews who

came to our meetings in this organization were pretty quiet about who they were, and they didn't stay. Maybe she can tell me why they wouldn't feel comfortable here. I don't want to offend her though.

When we examine the attitudes and beliefs about me, the Jewish trainer, we can see that, despite the knowledge and experience I brought to the training, my authority was relegated to anti-Semitism, and the validity of the very concept (i.e., anti-Semitism) was questioned by some and aroused anger in others. In fact, the identity of American Jews of my generation was called into question. There was almost an expectation or need for me to stay in the background and to leave a broad space for my African American colleague.

There is nothing shocking or unusual about these beliefs, attitudes, or misinformation. This is exactly the material, the "text," which should be the central focus of training to counter racism and oppression. Yet, as these beliefs played themselves out, June and I never named or questioned them directly. Instead we used the two-day training session to impart information as well as to guide participants through personal cultural histories, role plays, and an action plan for the organization. We used critical pedagogy to question and probe, but we never broached the subject of the group's relationship to the training team.

Looking back, I know June and I may have had a hunch about these beliefs, needs, and attitudes, and the way we were being objectified by some participants in the training session. Why didn't we follow those intuitions? Were we insecure about the new training relationship? Or perhaps we didn't fully realize that confronting the group with hypothetical or provocative questioning might lead to a far deeper level of work and more engagement with participants.

There were ways in which we both shared some of the needs, beliefs, and misinformation of the participants. I was idealizing June and her culture, and wanted to be a great ally. I believed that racism is the most devastating oppression in the United States, underpinning all others, and I was uncertain about how much time or attention I should give to anti-Semitism.

At the same time I devalued myself through an old strategy of diminishing my own power and visibility out of fear of confronting anti-Semitism. June and I both underestimated the hostility toward

Jews in this group of women. And we missed an opportunity to get beneath the polite interest and passivity that we found so suspect and unnerving.

Conclusions and Recommendations

Imagine the same scenario, but this time June and I are consciously seeking out the very attitudes, beliefs, and ideas that remained unspoken but evident in the dynamics of the group. Rather than a pragmatic, technical response to the group's focus on June (i.e., a tighter shared leadership structure), we are prepared to probe beneath surface politeness, quiet, fascination with June, and subtle avoidance of me. We recognize the dynamic, and use the participants' text as the basis of our work with them: that is, what we can know from what is spoken and unspoken, from body language, and from the emotional tone of the individuals and the group and their interactions with us. This is the approach of critical pedagogy.

Brazilian philosopher Paolo Freire proposed a critical pedagogy to teach literacy and social and political empowerment. He inspired radical educators to promote social consciousness through student-generated learning in a wide variety of settings. In his work with impoverished adults in Brazil, Freire used students' life experiences as the starting point for conversations that produced literacy and politicization.[8]

Freire contends that knowledge is socially constructed and furthered through problem-posing dialogue.[9] Critical educators in antiracism and antioppression work are engaged guides. They question and help unravel the sources of knowledge and beliefs, and propose hypothetical questions and situations, with the goal of moving participants toward deeper understanding and an active response to racism and oppression.

Using "everything as text"[10] not only enables us to surface the personal and intragroup dynamics, but to relate these phenomena to a larger understanding of history and human agency, and to a critique of hierarchical and oppressive social, economic, and political structures.

In practice, critical pedagogy presupposes an openness to participants, flexible thinking, spontaneity, persistence, and a belief that the real guts of the work will be presented by the participants. When June and I become aware of quiet, reluctance, or an absorbing interest in June, the African American trainer, we would begin to name the problem, to explore its meaning to individuals and to the group. We would encourage participants to reflect on the following questions: Why is it so important to connect with the African American trainer? Do we counter racism through interpersonal connections? Can European American people become knowledgeable about racism? Can Jews be knowledgeable about non-Jews, or women about men? Should they be? Is there a responsibility implicit in learning? And what does it mean to connect with the European American Jewish trainer? What do you believe about anti-Semitism?

In this approach we consciously use ourselves, and our relationship with one another and with participants, as the means of surfacing a range of beliefs, attitudes, misinformation, and confusion. And with the dynamics of the group in sharper focus, we can easily move to a discussion of the systemic nature of racism and oppression.

Critical pedagogy is a methodology that can and has been separated from its philosophical roots for purposes other than social and political transformation or the empowerment of oppressed peoples.

It is possible, therefore, to imagine that critical pedagogy could be used to promote prejudice reduction and cross-cultural understanding. The trainers still use participant text as a starting point, and dialogue and questioning to pursue a deeper understanding of the existence of prejudice in the group. Problem posing and critique would draw from a theoretical base supporting the view that there are solutions to prejudice within the group. In this model such solutions work in an additive way: as more individuals and groups undergo prejudice reduction, a society is created in which prejudice is eliminated.

Antiracist educators embrace the philosophical base of critical pedagogy, its critique of the roots of injustice, and the hope it offers for social transformation through alliances for social change. Whereas the method of critical pedagogy coupled with prejudice reduction appears to provide answers, when coupled with antiracist education it brings to light the enormity of the problems of racism and oppression in our history and in contemporary life.

As a cross-cultural training team June and I embodied the possibility of mutually respectful partnerships across race and ethnicity. We demonstrated that Jews and African Americans are likely partners when they work toward social change. No matter how new and tenuous that relationship was and no matter how dissatisfied we were with the outcome of our training, we shared a vision of a just world and a perspective on how to pursue social change. Our work together that weekend, and subsequently, gained its strength and resilience from our commitment to that purpose.

As a Jewish critical educator I must be prepared to explore the range of internalized and overt forms of oppression that will manifest themselves in groups. I must be aware of myself as an actor on this stage where risk, discomfort, and painful emotions can be expected among participants and trainers alike. And I must be willing and able to put myself forward as a Jew in the most public and vulnerable way, in the training and in my relationship with African American colleagues.

To be able to do this work, and to understand the dynamics that may arise when training with an African American colleague, a strong support network with other Jewish trainers is crucial. The educational potential in the cross-cultural training relationship cannot be met through antiracist, critical pedagogy alone. As a Jewish trainer my ability to be an effective educator rests on a thorough and continuous examination of the personal impact of anti-Semitism and racism in my life.

There was a powerful opportunity to explode the myths and long-held beliefs of the participants and trainers in the training scenario. Each training session holds that potential. The Jewish critical educator who enters this arena with an African American colleague, and with the strong support of other Jewish trainers, brings understanding and knowledge that tremendously enriches the educational project.

Notes

1.   This essay is a composite of several training sessions I conducted as the Jewish member of a training team. My partner in each case was an African American. The training took place at conferences, universities, and grassroots organizations.

2.   P. Freire, *Pedagogy of the Oppressed* (New York: Continuum, 1970); idem, *Education for Critical Consciousness* (New York: Continuum, 1982); E. Lee, *Letters to Marcia: A Teacher's Guide to Anti-Racist Education* (Toronto: Cross-Cultural Communication Center, 1984); M. Okazawa-Rey, *Training Proceedings, The Washington School* (Washington, D.C.: Institute for Policy Studies, 1991).

3.   James A. Banks, *Multiethnic Education: Theory and Practice*, 2nd ed. (Boston: Allyn and Bacon, 1988).

4.   Lee, *Letters to Marcia*, p. 9.

5.   Ibid., pp. 8–9.

6.   Conversos were Jews living in the Iberian Peninsula, or in Spanish and Portuguese colonies, after 1492, who ostensibly converted to Catholicism but often secretly practiced Judaism and maintained Jewish traditions. This term is used rather than the more commonly known "marranos," which is a derogatory word for conversos, meaning "pigs."

7.   Ruth Behar, "What the Anthropologist Can't Tell: Being in Cuba, Turkey, and Spain, 1992" (Washington, D.C.: Proceedings of the American Anthropological Association, 1993); J. N Friedlander, "Christians, Jews, the Marranos and Me: In Mexico and Lithuania" (Washington, D.C.: Proceedings of the American Anthropological Association, 1993).

8.   Freire, *Pedagogy of the Oppressed*.

9.   Ibid.

10.   Okazawa-Rey, *Training Proceedings*.

Making Room for Jews in Multicultural Public School Education

LEORA SAPOSNIK
ELLEN OSTERHAUS

The Civil Rights Movement of the late 1960s and early 1970s spawned a variety of efforts to increase equity throughout society. Educational institutions and organizations, as well as individual teachers and parents, began to note inequities in K–12 schools and devise plans to address them. Racism was an overriding issue, with sexism and handicappism added as the similarity of issues became apparent. Desegregation, bilingual education, and mainstreaming for students with special needs were some of the early efforts in educational reform. Unfortunately, creating educational institutions where students from diverse backgrounds with varying needs were brought together did not automatically eliminate bias and discrimination and result in quality educational experiences for all students. The complexity of social change was becoming apparent.

Over the course of the next two decades, educators developed a number of responses to these educational inequities. Human relations programs were developed to help students feel good about themselves and get along with others. Programs were developed to specifically help minority group students learn to fit in with students and staff from the majority, or mainstream, culture. Units and courses were developed on specific ethnic groups, such as Latino Studies and Black History Month activities. Each of these approaches tended to bring with it a new set of problems. The core curriculum continued to reflect the middle-class, Christian, Eurocentric perspective of the 1950s, as did teaching strategies and parent involvement efforts. Aspects of culture brought into the schools tended to be limited to holidays,

191

songs, folktales, and foods. Integration of history and culture was also limited. Generally one image was brought to the forefront for each group (for example, slavery became the defining aspect of African Americans). The experiences, accomplishments, literature, music, and art of African Americans beyond slavery were rarely included. Single group studies courses were generally electives and rarely selected by students whose background was not the subject of the course. There was little or no reflection on the importance of maintaining cultural identity for individual students. Counselors were often hired to work with minority students specifically rather than expecting the regular counseling staff to respond to the needs of all students or to learn about issues in the minority communities. The expression of culture tended to be encouraged when it involved the arts but discouraged when bias, discrimination, or conflict was involved. Clearly schools needed to reconsider these efforts and develop a more comprehensive plan.

In 1984 the Madison Metropolitan School District developed a position paper, "Multicultural Education in the Madison Metropolitan School District." The paper included the following definitions of multicultural education and a multicultural school.

Multicultural education is the process by which all students learn to participate fully in a pluralistic society, that is, (1) acknowledge and appreciate differences in themselves and others and (2) develop effective academic and social skills. A society which is pluralistic includes individual and group differences such as those of age, sex, race, ethnicity, cultural background, socio-economic status, health, physical and mental ability, sexual orientation, family structure, language, religious background and so forth.

A multicultural school is one in which the curriculum (formal and informal), leadership, staff (professional, para-professional, clerical, custodial, food service), parents and community groups respect and reflect the pluralism existing in society.

A multicultural school

—has a school environment which is physically and emotionally safe, nurturing and inclusive of all students

—has an integrated multicultural curriculum and library media collection

—has a pluralistic staff and

—provides opportunities for all parents to participate and become involved in the school.

Multicultural education has customarily been viewed as a response to issues of the African American, American Indian, Asian American, and Hispanic communities. As schools began to develop programs and strategies to respond to multicultural guidelines, it became apparent that diversity needed to be defined broadly if the schools were indeed going to respond to the needs of all students. For example, Jews were often viewed as white, European, and successful; therefore, there seemed to be no need for their inclusion in multicultural efforts. This commonly held stereotype does not accurately reflect the diversity of the Jewish community. Jews are in fact a prime example of a multicultural community: they have come from many places and represent the ethnic and racial makeup of those areas. The additional expectation that all Jews have achieved a level of economic success does not reflect the true socioeconomic picture. As in any community, there are working–class and poor Jews. The stereotype of Jewish involvement in money and banking more accurately reflects the longstanding insidious characterization of Jews as "money lenders" intent on controlling "worldwide money markets." Although Jews in America may not be identifiable by physical characteristics, nonetheless, the history, culture, and communal identification remain distinct. What is more, Jews continue to be targets of bias and discrimination.[1]

Upon their arrival in this country, Jews were advised to adapt quickly to the life and culture of the mainstream. In essence, Jews were presented with this offer: they could practice what they wished within the confines of their homes, as long as publicly they appeared mainstream. As a result, "Jews gained entrance to many professions, at many levels, and many chose to maintain a certain reserve in coming out as Jews, feeling it would be safer not to flaunt themselves."[2] Buying into the assimilationist theory, many Jews essentially evaporated into the American landscape.

Now, nearly seventy years after the major wave of Jewish immigration to the United States, Jewish Americans have begun to reevaluate their place in American society. This reevaluation is taking place largely as a result of the recent emphasis on multiculturalism, which has defiantly reversed the melting pot theory by declaring that differences cannot merely be smeared or merged; rather, they must be recognized and understood. American Jews, who have for nearly a century accepted that in order to succeed in American society one must "be a man outside and a Jew at home," to quote the famous assimilationist writer Y. L. Gordon, have now begun to shun that model. In essence, what some American Jews have begun to realize is that while other ethnic minorities in the United States have managed to preserve their cultures and cultural pride, much of the original language, theater, literature, and foods of the early Jewish Americans has disappeared (or, like the bagel, been mainstreamed). An article appearing in the March 8, 1995 *Wall Street Journal* attests to an awakening consciousness among Jewish Americans:

> Wendy Wagenheim never really thought much about anti-Semitism. The Birmingham, Mich., mother of two always felt part of the mainstream. . . . Then, a few months ago, Mrs. Wagenheim learned that political conservatives newly elected to the Michigan Board of Education had passed a "mission statement" laced with references to God and prayer. Parents in her son's sixth-grade class began complaining about rules that prohibited children from singing "Silent Night." Classmates told her 12-year-old son they didn't like having to learn about Hanukkah. Mrs. Wagenheim watched with growing alarm as Washington politicians proposed reintroducing school prayer. "I thought I could be like everyone else," Mrs. Wagenheim says. "But now we seem to stand out more. I never felt like this before."

In accordance with the definition of a multicultural school, public schools must consider the diverse voices of their student body and pay attention to the needs of each child they endeavor to educate. Madison, Wisconsin schools have attempted to depict minority children's own perspectives on their ethnic identity and determine how well the school district is addressing their needs. As such, the district has produced a number of videos such as "Perspectives of Black Children in the Madison Metropolitan School District," and most recently, "Jewish Lives: A Look at Contemporary Jewish Life in Madison, Wisconsin." In our interviews with Jewish schoolage children they have defined themselves as an eclectic group of people with widely varying opinions and beliefs. Udi, a middle-school student, defined his identity: "Being Jewish means to me that it's something special that I have for myself. . . . Being around Jewish friends and just participating in it . . . makes it feel like it's not going to die and it makes the culture just live on and that's very special. . . . People think that Jewish people are different, or just that different cultures are different from themselves . . . , and it's really not, it's just a culture that you have inside of you." A senior in high school elaborated: "I see it more as a community than a religion, because from a religious point of view there are a lot of differences. . . . Jews are hard to classify. What I like about Judaism is that there is a lot of freedom for self-expression for people to believe what they want to believe, I mean there are a lot of different opinions and they don't always agree, but freedom of thought and individual beliefs are always very important in Judaism. But what they all have in common is, first of all they belong to the Jewish people and identify themselves with them and secondly they participate in a Jewish community." The challenge, then, for teachers in the public schools is to incorporate these perspectives into their curricula. Jewish children, like all children, must see themselves reflected in the curriculum in order to reach their fullest potential.

Due to the diversity within the Jewish community, one cannot assume that any individual will hold a particular perspective. An individual within the Jewish community may be more or less aware of Jewish communal issues, Jewish practice, Jewish history, cultural roots, or national aspirations. Similarly, what each member of the community chooses to do with that awareness has manifested itself in diverse levels of religious observance, and has given rise to varying responses to Jewish ethnic and cultural identification. Regardless of the differences within the community, Jewish children in the public schools may have perspectives and needs different from those of mainstream and other ethnic/cultural groups.

Jewish issues should be considered as schools implement multicultural education for several very specific reasons. Certain topics of European history and contemporary conflicts in the Middle East may be viewed by some Jewish children from perspectives different than those of their classmates. The basis for understanding religious holidays will also differ. Additionally, Jewish children may be frustrated by their inability to find books in the school library that reflect their experiences. The children confront further disappointment when they realize that staff often are unprepared to provide multiple perspectives on history or information on Jewish holidays and culture. Jewish parents often feel reluctant to suggest curricular changes because of possible repercussions. By defining their children's needs as distinct from the larger group, Jewish parents may fear their children will be alienated from the group. Occasionally when staff have attempted to respond to parental concerns, the resulting activities have been superficial and have only served to reinforce stereotypes of Jews. Any of these situations can result in alienation of Jewish students from public school education. However, there are steps schools can take toward providing a more inclusive educational environment.

Jewish culture in the elementary schools has traditionally been limited to the topic of Hanukkah. Hanukkah activities became increasingly popular as staff became aware of the imbalance in traditional instruction. These activities provided an effective response to charges of religious bias stemming from the emphasis on Christmas. Hanukkah, a relatively obscure holiday, was elevated to a position of prominence and often presented as the "Jewish Christmas." Non-Jewish students would also notice the absence of Jewish students on particular days that were generally identified as religious holidays. Thus non-Jewish students learned that the difference between Jews and non-Jews is basically a religious difference, similar to the difference between Jehovah's Witnesses and Catholics. The fact that many Jews are expressly secular is not generally communicated by teachers and in fact is not generally known by non-Jewish teachers. Therefore, essential elements such as ethnic and national identity and cultural traditions tended to be ignored by the schools.

Non-Jewish teachers desiring to teach about Jewish culture generally turn to school libraries, school supply stores, and Jewish parents. Libraries and stores offer a very limited range of materials. Hanukkah is invariably showcased as representative of Jewish culture. Occasionally materials on Passover and Anne Frank are included, but rarely are other topics covered. To respond to the recent interest in multicultural education, publishers and distributors have been increasing the ethnic and cultural representations in their materials. Unfortunately, rather than increasing the quality of the information on cultures and histories, many companies simply provide more token representations. For example, a 1993–94 catalogue entitled "Culturally Diverse Materials for Antibias Curriculum," which certainly has adopted the language of multiculturalism, provides many traditional educational materials, altered only by changing skin color and clothing. In this particular catalogue fifteen items were included that reflected Jewish culture: twelve were related to Hanukkah, one to Passover, and two sets of Hebrew letters. Interestingly enough, there was only one item, an Advent calendar, relating to Christmas. The calendar was pictured next to a very similar item with a Hanukkah theme. The Advent calendar features twenty-five "multicultural" dolls; a doll is placed on the Christmas tree each day in December leading up to Christmas. Similarly, the Hanukkah wall hanging provides nine candles to be attached to the menorah daily. The similarity would lead teachers to assume an affinity. Since no such tradition exists in Jewish practice, such materials are misleading to teachers and students alike, serving only to blur the distinctions between cultures.

Unfortunately, many materials marketed to teachers place a heavy emphasis on Christmas activities and suggest few alternatives. Since Christmas activities are so routine, many teachers do not question their role in the curriculum and believe they are addressing the goals of multicultural education by providing "multicultural Christmas activities." A typical activity is the International Christmas Tree. In *Ethnic Celebrations around the World* the authors suggest that teachers decorate Christmas trees with a variety of symbols taken from many countries. The suggested symbols for Israel, where Christmas is not generally celebrated, is the dreidel (or top) and menorah. In effect this practice encourages students to equate candy canes, the crèche, and stars with the dreidel and menorah, thereby negating the distinctiveness in cultures, histories, and doctrinal approaches. This rendition of multicultural education attempts to neutralize differences and paint an image of an essentially harmonious world in which all people are alike.

Jewish parents are often contacted in December to provide presentations in their children's classrooms. Teachers may be making the request because of the desire to provide instruction on new topics, to counter the amount of Christmas-related activities, or possibly to make the Jewish students feel more comfortable. Because these requests come in December, parents tend to present information on Hanukkah. Often this is the only invitation extended to them. Once again, Hanukkah is seen as representing Jewish culture. The timing suggests to non-Jewish students that Christmas and Hanukkah are comparable. Typical presentations rarely include a discussion of the historical background that is fundamental to the distinction between the two holidays. Students comparing the holidays generally focus on decorations, foods, and gifts, and then conclude that Christmas is more exciting. In the children's book *There's No Such Thing as a Chanukah Bush, Sandy Goldstein* by Susan Sussman, a fourth-grade girl expresses discontent with her own people's celebration in the face of the glamour of Christmas. She cries herself to sleep, saying, "It isn't easy being Jewish at Christmas time." Many Jewish children can identify with this feeling; however, they may not identify with the author's solution. In response to her sadness, her grandfather takes her to a Christmas party where she dances, decorates the tree, and visits with Santa. In effect, the child's happiness hinges on active participation in Christmas activities. It's hard to see how this solution would help a Jewish child feel better about her or his own holidays.

The focus of representation of Jewish history and culture in elementary schools needs to be broadened. An inclusive curriculum that more realistically reflects Jewish culture would be far more interesting and stimulating for Jewish and non-Jewish students alike. Curriculum should include the many facets of Judaism—historic heritage, cultural distinctiveness, contributions to American society, and issues of prejudice and discrimination. Although there is not an abundance, instructional materials and resources that effectively represent these facets are available.

The curriculum in the early elementary grades tends to focus on self, family, and community. Typical activities incorporate folktales and family traditions. Two recent books that accurately and sensitively reflect these themes are *The Three Riddles: A Jewish Folktale* by Nina Jaffe and *The Keeping Quilt* by Patricia Polacco. *The Three Riddles* illustrates Jewish cultural heritage and the means by which it has been preserved over the course of many generations. As Jaffe points out, folktales often reflect cultural values as well as concerns affecting a community at a particular time. Such stories work well in multicultural folktale units; they provide a content in which even very young students can identify similarities and distinctions of cultures and traditions. They are also entertaining. *The Keeping Quilt* suggests a wide range of strategies for discussing family and ethnic traditions, as well as immigration. The story, which begins on a boat coming from Russia, traces five generations of a Jewish family in America. The quilt becomes symbolic of the importance of valuing and transmitting cultural heritage through the generations. This book has been used quite successfully in thematic units focusing on quilts made in the United

States or brought here, representing many cultural traditions including African American, Hmong, and American Indian.

Teachers in elementary grades often use holidays as a vehicle for teaching about traditions. A great variety of material on holidays is available. An example of an instructional kit is *Multicultural Celebrations*, distributed by Modern Curriculum Press. It includes picture-books on holidays from a wide range of religious and cultural traditions. The accompanying teaching guides furnish staff with background information as well as appropriate activities. Although holidays can be difficult subjects to address, teachers can model respect for diversity by using accurate and authentic materials, which can provide students with a greater understanding of holiday traditions. Recognizing the traditions of students in the classroom and in the larger society creates an atmosphere where all students can be comfortable expressing their traditions. Students who need to be absent from school for religious holidays will feel more at ease knowing that their classmates are familiar with the celebration and the reason for their absence.

An integrated approach goes beyond folktales and holidays; materials that reflect aspects of Jewish life can be used throughout the curriculum. *Bar Mitzvah: A Jewish Boy's Coming of Age* by Eric A. Kimmel is an up-to-date guide to contemporary celebrations of this rite of passage and its historical significance. As children approach the age of thirteen, they are often curious about how cultures mark this transitional period. *The Gift* by Aliana Brodmann, which takes place in Germany during Hanukkah, focuses on the Jewish tradition of Tzedaka, or giving. It affords the teacher an opportunity to discuss social responsibility and the value of sharing. The appealing and non-stereotypical illustrations provide an additional benefit. In the upper elementary grades, the curriculum usually includes information about pioneer life. Esther Silverstein Blanc's book, *Berchick*, introduces the reader to a very nonstereotypic family homesteading in Wyoming at the turn of the century. This delightful book will introduce the reader to Yiddish and Hebrew terms such as Challah (the traditional Sabbath bread), Chochim (a Yiddish term meaning "wise"), and Talmud, by contextualizing the material. Children will enjoy the depictions of family life on the ranch. As these few examples illustrate, there are many opportunities to incorporate aspects of Jewish culture into the elementary school curriculum.

In the upper elementary grades students begin to develop an awareness of history. At this level the curriculum tends to focus on the history of the United States with a sampling of world history. The most effective activities provide students not only with a sense of time and place, but more so, suggest avenues for interacting with the information. *Joseph and Anna's Time Capsule* by Chaya Burstein exemplifies this approach to history. The story provides a glimpse of life in a Jewish family in Prague during the 1840s. But its real strength is its approach to historic documentation. Joseph and Anna make a "time capsule," collecting family heirlooms and objects of ritual that reflect their daily life. The illustrations include photographs of objects from the collection of the Jewish Museum in Prague. Teachers concerned about the authenticity of the materials they use will find such attention to accuracy reassuring. This innovative approach allows children to view history as both personal and interactive. Equally important is the portrayal of Jewish ritual through explanation of the objects. This book can be used as an effective introduction to Judaism.

It is important for students learning about the history of people around the world to understand that history is vibrant and continuous. The study of contemporary cultures helps students grasp the effect of the past on the present. They can begin to see themselves as cultural beings carrying on beliefs and traditions, tying the past to the future. *A Tree Still Stands: Jewish Youth in Eastern Europe Today* by Yale Strom uses photographs and interviews to convey contemporary life in Eastern Europe from the perspective of children ages seven through eighteen. These personal narratives, in a sense, allow American students to meet peers who are growing up in a cultural setting different from their own. Students will be able to discern aspects of contemporary life that have directly resulted from the distinct history of the Jews of Eastern Europe. This book could also be used in conjunction with *Joseph and Anna's Time Capsule* to demonstrate cultural continuity; the books show the same geographic area separated by 150 years. Children in the 1980s maintain many traditions and rituals similar to Joseph and Anna. However, the historical events between the two periods had a devastating effect on the communities. The Holocaust could be introduced through use of these materials. Rather than concluding with the destruction of European Jewry, these two books offer a view of a vital and flourishing community despite the hardships.

Elementary students are often expected to research famous

people and write short biographies. The subjects tend to be the tradi-tional famous people—presidents, explorers, and scientists. This can be an opportunity for teachers to introduce students to a wide array of Jewish men and women who have made significant contributions to culture in the United States. A 1991 biography of Hank Greenberg by Ira Berkow, entitled *Hank Greenberg: Hall of Fame Slugger*, explores Greenberg's successful career and the difficulties of being one of few Jews in the game of baseball. The author also presents the friendship between Greenberg and the first African American major league ballplayer, Jackie Robinson. A few recent collections of biographies on notable American Jews have redressed the previous imbalance, which often slighted women and Jews of Sephardi origin. Although these newer biographies certainly offer more diversity of representa-tion, up-to-date biographies on recent Jewish immigrant groups from non-European countries have yet to be published. Nonetheless, *The Mystery of Being Jewish*, as one collection is entitled, includes Golda Meir, Natan Sharansky (refusnik, author, and human rights activist), Andrew Goodman (Civil Rights volunteer), Betty Friedan, Laura Geller (a woman rabbi), Barabara Streisand, Maurice Sendak (illustra-tor), and many others. Other books, such as *Heroes of American Jewish History* by Deborah Karp and *The Junior Jewish Encyclopedia* edited by Naomi Ben-Asher and Hayim Leaf, can also provide teachers with some of the background they need.

The inclusion of accurate and sensitive reflections on Jewish his-tory and culture will contribute to a reduction of misconceptions and discrimination. However, such activities do not eliminate the need for instruction that deals directly with bias. Many elementary school teachers are aware of the biases and prejudices of even very young children, and have begun to incorporate teaching units to directly ad-dress the issues. Materials have been developed to assist teachers in combating group stereotypes. *The Anti-Bias Curriculum* by Louise Derman-Sparks and *Teacher, They Called Me a _____!* by Deborah A. Byrnes provide both background information for teachers as well as student activities. Generally these approaches do not specifically teach about culture; rather, they promote an environment of respect for differences. Students are taught to identify prejudice and to respond appropriately.

As students enter the upper grades, holiday activities become less prevalent and the curriculum provides more opportunities for inclusion of Jewish culture and issues. Regardless of the opportunities, immigration and the Holocaust tend to be the only units that broach the subject. As Hanukkah has become central to Jewish identity in the elementary grades, the Holocaust has come to embody the Jewish identity at the secondary level.

Immigration is generally presented by comparing reasons for immigration and the similarities of experiences upon entering the United States. Reasons given for leaving other countries are usually universalized as "the search for freedom and a better life." A detailed study of an individual or a group's experience would do more to enhance the students' grasp of the immigration experience, as well as add to their understanding of the realities of political and economic pressures. Resources that vividly reflect the Jewish immigration experience for the secondary level include *The World of Our Mothers* by Sydney Stahl Weinberg and *World of Our Fathers* and *How We Lived* by Irving Howe. Another resource is *Hungry Hearts* by Anzia Yezierska, a collection of stories about the lives of immigrant Jews. This book, first published in 1921, is an excellent example of literature that can personalize the history curriculum. Two relatively new autobiographical picturebooks can add personal stories of immigration presented in a very fun and readable way. *Passover as I Remember It* by Toby Knobel Fluek is a lovely portrayal of what life was like in rural Poland prior to the destruction of Polish Jewry. The author, now living in the United States, compares her childhood memories of preparing for Passover to her current celebration of the holiday in America. *Leaving for America* by Roslyn Bresnick-Perry intersperses paintings and photographs of a young girl's journey from Russia to America during the earlier part of this century.

Although the topic of immigration is generally taught as part of the history of the Unites States at the turn of the century, as new immigrant groups continue to arrive their stories of immigration are beginning to be included as well. Thus, the recent immigration of Hmong people from Laos has been increasingly included in the study of immigration. This will undoubtedly open up new avenues for the inclusion of other more recent immigrant groups such as Arab Americans, and Jews of North African and Israeli descent. As of now, there is simply a paucity of materials available on these groups, and thus no examples could be cited.

As the topics of immigration and cultural traditions are essential to understanding the Jewish experience, so too is the Holocaust. More broadly, a grasp of the significance of the Holocaust is necessary for an understanding of world history in the twentieth century. The Holocaust can be a complicated subject to teach. The teacher must consider the knowledge and maturity of the students in selecting materials and planning activities. Students may find the violence fascinating, or they may find the presentation of events too overwhelming. Teaching the Holocaust requires a delicate balance between giving accurate information and supporting students' emotional reaction to the material. Teaching the Holocaust within the context of multicultural education in which students have already been exposed to issues of prejudice, social responsibility, and Jewish culture tends to be easier and more successful. Both literary and documentary accounts of the wide range of experiences of survivors and victims are readily available. In many communities survivors are available to speak in classrooms. Survivors or children of survivors can provide students with a sense of the vitality of history and the impact of history on individual lives. Written testimonies provide students with an in-depth, personal view of the Holocaust. *Dry Tears* by Nechama Tec, *Eva's Story* by Eva Schloss, and *Hidden Children* by Howard Greenfeld detail the experiences of children during the Holocaust. All of these are appropriate for the secondary level. Visual testimonies can be even more compelling than written ones; for many students sound and motion add to the sense of reality. "Daniel's Story," a video produced by the U.S. Holocaust Museum and developed for students grades 4 and up, is a fictional account drawn from the experiences of many survivors; it effectively represents the difficulties of childhood during the Holocaust. Active gathering of historical information can effectively involve students in personalizing the experiences. Students have access to documents and photographs through interlibrary loan systems. Copies of original documents enhance the learning experience. A 1992 Jackdaw kit simply entitled *The Holocaust*, published by Golden Owl Publishing Co., provides primary source exhibits including letters, maps, aerial photos, and newspaper accounts as well as a glossary and timeline of the Holocaust. Students can also talk with survivors and even create their own video accounts using photographs, maps, and testimonies.

Holocaust material is generally reserved for history but certainly can be integrated into other subject areas. Several books have combined history, literature, and artistic expression. An excellent example is *Maus: A Survivor's Tale* by Art Spiegelman. Through this cat and mouse story the author reveals the story of his father's horrifying experience in war-torn Poland and the impact of the experience on his postwar life and his relationship with his son. The cartoon medium, usually associated with childhood innocence, has a shocking effect when used to convey this material. The evil monsters of the cartoon world are mild compared to real life. Poetry and art come together in *I Never Saw Another Butterfly* by Hana Volavkova. The drawings and poems of the children who passed through the Terezin concentration camp reflect their daily misery as well as courage and optimism. The poems and drawings appear to be normal expressions of childhood yet all 15,000 children that entered the camp died there. Art becomes a vehicle for students to understand the experience of the individual survivor as well as the role of personal expression in overcoming crisis. A book that exemplifies this need for expression is Ruth Minsky Sender's *The Cage*. As a sixteen-year-old the author risked her life to steal scraps of paper and pencils from the Nazis in order to write poetry.

Comparison is a strategy teachers often use when introducing new material. However, comparing the Holocaust to such events as slavery, Cambodia, or Armenia can muddle the distinctions of each event. Students may begin to generalize the experiences of Jews, African Americans, and other victims of genocide rather than learn about specific events and people. If a goal of history is to learn about the past in order to avoid repeating mistakes, broad generalizations fail to prepare students for the future. Students must understand the specific political and social environment, timing, and economic circumstances that led to the Holocaust and other attempts at genocide. Comprehensive accounts of the history of the Holocaust for the secondary level are available through a variety of sources. An outstanding example is *Smoke and Ashes* by Barbara Rogasky, which provides an excellent overview of the history of anti-Semitism, events leading up to the Holocaust, and the lives of the victims, survivors, and those who helped them. The U.S. Holocaust Museum offers bibliographies of recommended resources for teachers as well as specific materials for use in classrooms.

Care should always be taken, however, to keep the Holocaust in its proper historical place in Jewish history. Although this event is certainly significant in world history and has become central to questions of Jewish identity and survival, it is not the end point of Jewish history. The reliance on the Holocaust for inclusion of Jewish culture was recently exemplified by a local middle school. The school requested a Holocaust survivor for the "Jewish booth" in a multicultural fair. While other cultures were represented by foods, dances, and art, the element of Jewish culture seen as representational was the victimization of Jews during World War II. The fact that Jews were not asked to bring ethnic foods, to share rituals, or to display their art serves to demonstrate that little is known about the joy and so much is known about the destruction. To counter these preconceptions an alternative representation was offered. A Jewish wedding was performed, complete with klezmer music, cake, huppa (or wedding canopy), ketubah (the Jewish marriage certificate), and wedding attire. The students became active participants in the joyous occasion; they held the huppa and the rings and danced around the bride and groom. The ceremony was followed by an opportunity for students to ask questions and draw parallels to their own experiences. Staff and students both enjoyed the excitement of sharing in a cultural celebration.

Children's perception of the world hinges upon the way in which the world is presented to them in a variety of settings, including their schools. As public schools are attempting to build a multicultural environment, they hold the keys to defining what a multicultural school is and who is included. The process of definition sets the foundation for building curriculum and student services based on this model. Jews must be allowed to enter the doorway of multiculturalism, for in order to be truly inclusive and effective multicultural education must acknowledge Jewish history, culture, and identity.

Notes

1. For further documentation, see "Religious Fervor: Some Liberal Jews See a Rise in Bigotry," *Wall Street Journal*, March 8, 1995, p. 1. Examples cited there include increased fundamentalist Christians proselytizing in Phoenix, aimed specifically at Jews. In Texas, a Jewish school board member was heckled for his support of condom distribution in the schools, and was repeatedly called "a dirty Jew"; he had to be escorted out of the meeting by the police.

2. Michael Galchinski, "Glimpsing Golus in the Golden Land: Jews and Multiculturalism in America," *Judaism* 43, no. 4 (1994):360–68.

Selected Bibliography

Ben-Asher, Naomi, and Hayim Leaf. *The Junior Jewish Encyclopedia*. New York: Shengold Publishers, 1991.

Berkow, Ira. *Hank Greenberg: Hall of Fame Slugger*. Philadelphia: Jewish Publication Society, 1991.

Blanc, Esther Silverstein. *Berchick*. Volcano, Calif.: Volcano Press, 1989.

Bresnick-Perry, Roslyn. *Leaving For America*. San Francisco: Children's Book Press, 1992.

Brodmann, Aliana. *The Gift*. New York: Simon and Schuster, 1993.

Burstein, Chaya. *Joseph and Anna's Time Capsule*. New York: Dell, 1984.

Byrnes, Deborah A. *Teacher They Called Me A _____!* New York: Anti-Defamation League, 1988.

Cone, Molly. *The Mystery of Being Jewish*. New York: UAHC Press, 1989.

Derman-Sparks, Louise. *The Anti-Bias Curriculum*. National Association for the Education of Young Children, 1989.

Fluek, Toby Knobel. *Passover as I Remember It*. New York: Alfred A. Knopf, 1994.

Greenfeld, Howard. *Hidden Children*. New York: Ticknor and Fields, 1993.

Howe, Irving. *World of Our Fathers*. New York: Pocket Books, 1978.

_____. *How We Lived*. New York: Putnam, 1983.

Jaffe, Nina. *The Three Riddles: A Jewish Folktale*. New York: Bantam, 1989.

Karp, Deborah. *Heroes of American Jewish History*. Hoboken, N.J.: Ktav, 1972.

Kimmel, Eric A. *Bar Mitzvah: A Jewish Boy's Coming Of Age*. New York: Viking, 1995.

Modern Curriculum Press. *Multicultural Celebrations*. Cleveland, Ohio: Modern Curriculum Press, 1992.

Phillips, William. *The Holocaust*. Lexington Park, Md.: Golden Owl Publications, 1992.

Polacco, Patricia. *The Keeping Quilt*. New York: Simon and Schuster, 1988.

Rogasky, Barbara. *Smoke and Ashes*. New York: Holiday House, 1991.

Schloss, Eva. *Eva's Story*. New York: Berkley Publishing Group, 1990.

Sender, Ruth Minsky. *The Cage*. New York: Bantam, 1988.

Stahl, Sydney. *The World of Our Mothers*. New York: Schocken Books, 1990.

Strom, Yale. *A Tree Still Stands*. New York: Philomel Books, 1990.

Tec, Nechama. *Dry Tears*. New York: Oxford University Press, 1984.

U.S. Holocaust Memorial Museum. *Daniel's Story*. U.S. Holocaust Memorial Museum, 1991.

Volavkova, Hana. *I Never Saw Another Butterfly*. New York: Schocken Books, 1979.

Yezierska, Anzia. *Hungry Hearts*. New York: Persea Books, 1985.

The Tree of Knowledge and the Tree of Life

JONATHAN BOYARIN

A lluding to, but I fear not quite making good on, the promise of my title, I start at the beginning, in the Garden, with the two trees. One tree grants to those who eat its fruit eternal life; the other, knowledge of good and evil. I will say nothing of the subsequent tale, the eating of the fruit of the tree of knowledge that initiates history and literature, if not language. The description of the trees suggests various puzzles. What is the significance of the contrast between the two trees? Why is the tree of knowledge—the forbidden one—eaten? Why is it that the Torah—the sum of our knowledge—is subsequently referred to as a tree of life, and why is it inconceivable that a yeshiva could ever be called *Etz HaDaas*, "Tree of Knowledge?"[1]

But the most urgent question in my mind is why there are two trees in the first place. In my understanding of Judaism, life and knowledge have always been one; and this is what calling the Torah (literally, teaching) a tree of life rather than a tree of knowledge would suggest. The separation between the two, and the elevation of life above knowledge, seems more consistent with Platonic idealism. But, of course, Plato could not have endorsed the scenario according to which knowledge is punished by mortality. I won't try to resolve these riddles here, but only use them to suggest on one hand that the very content and range of what the European Christian tradition calls "learning" may be quite different from that found in Jewish communities through the centuries, and on the other hand that the relationship between the two conceptions is certainly not one of neat or direct opposition. It would seem my own understanding has been too simplistic, too self-reassuring, and Judaism, too, recognizes and struggles with a tension, though not a hierarchical opposition, between learning and life, as between the reproduction of students and of children.

The university is faced now with a great challenge to rethink and to reinvent its relation both to the life outside it and to the lives that its members bring to it. Even if we acknowledge that Jewish tradition does not simply conflate learning and life, the promise contained in the assertion of Torah as a source of life must be one of the resources we seize upon in meeting this challenge.

But who is this "we" of whom I presume to speak? If the relationship between knowledge and life is so complex, we can no more take for granted the relationship between Judaism and Jews, between a historical civilization and an ethnic or religious identity. Especially in the university, these relationships are always being questioned, and rightly so. Is a "Jewish approach" one taken by Jews, one taken in the name of Jews, or one that employs Jewish cultural resources and strategies? Some of the possible kinds of relation between those called Jews on one hand, and Jewish references on the other, might become clearer if we try to imagine various efforts at establishing what we might call a "Judeocentric" space in higher education.

My use of the term "Judeocentrism" here is inspired by, and partly analogous to, Afrocentrism. At the level of primary education policy, Afrocentrism is explicitly designed to promote general social success through an education stressing self-esteem.[2] It is based on the assumption that skin color and social situation predetermine what the collective "self" is; hence the significance of the change in ethnic name from the neutral descriptor "Black" to the historically and territorially significant "African American." My own education, at least since the years when, as an undergraduate, I decided that the fact of Jewishness was foremost in the definition of my own identity, has been "Judeocentric," and indeed in a loosely analogous way: I decided that, since so much of my identity had evidently already been shaped by the fact of being born Jewish, my best chance at autonomous adulthood lay in developing, exploiting, and shaping those resources.

Any exploration of self based on particular histories and identities may well develop in defensive and chauvinistic ways.[3] Yet I argue that on the whole, taken in the more open sense of multiple "centers" of identity or bases for exploration and learning, there is little to fear from ethnic or other group articulations in education. Beyond that, as Amos Funkenstein reminds us, the alternative ideal of disinterested, objective "academic freedom," which claims universality for itself, actually has its own very particular history. Medieval Christian European intellectuals claimed their right to debate issues of theology and epistemology "purely academically," that is, in explicit denial that these debates had any bearing on effective church dogma or law.[4] Support for this possibility of a sphere of autonomous, ineffectual theoretical debate doubtless came from Platonist idealism. Those who still uphold it today seem often motivated as well by that "fear of diversity" that the classical scholar Arlene Saxonhouse has recently identified in ancient Greek thinking.[5]

The separation between the academy and the "real world" thus stems from the Middle Ages. My bafflement at this notion when I reached college was perhaps the clearest signal that even in childhood I had been imbued with a different notion of learning. Yet curiously, even approaches that respect and promote diversity can reinforce this notion of the university as a world apart, something separate from the "real world." Thus Edward Said has written,

> our model for academic freedom should therefore be the migrant or traveler: for if, in the real world outside the academy, we must need be ourselves and only ourselves, inside the academy we should be able to discover and travel among other selves, other identities, other varieties of the human adventure. But, most essentially, in this joint discovery of self and other, it is the role of the academy to transform what might be conflict, or context, or assertion into reconciliation, mutuality, recognition, creative interaction.[6]

This statement contains the oddly conventional implication that migrants and travelers are only in the real world, only "themselves," when they are at home, and it is only when they move away from home that they are free to become something different—a notion that Said, who has written eloquently on Diaspora, should be wary of. But more on Diaspora below. For now let me state that in our interdependent world, where each day's headlines show the bloody consequences of the attempt to place everyone at home, it is too much of a luxury to say that outside the academy we can possibly be "ourselves and only ourselves." The academy could, instead, become a model and a testing ground for experiments in simultaneously being self and "Other."

One option for Judeocentrism in the university that is in any case ruled out is an approach aimed solely at reinforcing the neat boundaries of Jewish collective selfhood. That caveat aside, there are several models for a possible Judeocentrism, all of which are in fact being tried out in various contexts and to varying degrees.

1. One model places more emphasis on "Jewish content" as an option within, for example, an undergraduate liberal arts curriculum. This is not invalid in itself; there is plenty "within the tradition" that can be utilized to serve the aims of liberal education without testing the model in fundamental ways.

2. Another model works "outward" toward the world in general from a perspective of primarily Jewish identities and interests or references: this would be analogous to the kind of "Afrocentrism" (even if it doesn't call itself that) I find most exciting, the kind exemplified by *Transition* magazine. Most of the articles in *Transition*, which was originally actually published in Africa and has now been revived under the editorship of Henry Louis Gates Jr. and Anthony Appiah, focus on issues of critical interest to African and African American intellectuals, but its pages also find room for the same critical energy applied to a wide range of topics, and its language is not restricted to specialists in critical theory. This model could also serve as a focus for Jewish intellectual socialization: meeting informally to address world issues as Jews, but not only vis-à-vis whether they are good or bad for the Jews—a question, by the way, which might not especially interest younger generations of Jewish students.

3. Then there is a more ambitious, decentralized, and yet articulated project, among scholars officially housed in many different disciplines, of Jewish cultural critique. This project has one eye, certainly, aimed at the renewal of Jewish intellectual life conceived *as* social life. It must incorporate the previous two levels of (1) specific references and resources and (2) the notion that Jews as Jews can and should be critically involved with everything that goes on in the world. But it goes beyond, to a ramified critique of power and knowledge in our times that is grounded in the double recognition of the ambivalent and partial Jewish sources of Christian progressive, imperial universalism on one hand, and the agonistic persistence of Jewish specificity within that universalizing framework on the other.

Central to the "approach to the disciplines" implied by this third notion of critical Judeocentrism is a high degree of skepticism vis-à-vis the various disciplines' historically contingent, not to say arbitrary and often dysfunctional boundaries, along with a willingness to be *masig gvul*, to transgress those boundaries when necessary. All the same,

both the Jewish historical situation and the Jewish textual and memorial tradition offer more specific resources that can be used to address
the constituted disciplines in fairly specific ways. I focus below on
three examples.

1. *Literary Theory.* Here the Rabbinic reading model called
midrash joins, complicates, and enriches the broader critique of the
assumption of fixed meaning, or of authorial intent as the ultimate ar-
biter of meaning and the goal of literary scholarship. This same issue,
and the range of available Jewish responses to it, is even more relevant
perhaps to legal theory—I note that the U.S. Supreme Court is still referring to the "probable intent of Congress" in making many of its
rulings! Jewish literature is replete with discussions of the problem of
authoritative meaning in the absence of a stable referent. The standard
reference for this in the Talmud is the story about the debate between
Rabbi Eliezer and the rest of the rabbis over a certain technical point
in Jewish law. Rabbi Eliezer several times calls heaven as his witness,
and the Divinity obliges by performing various miracles. The rabbis
are not impressed, quoting Torah against Divinity: "It is not in
heaven!"—the "it" here being the Torah itself.[7] Indeed, when we consider the context of that citation, "It is not in heaven!" the story becomes even more relevant to contemporary demands for a democratic
approach to the question of meaning, for there the sentence serves to
deny the possible excuse that the Torah cannot be observed because it
is so remote. Thus, we might say today, the works of Shakespeare too
lehavdil[8] are not ensconced in some immortal Pantheon, remote from
our own concerns;, but their critical, humane, educational potential
can be realized only by engaging them with our own concerns.

2. *History.* One Jewish approach is to be found in the work of Walter Benjamin. I would hazard a one-sentence summary of that approach as an unremitting struggle to synthesize the conviction of
participation in the life of previous generations—our own and others—with a sense of responsibility for the ways in which the past informs us.[9] Benjamin himself famously captures the idea in the vision
of the Messianic age as a time when the "past is citable in all its moments." In this view, our own lives extend backward and outward to
the extent that we are able to identify imaginatively with ancestors.
One might ask how different this is from the conception implicit in
the so-called ancestor worship of nonstate peoples. Nevertheless, this
is not a mystical approach to the academic discipline of history, nor

does it denigrate or ignore professionally established standards of research, evaluation, and interpretation. Rather, it conclusively replaces the elusive ideal of a reconstructed actual past with the most exigent standards that follow on the recognition that our own lives not only are linked to, not only depend on, but in a sense *are*, the history that we make as we are made by it. Since ultimately there is no neatly defined "we" that can be set over and against "history," only the most rigorous agenda, consisting simultaneously of imaginative research and critical openness, can help make us as fully developed and as generous as we can be. Thus, to take a handy example, it will not do to take Michael Walzer's *Exodus and Revolution* as a model for a "Jewish approach to history." Although Walzer's recognition that the exodus myth model is effective in contemporary Zionist politics is important, it does not authorize the strategy of his book: a slanted reading of selected episodes in the cultural history of that myth model to support a particular tendency today. True, such an approach recognizes that history remains effective, that it is not dead; but in its slipshod attitude toward the past, it betrays a fundamentally progressivist stance toward the past far from a traditionally Jewish sensibility. On the other hand, critical, indeed self-critical reading of sources and the highest respect for the dead, such that their images and their very names are not to be evoked opportunistically or univocally, are parts of what such an approach might be.[10]

    3. *Philosophy.* Much contemporary philosophical theory—including so-called cutting-edge French critical theory—somehow manages to maintain the pretense of speaking as an ungrounded, unbounded universal subject, as if the philosopher himself had no history, no body, no comrades with names, no mortality. Inevitably, as with academic freedom, such efforts betray their own grounding in precisely the Greco-Christian tradition that assumes the possibility and desirability of such universal subjecthood. Thus an otherwise worthy book such as Jean-Luc Nancy's *The Inoperative Community*, which addresses the problem of how to think about the possibility of a universal community that would not be grounded in some form of coercion, includes the remarkable claim that "The true consciousness of the loss of community is Christian."[11] Nancy also traces the collective history of the "we" to whom he addressed his book back to the story of Ulysses. There is thus a linkage of the notions of universality, Christianity, Greek origins, and philosophy. Nancy thus effectively on

one hand precludes anyone's consciousness of the loss of particular communities as having genuinely philosophical significance, and on the other reinforces the preeminence of even an abandoned Christianity as the tragic ultimate in philosophical consciousness of community. I have written an essay confronting Nancy's text with a portrait of a different, fragmentary, perhaps "inoperative" community, my morning *minyan* on the Lower East Side.[12]

4. *Anthropology*. I must begin with a caution here. When I did my doctoral fieldwork with Polish Jews in Paris,[13] my explanation that I was a specialist in "Jewish anthropology" was more than once met with the shocked response: "But that's what the Nazis did!" Of course, "what the Nazis did" was not the empathetic study of Jewish communities following the same principles as applied in all cultural anthropology, but rather the application of racist pseudoscience in support of a murderously exclusionary state policy. The first duty of a "Jewish approach to anthropology," then, responding to the specific ways in which the misuse of anthropology was employed to make Jews suffer, is probably to combat racism.

More specifically perhaps, one of the most important challenges posed by the Jewish tradition linking identity, text, and scholarship is to the organization of cultural anthropology by so-called culture areas. While the development of area studies in post–World War II academic life has certainly been one of the crucial bases for democratizing and diversifying scholarship, it is also grounded in the "cultural geography" developed by Friedrich Raetzel—the man who also popularized the *Lebensraum* notion.[14] Area studies in anthropology generally still rely on the outmoded notion that territory and group identity are essentially, properly, and inevitably matched with one another. Jews don't make it as an ethnographic specialty in cultural anthropology because they fit none of the culture areas of the world. On the other hand, studies of and by Jews should be in the forefront of the current corrective wave of work on Diaspora—work that both furthers and responds to the recognition that, as often as not, people are to be found outside the territory to which they nominally owe their identity. The point here is neither that area studies, in anthropology and beyond, should be done away with, nor that Jewish Studies should necessarily simply find its place as one of the certified areas. Within anthropology, the demand for recognition of Jews as a legitimate specialty runs up against other legitimate calls for diversification at a time when the overall resources of the discipline have shrunk drastically. A Jewish approach—typically restless, hopeful, questioning—should thus serve at least to make the disciplines try to be more than they are, constantly aware of their own contingent histories and indeed their gross inadequacies.

Conclusion

I want to conclude by turning the tables—sort of. We've had more than a century of the history of the Jews, decades of sociology of the Jews, and certainly many studies of Jewish philosophy. Such work—disciplinary approaches to Jews—will continue, but it is far from obvious that they will provide fundamental insights into the dynamics of Jewish life. What seems at any rate more urgent to me are approaches that themselves transgress disciplinary boundaries: "Is There a Feminist Approach to Jewish Studies?" "Is There a Postcolonial Approach to Jewish Studies?" "What Are Jewish Cultural Studies?"

For one thing, such perspectives help guard us from the danger of self-righteousness at any level of Judeocentrism in the university. If we bear in mind the subordination of Jewish women, then we will learn to be wary of philosemitic descriptions of "the Jew" as the very embodiment of rational, nonoppressive freedom. If we bear in mind the global phenomenon of European colonialism and its aftermath, we will avoid hanging our identity on the image of Jews as the supreme victim. More generally these critical perspectives offer a way of responding to the assigned question: "Is There a Jewish Approach to the Disciplines?" that moves beyond yes or no. These discourses have developed their own explorations of the ways in which particular identities are historically grounded, yet not eternally or objectively fixed, and they have also examined in detail the links between universalist, scientific knowledge and structures of power.[15] Hence on one hand they suggest by analogy that there cannot be a single, univocal "Jewish approach" (*that* precisely would not be Jewish!)—and on the other hand they undermine the impression that the disciplines themselves are objectively fixed and established. These discourses likewise share with critical and traditional Jewish perspectives the tendency to move away from an emphasis on originality and progress toward critical commentary and dialogue. As feminism challenges the fixity of the sex-gender system and postcolonial voices challenge the Eurocentric vision of enlightenment, civilization and universalism, Jewish diasporic existence and creativity challenge simultaneously the fixity of the nation-state and the divorce of knowledge from life. To return to the trees by way of conclusion, voices such as those of feminists and postcolonial thinkers may help us, Jews committed to the university— that is, to the world—shake off the tragic view of the events in the Biblical Garden. We may find we don't even want to get back to that first, God-given garden, but rather to learn how we can better tend our own gardens, and invite others to share them with us.

Notes

1.   "It is a tree of life for those who grasp it, and its supporters are praiseworthy" (Proverbs 3:18). That "it" here refers to the Torah is both evidenced and reiterated by the practice of reciting this verse as the Torah is lifted after being publicly read in the synagogue, and by the use of the term *etz khayem* ("tree of life") to refer to the two wooden poles around which the Torah scroll is wound. One of the great European yeshivas, now relocated in Brooklyn, is called *Ets Haim*.

2.   I refer here generally to schools established in inner-city neighborhoods, often stressing not only the central positive value of African American identity but the need to reinforce African American "manhood" as well.

3.   For several exemplary explorations of this issue, see the special issue of *Critical Inquiry* on "Identities" (18, no. 4 [Summer 1992]), edited by Kwame Anthony Appiah and Henry Louis Gates. Especially germane is the sustained critique of deterministic notions of collective identity mounted by Walter Benn Michaels ("Race into Culture: A Critical Genealogy of Collective Identity," pp. 655–85). See, however, in part as a rejoinder to Michaels, the essay by Daniel Boyarin and myself, "Diaspora: Generation and the Ground of Jewish Identity" (*Critical Inquiry* 19, no. 4 [Summer 1993]:693–725).

4.   Amos Funkenstein, *Intellectuals and Jews*, The Albert T. Bilgray Lecture, University of Arizona (Tucson: Temple Emanu-El, 1989).

5.   Arlene W. Saxonhouse, *Fear of Diversity: The Birth of Political Science in Ancient Greek Thought* (Chicago: University of Chicago Press, 1992).

6.   Cited in Gates, *Critical Inquiry*, pp. 17–18.

7.   Babylonian Talmud, Tractate Baba Metsia, fol. 59a–b. One recent discussion of this famous passage is in Daniel Boyarin, *Intertextuality and the Reading Midrash* (Bloomington: Indiana University Press, 1990), pp. 33ff.

8.   This Hebrew term, the infinitive "to make a distinction," is used by observant Jews to avoid the implication that in comparing something sacred within Judaism to something secular or to something pertinent to a different religious tradition, they are according the two equivalent value.

9.   Another way to say this, and one certainly pertinent to Benjamin's historical situation, is that he strove to articulate a *nonfascist* mode of identification with the past— actually a much harder task than it may seem at first. The locus classicus for this is, of course, Benjamin's Scripture-like manifesto (which he declined to publish in his

lifetime, fearing misunderstanding), "Theses on the Philosophy of History," in *Illumina-tions* (New York: Schocken, 1969), pp. 253–64.

10.   Michael Walzer, *Exodus and Revolution* (New York: Basic Books, 1985). For a critique of both Walzer's book and Edward Said's response to it, see my essay "Reading Exodus into History," *New Literary History* 23, no. 3 (1992):523–54.

11.   Jean-Luc Nancy, *The Inoperative Community* (Minneapolis: University of Minnesota Press, 1991), p. 10.

12.   Not surprisingly, that essay was rejected by the editors of the prestigious *An-nales* journal as being hopelessly egoistic and subjective. Do not suppose that attempts to assert "Jewish approaches to the disciplines" are generally accepted! It was subsequently published as "Death and the Minyan," *Cultural Anthropology* 9, no. 1 (1994); and is also forthcoming in my *Thinking in Jewish* (Chicago: University of Chicago Press, 1996).

13.   See *Polish Jews in Paris: The Ethnography of Memory* (Bloomington: Indiana University Press, 1991).

14.   Friedrich Ratzel, *Der Lebensraum: Ein biogeographische Studie* (Darmstadt: Wissenschaftliche Buchgesselschaft, 1966). For a discussion of Jewish Studies, an-thropology, and the mixed legacy of area studies, see the chapter entitled "Jewish Ethnography and the Question of the Book," in my *Storm from Paradise: The Politics of Jewish Memory* (Minneapolis: University of Minnesota Press, 1992).

15.   See, for exemplary studies in feminism and postcoloniality, the following: Judith Butler, *Gender Trouble: Feminism and the Subversion of Identity* (New York: Rout-ledge, 1990); Gayatri Chakravorti Pivak, *In Other Worlds: Essays in Cultural Politics* (New York: Methuen, 1987); Homi Bhabha, *The Location of Culture* (New York: Routledge, 1994); and Paul Gilroy, *The Black Atlantic: Modernity and Double Consciousness* (Cam-bridge, Mass.: Harvard University Press, 1993).

"But Is It Good for the Jews?" Challenges and Jewish Responsibility in a Multicultural World

Hearing the Call
Solidarity with Ethiopian Jews

EPHRAIM ISAAC

Jewish contact with Ethiopia, as both legend[1] and history suggest, goes back at least to the First Temple period. Since that
time, Jews have sought out the land of Ethiopia and its South Arabian
(Yemeni) colonies[2] as a commercial venue in peaceful times and as a
refuge during times of war and destruction in the land of Israel.[3] It is,
therefore, not surprising that world Jewish solidarity, encompassing
Jews living in Ethiopia (and Yemen), echoes back to antiquity. This
early relationship, however, began to be eclipsed already in the sixth
century.[4] Although some contact remained,[5] Sir Gibbons' overused
quotation, that "the Ethiopians slept for near a thousand years, forget-
ful of the world by which they were forgotten," expresses the historical reality remarkably well.[6] The reconnection between European and
Ethiopian Jews beginning in the medieval period generated a new
sense of world Jewish solidarity to which recently American Jews in
particular have begun to respond.

The Age of Exploration to the Ninteenth Century

Reports brought by Portuguese missionaries in the sixteenth and
seventeenth centuries contributed to animating international curios-
ity about Ethiopia. These missionaries not only wrote about the
prominent role of the Jewish religious practices in the Ethiopian
church, but also referred to "the Jews of the mountains" whom Jesuit
theologians such as Jeronym Lobo distinguished from the Judaizing
Ethiopian Christians. Subsequently, late-eighteenth-century reports

This essay is an abbreviated and modified form of an article first published in Hebrew as
"Ha'solidariyut Ha'yehudit Wa'yehudei Ethiopia," in *Solidariyut Yehudit Le'vmit Ba'et
Ha'hadashah*, ed. Benjamin Pinurs and Ilan Troen (Ben Gurion University Press, 1988).

of James Bruce, who introduced the first Ethiopic manuscripts of the lost Jewish *Book of Enoch* to Europe, and of early-ninteenth-century explorers such as Henry Salt, Charles T. Beke, Antoine Thomson D'Abbadie, and others, heightened the interest in Ethiopia and its Jews.[7]

It was in the early nineteenth century, after the ascendancy of Emperor Theodore II (1855–68), that direct and permanent contact between world and Ethiopian Jewry was made. This new contact primarily came as a result of a strong Jewish reaction to modern European Christian missionary activities in Ethiopia.[8] Although Jewish journalists brought news of this campaign to the attention of European Jews, causing much concern,[9] very little was done immediately to actually aid Ethiopian Jewry.[10]

The visit by Joseph Halevy (in 1827), the first European Jew to establish personal contact with Ethiopian Jews in modern times, was thus a breakthrough in world Jewish solidarity. The central committee of the French-based Alliance Israelite initiated and authorized Halevy's expedition and British Jewry supported it. The trip, whose objective was chiefly to counteract the said Christian missionary activities among Ethiopian Jews, cost about ten thousand francs, not a small sum of money then.

Halevy reached the port of Massawa on the Red Sea in October 1867, coinciding with the 1867–68 British military offensive in Ethiopia. The trip was no mean undertaking, as the then prevailing atmosphere was hostile to Europeans. But Halevy successfully worked his way into the highland regions, and for three months visited Jewish villages in the Wolqayet, Armachoho, Djanfancara, and Qwara districts (he did not reach the town of Gondar). Upon his return, Halevy wrote on the history, religious practices, and socioeconomic conditions of Ethiopian Jews.[11] He also edited Ethiopic Jewish texts and translated them into a European language for the first time.[12]

The Twentieth Century

There is no doubt that the foundation for modern Ethiopian and world Jewish solidarity was laid by Halevy, culturally a Sephardi Jew brought up in Adrianopole. Unfortunately, Halevy's plea for action to aid Ethiopian Jews was not acted upon expeditiously by the leaders of the Alliance. Building the solidarity bridge between the two communities was left to one of his intellectual heirs, a Polish Jew named Jacques Faitlovitch (1880–1955).

Armed with the knowledge of modern Ethiopian languages, which he studied with Halevy at the Ecole des Hautes Etudes (the Sorbonne), Faitlovitch made his first trip to Ethiopia in 1904. The trip was sponsored by the Alliance and subsidized by Baron Edmond de Rothschild. Altogether Faitlovitch made six successive trips between 1904 and 1955 (1904, 1909, 1913, 1920, 1924, and 1946) and his missions received the support of many world Jewish leaders (including Chief Rabbi Zadok Kahn of Paris, Chief Rabbi Hertz of England, and Chief Rabbi Abraham Kook of Israel). His life and mission together represent another whole chapter in the history of world Jewish solidarity.

Historically, the motivation for world Jewish solidarity had been to counteract evangelization. Despite initial fears that he was a missionary, Faitlovitch was able to combine anti-evangelization work with a new socioeconomic objective including introducing Ethiopian Jews to European Jewish culture and Western education. To this end, he returned to Europe in 1905 with two Ethiopian young men, named Gete Eremyas and Taamrat Emanuel, both of whom he enrolled in the Ecole Normal of the Alliance in Paris. Through his influence, the "Hinfscerein der Deutschen Juden" decided to sponsor other young Ethiopian Jews to study in Europe and at its training school in Jerusalem.

Faitlovitch also used his diplomatic skills to cultivate friendship with Ethiopian authorities. In Europe Faitlovitch launched an aggressive lecture tour to raise funds, primarily for educational purposes. In addition, Faitlovitch was able to convince forty-five leading Orthodox rabbis to put their signatures on a letter reaffirming Jewish kinship and supporting the idea of a common destiny, unity, and solidarity with Beta Israel.

In the 1920s Ethiopian and world Jewish solidarity seemed to grow. Faitlovitch organized spiritual and financial support from another corner of the world: the American Pro-Falasha Committee. This organization became prominent in the world Jewish solidarity effort and existed in North America until the early 1970s. In addition, in 1921 the respected mystic Chief Rabbi Abraham Isaac Kook of Palestine proclaimed an appeal to world Jewry to support Ethiopian Jewish *aliyah* (immigration).

The 1935–45 period, the Holocaust decade, is one of the gloomiest in modern European Jewish history. It was no different for Jews living in Ethiopia, both Yemenites and native-born.

The postwar period opened a new chapter for Ethiopian Jews, as it did for world Jewry as a whole. Ironically, however, the new era did not hold the same reconstructive prospects for Ethiopian Jews as it did for the rest of the world Jewry. Just before World War II, when most European Jews showed little, if any, genuine enthusiasm in *aliyah*, there was a serious plan to populate the land of Israel with Jewish immigrants from Ethiopia. (The plan undoubtedly got momentum from Rabbi Kook's historic declaration.) Unfortunately, it never got off the ground. Jews from other areas of the world were given a higher priority for immigration into Israel. In addition, the policy of the emperor of Ethiopia, whose friendship the Israeli government sought, was hostile to emigration of Ethiopian citizens.

The 1950s and 1960s—Tokenism and Apathy

In the period following the birth of Israel, the Jewish Agency decided to aid Ethiopian Jews primarily at home. It set up a token teacher-training boarding school in Asmara and elementary schools in the Gondar region. The school in Asmara opened in January 1954 with fifty-seven students, and in 1955–56 twenty-seven of those students were sent to Israel to study in the Youth Aliyah village of Kfar Batya, sponsored by the Mizrachi Women of America. Sadly, the Kfar Batya program was short-lived. In the end, most of the Kfar Batya students returned to Ethiopia in 1957, and no additional ones were sent to Israel. Unfortunately, about the same time, the school in Asmara was closed and moved first to Wuzaba and then, after its facilities were vandalized by hostile villagers, to Ambobar. Ethiopian Jewish education was shrinking rather than growing.

In February 1960 Ethiopian Jews sent an open letter to world Jewish leaders expressing their disappointment concerning the lack of action on the part of their fellow Jews. In this letter they requested help for *aliyah* to Israel and for medical and educational assistance at home. Perhaps as a response, in 1962 an Israeli doctor named Har-El and his wife were sent by the World Jewish Congress to serve in the Gondar region, providing some modest social service. The British Jewish community also organized some services. Unfortunately, these praise-worthy individual efforts were so modest that their effects were hardly felt by most Ethiopian Jews.

Throughout this period, Ethiopian Jews continued to struggle for survival. In most areas, as Ethiopian Jews were not allowed to own land, they worked as sharecroppers for landlords who exacted high rents. In the late 1950s their leaders laid the main grievances before Emperor Hayla Sellasse in palace audiences at least three times. They asked for protection from the high rents and taxes that were being exacted and brought complaints against local people who falsely charged them of sorcery (these charges sometimes resulted in their being murdered and also in attacks of arson). Even when the restrictions against their buying land were lifted, most owners were reluctant to sell land to Jews. Ethiopian Jews continued to be harassed and driven off of the land at will.[13]

Following the historic revolution of 1974, many oppressed minorities, including Jews, sought religious equality and land reform. On March 3, 1975, these groups got the Land Reform Declaration of the Provisional Military Government: land was nationalized and cooperative farms were instituted, though farmers were allowed to own up to twenty-five acres. Although this was welcome news for Ethiopian Jews, in fact, their economic and political conditions deteriorated. The government did not have firm enough control in the countryside to enable the Jews to benefit from its declaration. If anything, the areas inhabited by Jews became veritable battlefields between the government and three of its staunchest enemies: the rival socialist Ethiopian People's Revolutionary Party in Woggera, the anti-Marxist and Muslim-backed Ethiopian Democratic Union in the Gondar area, and the nationalist Tigrai People's Liberation Movement in the north. It has been argued that the Jews were not "specifically selected for persecution," but the fact is that many found themselves directly in the line of fire. Rebellious landlords also individually formed bandit gangs and increasingly harassed the farmers, kidnapping or killing many of them.

In spite of these problems, solidarity efforts such as Ethiopian Jewish immigration to Israel were not put on any official Jewish agenda. From the time that I came to the United States as a student in the late 1950s, I was invited to give numerous lectures in synagogues and Hillel houses here and in Canada. In 1974–75 I was a visiting lecturer at the Hebrew University, and was interviewed on radio and television. I found world Jewry as a whole eager to learn about Ethiopian Jews. Concrete action toward their actual rescue, however, was only a late 1970s development.[14]

The Revival of Ethiopian Jewish Aliyah

The late 1970s represent a turn in the history of the Ethiopian-world Jewish relationship. The British Jewish community established more schools after the 1974 Ethiopian revolution. Israeli agronomist Gershon Levy expanded the educational and communal projects.[15] Also at this time, American solidarity workers regrouped under the American Association for Ethiopian Jews (AAEJ),[16] which came to be known as an activist organization committed chiefly to *aliyah* with (in contrast to other American organizations) little interest in social or educational activities in Ethiopia.[17] The American Jewish Joint Distribution Committee, in conjunction with the World Jewish Congress, also retained contact with Ethiopian Jews. Finally, beginning in July 1977, Organization for Rehabilitation through Training worked with the Joint in Gondar on a program emphasizing technical education and community development.[18]

The Difficult Road

In Israel a committee was formed in the early 1970s to assist Ethiopian Jews. Chaired by Professor Arieh Tartakower, among its members were Ruth Dayan and Ovadia Hazzi, the most active member of the committee.[19] When in 1973 the Sephardi Israeli Chief Rabbi Ovadiah Yosef made his historic affirmation of the Jewishness of Beta Israel and called for their immigration to Israel, it was in the form of a response to Ovadiah Hazzi. Ethiopian Jews were thus deemed eligible for immigration under the Israeli Law of Return. With the rabbinic decision and international, particularly American, pressure, the *aliyah* of Beta Israel was under way.

There were, however, other obstacles to overcome in order to bring about this wave of Jewish immigration. First, there were no official ties between Israel and Ethiopia. Second, the Ethiopian government was opposed to mass migration, fearing, among other things, general minority group unrest. There were also other, outside, pressures on the Ethiopian government to keep Israel at arm's length. But Ethiopia also needed the support of Israel against its Arab-supported enemies. Thus, "unofficial" channels of communication were opened between the two countries, and the Ethiopian government "turned a blind eye" to the emigration of "two groups of between fifty and sixty" who arrived in Israel by air in 1977 in exchange for "a small supply of arms." This process ended when Minister of Defense Moshe Dyaan confirmed reports of the deal in an interview. In spite of the damage, a few other Ethiopian Jews continued to reach Israel independently after 1977.

About this time, the criticism directed at the Israeli government by AAEJ, Canadian Association for Ethiopian Jews, and the North American Jewish media began to grow. Stories and editorials appeared in Jewish newspapers about Israeli inaction. Lectures critical of Israel were given in North American institutions from Yeshiva University to Hillel houses. In local speeches, G. Berger, the founder of AAEJ, outlined the plight of Ethiopian Jews and accused the Israeli government of being indifferent. Later AAEJ chairpersons Howard Lenhoff and Nate Shapiro argued for pressure on the Israeli government to increase immigration. It was argued also that Israeli government records from the 1950s revealed a policy against Ethiopian immigration.

The criticism of the Israeli government by AAEJ and CAEJ escalated when, beginning in 1979, the Council for Ethiopian Jews, a group consisting primarily of 1970s immigrants to Israel, protested over the slow rate of immigration.[20] The immigrants held that the Israeli government was stalling on the issue, hiding behind a concern for secrecy. They then met with Prime Minister Begin, who promised to act. As Israeli officials claimed to be on top of the problem, Ethiopian Jews in Israel proclaimed the death of some three thousand in refugee camps. To assure that things would move forward, they sent letters to American Jewish organizations asking them to increase pressure on Israel to help Ethiopian Jewish *aliyah*. This appeal to world Jewry further brought the matter to wider international attention. The climax came in October 1979, when Yona Boagale made a historic appearance at the annual meeting of the Jewish Federation in Montreal; by 1981 larger numbers of Ethiopian Jews were beginning to reach Israel by "circuitous routes."[21]

Ethiopian policy toward Beta Israel itself became a bone of contention for the opposing forces. Many Israeli and Jewish leaders regarded the policy as benign; others condemned it. The report of WJC visitors to Ethiopia that Jews were no worse off than other Ethiopians infuriated even some Knesset members. Journalists who visited Ethiopia reported stories of persecution, the closing of synagogues, imprisonment, and torture. The threat was said to be from antigovernment forces, by some, and from the Ethiopian government itself, by others. There was one thing on which all sides seemed to agree: Jews were subjected to abuses by rebel forces and active government persecution originated from local rather than national authorities.

In the meantime, the dispute escalated in North America. A National Jewish Community Relations Council tour group claimed to see improving conditions in Ethiopia and criticized stories of mass extermination. A group of four social workers returning from an Ethiopia trip, sponsored by the State Tourist Corporation, also claimed that there was no government persecution or anti-Semitism. A freelance reporter, M. Winn, visited Ethiopia and wrote that Jews were better off under the current government than under the past one. He claimed that the government was in fact helping Jews, but prevented their emigration to avoid charges of favoritism by other groups. He asserted that Jews faced threat of extinction but not from persecution and advocated a "long-term approach" rather than emergency measures. AAEJ criticized these various tour groups and journalists; it held that there was indeed an "emergency." An editorial response in the *Canadian Jewish News* disputed Winn's conclusions. One critical editorial response claimed that optimistic stories "Swept Facts under the Rug." A delegation of sixteen North American Jews to Ethiopia supported AAEJ; it reported pressure to assimilate, closing of schools, and discrimination.[22]

Operation Moses

In North America, Jewish solidarity with Ethiopian Jews and the determination to bring about their immigration to Israel led to various actions. Towns such as Natick and Newton in Massachusetts declared "Ethiopian Jewry Day." The New York State Senate voted to ask for U.S. help in rescuing Ethiopian Jews. In 1982 the U.S. government even proposed accepting Ethiopian Jewish exiles in the States (in case Israel was not prepared to receive them). A number of individual U.S. senators (Tribble) and congressmen (Lantos, Weiss) visited

Ethiopia or issued statements on behalf of Ethiopian Jews. In 1983 the House of Representatives introduced Resolution 107 in support of Ethiopian Jews and sent a letter to the State Department pressing Secretary of State Shultz on the issues of Ethiopian Jewish immigration to Israel and Ethiopian famine relief. The Senate joined in with its own Resolution 55 calling for Ethiopian Jewish emigration. (The Ethiopian government sharply repudiated the Senate resolution as an act of foreign interference and denied allegations of mistreatment of Jews.)

Eventually, immigration of Ethiopian Jews to Israel emerged as an "Urgent Priority." By the beginning of the 1980s, therefore, all conflicting Jewish groups set aside their differences and united in traditional solidarity. The initial efforts of Rav Ovadia Yosef and Rasar Hazzi bore fruit when Prime Minister Begin and members of the Knesset came forward with concrete immigration plans (which were completed under Prime Minister Peres). In North America, much credit goes to the United Jewish Appeal, the Jewish Federations, the Joint, Hadassah, AAEJ, CAEJ, and all the leading North American Jewish organizations.

By November 1984 Operation Moses, the massive airlift of Ethiopian Jews to Israel, was under way in full force. In some ways it was reminiscent of the Magic Carpet, the equally massive airlift of Yemenite Jews in 1948–49. It involved an unbelievable cooperation among many nations,[23] not to mention unusual arrangements with lukewarm Ethiopia and hostile Sudan. At first a secret operation, it was unwittingly revealed to the public by a member of the Jewish Agency before its completion. This caused its abrupt halt on January 6, 1985, and led to an international crisis: Sudan disavowed it and Ethiopia called it international piracy.

But the momentum could not be stopped. Secret negotiations ensued, with the U.S. government playing an active role. In the meantime, many Jews died in the holding camp; others gave up hope and found their way to Europe, America, or back to Ethiopia. In the end, Sudan let the Jews remaining in its territory leave, but not without the official stipulation that they not go to Israel. In the second phase of the airlift, which began in March 1985 and was dubbed "Operation Joshua" and "Operation Miriam" by some, an estimated 1,100 Jews were brought to Israel in a circuitous way.

By the time the operation was complete, there were over 15,000

Ethiopian Jews (mostly young people under the age of twenty) in Israel. Today there are some 16,000 Ethiopian Jews in Israel.

World opinion concerning the operation varied. There were
reports of some exploitation of the immigrants such as the one concerning unconfirmed plans to settle the immigrants in the West Bank.
Others wrote about prejudices. Anthropologists at a conference in
Israel charged that the Jewish Agency was destroying the culture of the
Ethiopian Jews and breeding dependence upon the government at the
absorption centers. These reports of abuse came simultaneously with
reports of increased support by Israeli officials for immigration. In
general, however, in speeches, news analyses, and editorials, most
praised Israel and this act of world Jewish solidarity.[24]

Conclusion

The *aliyah* of Ethiopian Jews to Israel is a remarkable event in
modern Jewish history. Among the specific exiled communities of
Jews mentioned in our Scriptures, we find the *golah* beyond the rivers
of Cush noted and a call for its redemption and return to the Land of
Israel. Ethiopia, a land connected with ancient Israel through legend,
history, language, and literature, has had a special relationship with the
Jewish people. It is a land that has preserved ancient Jewish customs,
where lost but important Jewish literary works such as the *Book of
Enoch* and the *Book of Jubilees* have been discovered and preserved in
their entirety. It is the land where everyone, including even the non-
Jews, calls Friday by no other name than its Jewish one: "the evening
[of Sabbath]."

Moreover, the *aliyah* has been a positive event in modern Jewish
history. It has brought Jews and Israelis from all walks of life together
and has generated a new Jewish zeal as well as heightened the Zionist
spirit. On the international level, it has deflated the pernicious claim
that Israel is racist. Interest in Ethiopian Jews has also generated wide
social and academic activities. A large number of Israeli educators and
social scientists are turning their attention to the intriguing and challenging absorption and integration of Ethiopian Jews and to the study
of their culture.

During the many centuries that Beta Israel lived in Ethiopia, they
never forgot their tie to the land of Israel. For example, their places of

worship must have at least two (large establishments must have four) entrances: one facing east, the other facing northeast to Jerusalem. The priests who officiate in the place of worship must stand beside the Torah facing Jerusalem. Those who enter the place of worship must turn toward Jerusalem and prostrate themselves before entering it.

With the *aliyah* of Ethiopian Jews, the Land of Israel becomes a veritable museum of living Jews coming together in one place, representing the vibrant and major Jewish cultural and historical periods: the Western Jews of the postindustrial and technological era, the Middle Eastern Jews of the medieval era, the Yemenite Jews of the pre-Islamic Rabbinic/Tannaitic/Amoraitic era, and now the Ethiopians of the Israelite priestly Temple era. It is thus important that this recent work of solidarity does not turn out to be a sour one. It should not obscure the potential for unpleasant failures.

One serious problem in Israel affecting life in general, not only concerning Ethiopians, is overburdensome bureaucracy; another is too much self-confidence. The existence of so many organizations trying to do the same thing is a problem. Furthermore, education is a basis of Jewish solidarity without which the Ethiopians cannot make a contribution to Israeli society. To integrate Ethiopians into Israeli culture is also to integrate them into all levels of university and technical education. Mistakes were made with the earlier absorption of Eastern Jews, funneling new Yemenite or Moroccan immigrants to the lower semiskilled or even unskilled level of industry. The consequence has been social polarization.

In this regard also, psychological tests (made for students from Western culture) and other culturally unfair requirements, particularly for Jews who wish to attend the institutions of higher learning, lead to cynical reports about their achievements. Theories once propounded about Eastern Jews—that they are antidemocratic, backward, and levantine in mentality—did not help the nation deal with real problems.

Not involving Ethiopians in leadership, taking responsibilities in all decision-making committees, organizations, and agencies that deal with them are other areas of potential problems. For example, the Faitlovitch library was perfunctorily dismantled some years ago without consulting the Ethiopian community.

Finally, and perhaps the most acute psychological problem faced by the Ethiopians, is the dismemberment of their families due to the

difficult conditions of their departure from Ethiopia. Such disloca-
tions cause depression, which negatively affects the stability of the
community. It generates agony and anxiety, has led some to commit
suicide, and remains an obstacle to the integration of Ethiopian Jews in
Israel. Until families are reunited, it is not possible to say that the rescue
of Ethiopian Jews has been successful.

Potential problems can develop also in the proper integration of
Ethiopian Jews into Israeli society and the *aliyah* of Jews remaining in
Ethiopia as a result of ill-conceived questions of identity or debate
over religious status. Therefore, Ethiopian Jews are rightly troubled by
these questions and angered by the refusal to recognize them as full
Jews. Religious or political authorities should not add to the psychological burden of the Ethiopians by making them feel that they are
neither Jews, nor Christians, nor Muslims. Ethiopian Jews sense in the
demands for renewal a differential treatment and resent it as a form of
religious discrimination. Jews have all lived in a Gentile world for over
two thousand years, and we should be the last to demand nonexisting
ethnic purity.[25]

The enthusiasm with which Ethiopian Jews are now received by
world Jewry reflects ancient Jewish wisdom and solidarity. But as one
begins to deal with real issues in a real world, the enthusiasm of solidarity can come to an end very fast. Ethiopian Jews may begin to
doubt the sincerity of Jewish solidarity if nothing is done soon to aid
their families now left behind in Ethiopia; if the authorities continue
to cast doubt on their commitment to Judaism; and if by the creation
of a poor ghetto society they are left out of an integrated Israeli society. In sum, the ability of the Jewish people to handle insurmountable
problems should be used creatively to assure that the rescue of
Ethiopian Jews enhances Jewish solidarity.

Notes

1.   Ethiopian legends claim that Jews settled in Ethiopia during King Solomon's
time. Certain Eastern Jewish legends claim that the queen of Sheba donated Ethiopia to
King Solomon. According to a certain midrash, however, the contact goes back even farther. This story, based on the intriguing Biblical reference to Moses' Ethiopian wife
(Numbers 12:1), relates that Moses found refuge in Ethiopia after he fled from Pharaoh's
palace; he became, first, a military leader and, later, succeeded the king who died in a battle against the Egyptians and married his widowed queen. According to Josephus, Moses

fought for the Egyptians against the Ethiopians, but conspired with the king's daughter, whom he later married.

2. The empire included pre-Islamic Yemen during much of the first six Christian centuries (cf. H. Z. Hirschberg, *Yesra'el Ba'Arab* [Tel Aviv, 1946], pp. 40, 49ff.).

3. In spite of some scholarly disagreements, a strong case can be made that the names Cush (Genesis 2:13; 10:16ff.; Isaiah 43:3; etc.), Sheba (Genesis 10:7, 28; 1 Kings 10:1ff.; Ezekiel 27:22f. etc.), and Havilah (Genesis 2:11; 10:7, 29; 25:18, etc.) refer to parts of northern and western Ethiopia, and indicate ancient Jewish contact with these lands. The discovery in Ethiopia of a number of important Jewish literary works (among them *The Book of Enoch* and *The Book of Jubilees*), the strong Jewish theological flavor of the Ge'ez language, and the overall Jewish molding of Ethiopian culture—as the German philologist August Dillmann already asserted in the nineteenth century—attest to the unquestionably strong Jewish presence in Ethiopia by early Christian times. Jews must have come to Ethiopia during later historical periods as well. These include the periods after the destruction of the First and Second Temples, in Hellenistic and Roman times, and, possibly, in pre-Solomonic times. Additionally, some Ethiopians converted to the religion of Israel. Ebedmelech (Jeremiah 38:7f.; 10ff.; 39:16) may have been such a convert; the Ethiopian eunuch of the Christian book of Acts (8:26ff.) another. The latter story points to the presence of Ethiopian Jewish pilgrims to the land of Israel.

4. This due to the suppression of the Jewish revolt in Yemen by King Kaleb (527–547) and before the Talmud had reached all of Jewry. Furthermore, the ascendancy of Islam accelerated the eclipse.

5. Sometime in the ninth century, a special sense of world Jewish spiritual solidarity emerged as a direct result of the activity of a certain Eldad ha-Dani, a Jew from Ethiopia (see A. Epstein's classical work *Eldad ha-Dani*, Presburg, 1891; cf. E. D. Goitein, "Note on Eldad", *JQR* 17 (1926–27):483).

6. In other ways, Ethiopian Jewry did not allow itself to be forgotten completely. Throughout the ages there has been a world Jewish obsession to establish contact with the exiles "beyond the rivers of Cush." The stories of Benjamin of Tudela (12th cent.), Elijah of Farrara and Obadiah of Bertinoro (15th), R. David ibn Zimra (16th), Abraham Ferussol (16th), Abraham Yagel (16th), Moses Edrei (17th), and others attest to this. In particular, Rabbi David Ibn Zimra affirmed the continuing Jewish solidarity in his response concerning an Ethiopian Jewish woman and her offspring. However, many years would pass before scholars would sift legend from history to describe the intense historical activity in Ethiopian-world Jewish solidarity.

7. The earliest Jewish scholarly work on Ethiopian Jews was that of linguist Filosseno Luzzato from the famous Italo-German scholarly family. Luzzato read Antoine D'Abbadie's narratives of his travels to Ethiopia, and published his first article in 1851 in the *Archives Israelites* of Paris. The London *Jewish Chronicle* published some translated portions of these articles. His history of Ethiopian Jews was published posthumously in 1854.

8. This action was led by Samuel Gobat, the second Anglican bishop of Jerusalem and a former missionary to Ethiopia. The London Society for Promoting Christianity among the Jews (founded in 1807) put forward, at their 1838 meeting, an aggressive plan for the evangelization of Ethiopian Jews. This group saw Ethiopian Jews as potential targets for conversion. Additionally, they believed that Jewish converts could be good evangelists similar to the early apostles, and could help "purify" Ethiopian

Christianity (meaning, make them "Protestants") and further the evangelization of Africa.

9.   Among those whose voices were raised was the distinguished Rabbi Israel Hildsheimer of Eisenstadt, Germany, who in 1864 pleaded for solidarity in the rescue of Ethiopian Jews.

10.   Some contemporary writers claim that this was due to doubts concerning the Jewishness of Beta Israel or because the notion of a "Jewish race" seemed to rule out the existence of Black Jews (David Kessler, *The Falashas: The Forgotten Jews of Ethiopia* [London: Geroge Allen & Unwin, 1982], p. 118). This, however, is reading modern reasons into past history. In fact, the nineteenth-century European theory of race put the so-called Hamites, to which the Ethiopian race was thought to belong, in the same Caucasian racial category as Europeans, Indians, and "Semites." At this time, the predominant view was that European Jews, unlike the white Arians, were descendants of dark-complexioned "primitive" Semites. Scholars like Renan, who looked down on the Semites, held that European Jews were non-Semitic; most European Jews of the nineteenth century, however, regarded themselves as Semites. In my judgment, the lack of immediate aid to Ethiopian Jewry cannot be separated from Jewish and world social, political, and economic conditions of the time. For West European Jews, political emancipation did not mean social equality and unlimited freedom in international operations and East European Jews were themselves needy. A major operation beyond the borders of the Ottoman Empire would have not been possible.

11.   "Rapport concernant la mission aupres des Falachas" (*Bulletin* of Alliance Israelite Universelle, Paris, 1968) and his "Excursion chez les Falachas, en Abyssinie" (*Bulletin de la Societe de Geographie*, Paris, 1869).

12.   *Prieres des Falachas* (1877), *Te'ezaza Sanbat* "Sabbath Commandments" (1902; the French version was the basis of Leslau's *Falasha Anthology*), and *La guerre de Sarsa Dengel contra les Falachas* (1907).

13.   Various other attempts were made by Ethiopian Jews to ameliorate their own condition. One such attempt was the participation in the Setit-Humera Development Project, organized by the Ethiopian government with the assistance of the United Nations and the World Bank. The project involved clearing malaria-infested lowlands in western Begemeder, near the Sudan border, and developing farms. Ethiopian Jews initially regarded this as an opportunity to acquire their own land and to grow cash crops. A group of people formed a commune and for five years worked side by side to clear and cultivate some five thousand acres of land. Unfortunately, it turned to be a sour experiment. At first, they were feared and harassed by some Sudanese as Zionist agents. Then, the general lack of safety in the area due to the various warring factions made life unbearable and they were soon forced off the land.

14.   According to some knowledgeable insiders and reliable sources, certain powerful and vocal leaders objected to Ethiopian Jews because of their color and supposed primitivity. Until the Yom Kippur War of 1973, Israel had strong and important diplomatic and economic ties with Ethiopia. The opponents of *aliyah* also held that raising the issue of mass immigration might endanger this relationship.

15.   For example, in cooperation with the Israeli government, Levy worked on a revolving credit fund for farmers. One of his more curious undertakings, however, involved a census of Ethiopian Jews: he found a total population of 28,189, consisting of 6,092 families in 490 mixed villages. Although his census was private and unofficial and did not take into account the traditional Ethiopian suspicion of counting people, it is surprisingly regarded by non-Ethiopians as the final word.

16.   In the 1960s, under the leadership of Martin Wurmbrand, the Pro-Falasha Committee evolved into the "American Friends of Beta Israel (Falasha) Committee," established by Jed Abraham, an Orthodox Jewish Peace Corps volunteer in Ethiopia. This organization was then absorbed into the American Association for Ethiopian Jews (AAEJ), established by Graenum Berger, formerly of the New York Jewish Federation.

17.   Because it came to be regarded as a controversial organization, its important contribution to the history of Ethiopian Jews has not yet been fully recognized.

18.   By 1979 ORT administered 19 village schools with about 1,660 pupils; in 1980 this number had grown to about 2,245 pupils. Clinics were also restored in Ambober and Tedda. A clear drinking water fountain and a flour mill were provided at Ambober. A road from Tedda to Wuzba and a factory for manufacturing hollow-block bricks were also built. The community "revolving credit fund" development program provided assistance to about 384 families. Religious institutions and programs were also supported. Hebrew prayer books were donated through the help of Yemenite Jews in Addis Abbaba. Fifteen synagogues, each having a Hebrew class, and about twenty-six priests were directly supported by ORT.

In the late 1970s ORT came under criticism by an association of Ethiopian Jews in Israel and by AAEJ in America; both groups advocated work toward *aliyah* as the best way of helping the Ethiopians. ORT also came under Ethiopian government criticism, ironically because some officials thought that it was encouraging *aliyah* via the Sudan. In October 1981 the government took over ORT's programs except the medical clinics.

19.   Hazzi himself was an Ethiopian Jew of Yemenite origin. He never lost contact with Ethiopia, and frequently visited the Jewish communities there. As a family friend (my parents shared his home for a year when they made *aliyah* to Israel in 1971), I have come to know him well. Few did as much for Ethiopian Jews at a crucial period in their history. An ardent Jewish Zionist, he used his extensive connections in Israeli official circles to get authorities to recognize Ethiopian Jews.

20.   See the exchanges in the many major newspapers around the United States: *Jewish Advocate*, Boston, February 11, 1982, "Exclusive: Leading Officials Clash on the Falasha Issue"; *Jerusalem Post*, March 31, 1983, "Call to Save Falashas Who Face Death in Refugee Camps," "Jewish Agency Officials Try to Muzzle AAEJ—MK BenPorat Comes to Its Defense"; *Sentinel*, March 24, 1983; *Jewish Telegraph Agency Daily News Bulletin*, January 25, 1983; *Moment*, "Truth-Telling and Leadership in American Jewish Life"; *New York Times*, May 4, 1985, "Falashas Emancipated by Ethiopia's Revolution" and Letter to the Editor in response to April 23 article entitled "Dying Ethiopian Jews."

21.   Simon D. Messing, *The Story of the Falashas: "Black Jews" of Ethiopia* (Brooklyn, N.Y.: Balshon, 1982), p. 93, n. 85; *New York Times*, November 15, 1981; *Sentinel*, March 24, 1983, "Why Doesn't Israel Do Something about Ethiopian Jews?", January 29, 1981, "After Shoah, Could We Live?", February 24, 1983, Letter to the Editor, "JTA Dispatch is Latest Effort in Campaign to Stall Falasha's Rescue," April 18, 1983, "What Is Involved in Actually Rescuing Falashas from the Refugee Camps," April 14, 1983, p. 16; *Jewish-American Examiner*, February 2, 1982; *Heritage*, April 17, 1981, "Falashas Appeal to U.S. Jewry"; *Jewish Post*, April 30, 1981; *Jewish Post and Opinion*, June 27, 1980, "Israel at Fault"; *Jerusalem Press International Edition*, May 1–7, 1983, "End the Silence on Falashas"; *New York Times*, March 2, 1984, "Exodus for a Twice-Lost Tribe"; *Wall Street Journal*, March 13, 1984, "The Endangered Falashas"; *Jewish World*, January 6, 1983, "Falasha Cry for Help"; *Globe and Mail*, September 26, 1981, "Black Jews of Ethiopia Nearly Extinct"; *The Journal*, April 23, 1981, "Jewry Warms Up to Falashas, but Doubts

Remain"; *Connecticut Jewish Ledger*, March 12, 1981, "JCC Series Speaker Urges the Rescue of Ethiopian Jews"; *Israel Today*, San Diego, December 1982, "Falasha Advocate Deplores Neglect"; *Detroit Jewish News*, April 23, 1983, "Silence on Falashas Deplored"; *Long Island Jewish World*, January 22–28, 1982; *Ha-Or*, March 25, 1981, "Israel's Falasha Policy Criticized"; *Intermountain Jewish News*, July 17, 1981, "If Jewish World Roused Itself, Falasha Jews Could Be Saved," December 25, 1981, "The Scandal of Silence on Ethiopic Jewry"; *Jerusalem Post* International Edition, December 20–26, 1981, "Against Quiet Despair"; *Israel Today*, January 28, 1982, "Documents Reveal Longstanding Policy against Falasha *Aliyah*"; *Jewish Week*, May 19–25, 1983; Kessler, p. 162.

22.   *Israel Today*, March 16–19, 1979, "Anti-Government Forces in Ethiopia Threaten Survival"; *Jewish Journal*, May 22, 1981; *National Jewish Monthly*, May 1981, "The Falashas: Doomed to Extinction?"; *Jewish Post*, May 28, 1981, "Ethiopian Jews Reported Tortured, Enslaved"; *New York Times*, October 21, 1981, "Ethiopic Black Jews, a Periled Community"; *Washington Post*, November 1, 1983, "Strangers in Their Own Land"; *Jewish Week-American Examiner*, May 16, 1982, "The Forgotten Falashas," June 6, 1982, "Poor, Isolated, Black Jews Yearn for Contact—ORT Schools Stand Half Furnished," February 17, 1984, "Doom Is Feared for the Falashas unless Their Rescue Is Quick"; *Ethiopian Herald*, January 12, 1982; *Jewish Advocate*, January 21, 1982, "Journey of the Falashas of Ethiopia"; *Genesis*, February 1982, "A Journey to the World of the Falashas of Ethiopia"; *Anti-Defamation League Bulletin*, May 1982, "Jounee to Gondar;" *San Diego Jewish Press Heritage*, May 28, 1982, "Journey to Save Falashas"; *Baltimore Jewish Times*, August 30, 1982, "Falashas: Not Persecuted, Israel Helping"; *Present Tense*, Summer 1982; *Jerusalem Post* International Edition, January 23–29, 1983, "Falashas Reputed to Be Living Well in Ethiopia"; *JCE*, November 8, 1983, "Falashas Describe Religious Persecution in Ethiopia"; *Hadassah Magazine*, January 1984, "Ethiopian Journey"; *JTA Daily News Bulletin*, March 12, 1984, "Special Interview—The Falashas: An Endangered People"; *Daily News Bulletin*, May 27, 1984.

23.   Operation Moses was a joint effort of many people and many organizations. World Jewry, particularly the U.S. and the Canadian Jewish community, responded generously. The United Jewish Appeal pledged $60 million toward the effort, and actually raised about $70 million by the time the campaign was concluded. It is believed that American rabbis as a whole had never responded with such financial commitment to an Israeli cause, not even during the Six-Day War. The government of Israel, the United States and other nations, the Jewish Agency, Israeli and international airline personnel, international negotiators, and many people in every walk of life helped carry out the historic operation.

24.   A speech given by Marvin S. Arrington, president of the Atlanta City Council, which was reprinted in the *Atlanta Journal and Constitution* expresses best the overall international reaction to world Jewish solidarity with Ethiopian Jews:

> Television news revealed that the Israeli government had airlifted thousands of starving black Jews from the Sudan and Ethiopia to a new home in the holy land. I sat dumbfounded. My logical, well-educated mind would not allow me to believe it was true. My knowledge of history, my understanding of Western culture, the recognition of powerful racism that still pervades our lives, both political and social, told me that this act of compassion and concern could not be occurring. . . .
>
> The Israelis have demonstrated to the world that there is brotherhood of man and that it is not bound to race. So many talk of love, but Israel has acted. It is relatively easy for the wealthy to send their money to feed the hungry of Africa for a

few weeks. For Israel, that is not enough. Israel has seen through the immediate problem to its cause and has taken caution to break the cycle of starvation by transporting these thousands into a new land where they can build new lives and become self-sufficient. That, in itself, would have been remarkable, but Israel has done more. . . .

As no group of people have ever done, the people of Israel have demonstrated that we are our brothers' keepers and that kinship transcends race. A tiny nation of approximately three million people has shown the world clearly that we can live by our loftiest ideals.

25.   So far the rabbinate has acted wisely by dropping its earlier demand that Ethiopian Jews undergo *hattafat dam brit* [symbolic] dripping of covenant blood, to the token ritual of circumcision for males. But the remaining dispute concerning *tebilah* or *mikveh* immersion or baptism ritual, in spite of its modification in February 1985, continues to embroil the community. *Tebilah* in water is actually a fine idea for all Jewish immigrants, not only for the Ethiopians. Perhaps a *takkanah* should be made requiring the immersion of all new Jewish immigrants to the land of Israel, including even the Hasidim.

Voices from the Field

Multiculturalism as Experienced in Jewish Social Service Agencies

NORA GOLD

Multiculturalism has made some very important social contributions by affirming the value of ethnic and cultural distinctness, articulating the way that power is used by the dominant culture against racial and ethnic minorities, and legitimizing ethnic-specific forms of expression, including communal institutions. In addition, the ideals and intentions at the heart of multiculturalism deserve nothing but praise. However, like any other social policy, multiculturalism has been forged and implemented through a political process, and as a result, its ideals and principles have become compromised in practice. In the process of "birthing" multiculturalism, people of color have played a major leadership role in defining the terms of reference and the agenda, and one result of this has been the implicit equation of ethnic "diversity" with "visible minority."[1] As this definition de facto excludes Jews from the multicultural agenda, relations between Jews and Blacks in particular have become very strained, which is ironic, of course, given the original intent of multiculturalism. This exclusion of Jews has also led many Jewish people who initially hailed the ideas of multiculturalism to become quite disillusioned and even cynical about it.

In academia, for example, the groups involved in promoting multiculturalism have responded with indifference, or worse, to Jewish issues and to anti–Semitism (Alexander, 1992; Beck, 1992). Specifically in my discipline, social work, there has been a laudable commitment not only to multiculturalism, but also to antiracism: there are task forces, conferences, and workshops, as well as considerable soul searching about how we can more effectively teach our students about racism and the importance of fighting it in an active and serious way. However, as many Jewish social work educators have noted privately (and as only a few have noted publicly), Jews and anti-Semitism are simply not on the antiracism agenda in schools of social work (Gold, 1996; Soifer, 1991). This is by no means unique to our discipline; on the contrary, it is typical of the current political climate in universities all across North America (Alexander, 1992).

As important as what happens in "the ivory tower" is, however, it is equally important to ask to what extent this experience reflects what is happening "in real life." Social work is very concerned with the relationship between theory and practice, and this led me to wonder whether *real people* (in this case Jews in need) are being adversely affected by multiculturalism. I wanted to know if Jewish communal institutions are being affected, and if so, how. Has it altered their capacity to care for Jewish people in need? their funding? their mandate? their "Jewish character"? Or is "the Jewish problem with multiculturalism" (ibid.) merely, in both senses of the word, an academic issue?

In order to begin answering these questions, I interviewed sixteen professionals (directors, supervisors, and frontline social workers) from a number of different Jewish social service agencies. These interviews, in which I asked what they thought and felt about multiculturalism, were quite informal, and their purpose was to begin to get some sense of what Jews out in the field were experiencing. The thoughts, anecdotes, and stories that I heard from these people led me quickly to feel that I had just dipped a toe into a vast and unexplored ocean, and that some in-depth research is urgently needed in order to adequately address this topic. I present here these first gleanings—not in the spirit of providing answers, but more in the hope that they will lead us toward some meaningful and useful questions.

Voices from the Field

Almost everyone I spoke to had something positive to say about multiculturalism and could identify ways in which it had enriched and improved their work. Simultaneously, however, there was a tone of disappointment regarding those things that they felt multiculturalism had promised yet failed to deliver. This mixed response of both praise and disappointment was strikingly consistent throughout the interviews, and created the tension of a piece of music written half in a major, and half in a minor, key. In some ways, it was like listening to a dialogue between their minds and hearts, or between their identities as professionals (excited by multiculturalism) and as Jews (disillusioned by it). This lack of integration in their responses indicated to me that there is some weakness in the phenomenon they are responding to, much as Jewish women often "split" (into "woman" versus "Jew") in response to the limitations imposed on women within Judaism. The weakness in multiculturalism as expressed by these professionals is the inconsistency between its theory and its practice, exemplified most obviously and painfully in its relationship to Jews.

In addition to disappointment and excitement, there was a third thread running through the responses (and maybe in a way a resolution of the first two): a kind of philosophical resignation combined with pragmatism. It is as if these senior professionals were saying, with almost a visible shrug of their shoulders, "Multiculturalism, shmulti-culturalism. Like all the other trends, ideologies, movements, it'll come, and it'll go. But Jews will remain—and we will do whatever we need to, to make sure that we remain strong." I will now elaborate on each of these three themes.

The Disappointment of Multiculturalism

The key disappointment of multiculturalism in the eyes of these professionals lay in its failure to promote greater understanding about Jews among non-Jews. Many of them commented on their frustration that multiculturalism had not achieved more, had not really improved anything at all, with regard to Jewish/non-Jewish relations. These people had hoped that multiculturalism would provide a social climate where Jewish uniqueness would be legitimized along with the uniqueness of other "diverse" ethnic groups. They expected that as Jews learned about other cultures, and others learned about ours, there would be an increase in mutual respect, understanding, and tolerance, perhaps even resulting in a decrease in anti-Semitism.

These things, from their perspective, did not come to pass. Anti-Semitism actually increased in Canada, and significantly so (B'nai Brith, 1995), and the hoped-for mutual understanding and respect was experienced as far from mutual. One supervisor noted bitterly that in workshops on multiculturalism, participants are taught about all kinds of cultures and ethnic groups, but never about Jews. Another re-marked that he works, as a representative of his agency, on several city-wide antiracism coalitions, yet none of his colleagues ever turn up to show *their* support when an action is taken to protest against anti-Semitism. He said that these colleagues, from various other "ethnic" agencies, perceived his agency as "mainstream," since theirs, which were relatively new and grassroots, had smaller budgets, and also because Jews were not a visible minority. In his view, although relations between them were fairly cordial, there was a real lack of understanding that Jews are something other than simply "white." Others felt this way as well. Only about half the people I spoke to believed that Jewishness was recognized, and respected, by their non-Jewish colleagues. Some expressed feelings of hurt and frustration on their clients' behalf, because of what clients often experienced outside the agency. One social worker said caustically: "Jewish clients do not receive 'ethnic sensitivity' out there." Another commented that Jewish social services were a necessity not only for positive reasons, but also because of the insensitivity of most non-Jews to central features of Jewish history and reality. This worker had a number of clients who had previously been in various therapeutic groups around town, but with all the talk about multiculturalism, nowhere had any of their experiences as Holocaust survivors, or as the children of Holocaust survivors, been addressed or even recognized as a significant issue. As a result, some social workers were ambivalent about referring their clients to non-Jewish agencies. This, of course, has serious implications for Jewish clients getting the kinds of care that they need, since Jewish services alone cannot possibly provide every specialized service that might be required; so one worker found an ingenious solution to this problem. She had a network of Jewish colleagues, some of whom had previously worked with her at a Jewish agency and were now working in non-Jewish settings. When she had to refer a client to a non-Jewish service, she would refer him or her specifically to someone from her network, and ask this colleague to keep an eye out for her client. "I shouldn't have to be doing this," she said. "I shouldn't have to be protecting my clients in this way. But this is the way it is."

The Positive Effects of Multiculturalism

In spite of the disappointments associated with it, multiculturalism was seen by these professionals as having had some positive effects on their work. For example, more than half of those I interviewed felt that multiculturalism had had a positive effect on "the Jewish character of the agency." Paradoxical as this may sound, it appears that although these professionals may have felt excluded as Jews by the day-to-day manifestations of multiculturalism, they also felt that what they were doing was legitimized and affirmed by the *theory* of multiculturalism, which justified and even supported ethnic-specific service delivery. Their comments regarding the uniqueness of their agency *as a Jewish agency* reflected contemporary multicultural parlance and perspective, and could have been made by social service providers from any number of diverse ethnic groups. They spoke about the need for social services provided within the cultural framework of Jewish tradition and values, and the psychological and communal importance of receiving care and assistance from other Jews, and "in the Jewish way." To illustrate this point, they offered two examples of services that existed in the non-Jewish sector, but where the absence of a *Jewish* service was keenly felt. One service identified as missing was a Jewish hospice for Jews with terminal illnesses so that people could be cared for in the context of the Jewish approach to death and dying. The other was a Jewish shelter for battered women. Some Jewish clients who had had to seek refuge "in church basements" told their social workers that they felt they had been betrayed by the Jewish community, which had refused to respond to their needs and instead had "sent them outside"; they had longed to be helped and cared for *as part of the Jewish community*. Obviously, Jewish professionals recognized long before multiculturalism came along how important it was for Jews to receive *Jewish* social services. However, what was striking here was the frequent reference to multiculturalism as a justification for this conviction, and the use of examples drawn from other "ethnic" agencies.

Another positive effect of multiculturalism, and perhaps its most significant contribution, was its sensitizing staff to ethnic diversity *within the Jewish community*. In the words of one supervisor, multiculturalism at her agency was primarily defined in terms of "multidiversity among Jewish ethnic groups." This particular interpretation of multiculturalism led agencies to recognize that they needed to reach out more to non-Ashkenazi Jews in the community, such as Sephardi and Ethiopian Jews, as well as those from the former Soviet Union and Yugoslavia. Yet some were frustrated by what were essentially the problems of cross-cultural outreach. For example, one woman felt that Jews from the former Soviet Union did not use her particular agency because they wanted to be helped only by other Russian Jews:

"They want their own people." Another worker cited an Ethiopian Jew who said she preferred to obtain help from non-Jews for fear that a Jewish agency would be "too Jewish," and try to impose on her "their kind" of Judaism. A number of those I spoke to were involved in outreach efforts to these particular groups; they clearly valued this work, although they found it difficult and met with varying degrees of success.

For a few individuals, multiculturalism opened their minds not only about ethnic differences, but about other differences and inequities as well. For example, one worker spoke of increased sensitivity to the issue of class as a result of multiculturalism, and gave examples of stereotypes that she and others had previously held about Jews who were poor or on welfare (e.g., that domestic violence is not "a Jewish problem" except among the poor). Similarly, one supervisor said it was because of the discussions about multiculturalism, diversity, and "inclusion" that she began to recognize that those at the highest echelon of the agency reflected only the "dominant [Jewish] culture" (i.e., Ashkenazi and middle-class) and none of the "minority" ethnic subgroups or the working class. Someone else said that multiculturalism opened up for her the whole issue of "difference," and she indirectly attributed to multiculturalism her learning about, and confronting her own, homophobia. Because multiculturalism was seen as increasing worker sensitivity, awareness, and responsiveness in these areas, a number of the people I spoke to felt that multiculturalism had helped improve the quality of service at their agency. Some identified specific areas of improvement, such as introducing new methods of intervention and changing the internal structure of the agency. Others felt that the intellectual and professional stimulation they received from the ideas associated with multiculturalism had made their jobs more interesting and challenging, and consequently had helped increase their job satisfaction.

The Management of Multiculturalism
(Or, "It hasn't helped, but it hasn't hurt")

From an administrative perspective, multiculturalism was less a disappointment or a source of professional stimulation, and more something to be managed so that the agency would not be hurt in any way. The senior administrators whom I spoke to seem to have been effective in this regard: they said that their agencies had not been hurt financially in any respect that could be directly related to multiculturalism, and they thought that their agencies were in stable financial condition. This is not to say that they did not experience any cutbacks; but they saw these as related to the recession, and not to multiculturalism or to indications of anti-Semitism in the general political climate. One senior administrator summarized his perception of the relationship between multiculturalism and the financial well-being of his agency by paraphrasing the punchline of an old Jewish joke: "It hasn't helped," he said, "but it also hasn't hurt."[2]

The administrators I spoke to suggested there were certain strategies that they employed that helped them succeed in protecting their agencies. One was the agency having a long-term involvement with organizations in the larger community like the United Way, an umbrella organization for a number of charities, cutting across ethnic and religious lines. This kind of participation was seen as the right thing to do because "Jews should take part in the life of their community," but also it was of practical benefit in terms of building positive relationships with other local organizations, including funding bodies and the government. From this perspective, managing multiculturalism was merely an old game with some new lingo, the purpose being the protection of Jewish interests by ensuring the continuity of Jewish communal institutions.

Similarly, supervisors and frontline staff employed specific strategies to protect the interests of Jewish clients. One example was the issue of intake. A Jewish agency known for its professional excellence as well as the fact that it did not have a waiting list was often in great demand from both Jews and non-Jews. The agency, of course, had a policy of serving anyone who applied to it for help, yet some of the social workers there had mixed feelings about this. "People are people," one of them said. "Of course, you would like to help everybody. But in some ways I would like to see our resources made available first to the Jewish community." One worker tried to resolve this conflict by explaining to new applicants that this was a Jewish agency and that it operated within this particular cultural framework. She made it very clear to me that her agency has never turned anyone away or refused to provide anyone with service. Just the same, it did often turn out that, after this explanation, clients elected to go elsewhere, sometimes to an agency of their own ethnic background. In this way, this worker felt that she helped preserve the Jewish character and mandate of her agency in terms that were consistent with the spirit of multiculturalism and yet did not violate her professional values and ethics. This example illustrates the complexity of trying to balance universalistic and particularistic commitments in the context of social service delivery, and the intersection of the idealistic and the pragmatic in the kinds of solutions reached.

Discussion

From this modest exploration of the topic, it appears that multiculturalism is experienced by at least some social workers in Jewish agencies in ways that are negative, positive, and neutral, all at the same time. On the negative side, multiculturalism was seen as a disappointment because of its exclusion of Jews and its failure to increase understanding about Jews and anti-Semitism in the larger community. Positively, it seems to have been "good for the Jews" by *theoretically* supporting the legitimacy of ethnic-specific agencies, and by introducing ideas that have resulted in services that were more responsive to client need and to the community as a whole. In terms of neutral effects, multiculturalism appears to have had no impact, either positive or negative, on the financial well-being of Jewish social service agencies.

The viewpoints, perceptions, and feelings voiced by these professionals have a number of implications. First of all, the comments "from the field" strikingly parallel, in their sense of disappointment and exclusion, the way that multiculturalism has been experienced by Jews in academia and elsewhere. While being cautious not to overgeneralize, this does suggest that the "Jewish problem with multiculturalism" is far from just academic, and that it should be taken seriously. Some work is being done now in social work education to try to address this problem. For example, Saunders, Gold, Johnson, and Garber (1995) have initiated an ongoing dialogue between Black and Jewish social work educators on the issues of anti-Semitism, racism, and "diversity"; and this author has critiqued multiculturalism from a Jewish perspective, and demanded that Jews and anti-Semitism be put on the agenda in schools of social work (Gold, 1993, 1996). Similarly, Jewish social workers in the field have an important role to play in educating their non-Jewish counterparts and putting Jews and anti-Semitism on the multicultural agenda. One way to do this might be to organize a work-shop entitled "Working with the Jewish Client," and offer it on a reg-ular basis to the professional community at large. Such a workshop, as one of many others on "social work and diversity," would be an im-portant first step in dealing with the invisibility of Jews within multi-cultural social work. Social workers in Jewish agencies are in an ideal position to perform this community education role, because they have support on these issues from their colleagues at work, as well as from the institution itself. On the other hand, Jewish social workers in non-Jewish settings often lack this support, and they can feel quite vulner-able, even "outnumbered," at work, especially if they have tried to raise the issue of anti-Semitism at their agencies. Sometimes these workers look to their colleagues at Jewish agencies to provide them with support, both moral and intellectual. In the words of one young woman, they need "weapons," considered arguments with which to fight anti-Semitism in the current multicultural climate.[3]

Anti-Semitism does need to be fought, and to do this it is essential that Jewish professionals remain engaged with non-Jews in dialogue and joint activism. This can be very difficult. For example, Black-Jew-ish relations are very strained at the present time; yet even now there are Blacks and Jews who recognize their commonalities of interest, and are doing some important work together (Hooks, 1992; Pogrebin, 1991; Saunders et al., 1995; West, 1993). When we work *as Jews* with other groups, we need to ask ourselves questions like: What does it mean for building alliances with others that Jews are predominantly white and middle-class, unlike most of the other ethnic groups around the multicultural table? What can we share with them from our expe-rience to help them in their struggles, and how do we do this without being patronizing? What can we learn from *them*? And how can we work together, responsibly acknowledging our relative privilege without allowing others to deny or trivialize the oppression that we have experienced as Jews? These are hard questions, and when faced with them, we can feel the temptation to withdraw into ourselves—a temptation that is especially strong at times like these, when we feel excluded and marginalized. But we must not succumb to it. *Tikkun olam*, repairing and transforming the world around us, is now (as ever) both a moral and a pragmatic imperative.

In addition to changing other people and their communities, we need to look inward and work to transform our own. This means confronting the real tension between the universal and the particular, and beginning to articulate more clearly than we have until now on what ethical and practical bases we balance "If I am not for myself, who is?" with "If I am only for myself, what am I?" These are questions that not only individuals, but Jewish social service agencies as collectivities, should be actively struggling with. Issues of how intake is managed, and how priorities are set when resources are scarce, are issues of not only practical, but also ethical and cultural, significance.

We also need to find ways to make Jewish social services, and the Jewish community in general, more inclusive, responsive, and democratic. This may be difficult to achieve, but citing one or two unsuccessful experiences with non-Ashkenazi employees (as one supervisor did) is simply not sufficient justification for having only Ashkenazi Jews at the upper echelons of our institutions. What can we do differently so that Ethiopian, Russian, and Sephardi Jews are more equitably represented in social services, not only among our clients, but also as staff, supervisors, and agency directors? And if we think about inclusiveness in its broadest sense—in terms not only of ethnicity, but also of gender, class, age, ability, and sexual orientation—what are the implications for trying to create a Jewish community and Jewish communal institutions that are truly inclusive, and reflective, of all *am Yisrael*, the whole Jewish people?

Finally, further research is necessary. Future studies should examine the impact of multiculturalism not only on Jewish social service agencies, but on a wide variety of other communal institutions, including Jewish day schools, hospitals, and homes for the aged. Both quantitative and qualitative methods should be used to explore how these institutions have been affected in terms of their internal structures and processes, their quality of service, their funding, and their relationships with government bodies and other organizations in the community. We also need to explore more fully the ways that Jews have experienced multiculturalism, in terms of both its positive and negative effects. Research, critical questioning, open discussions of these issues among ourselves and with others, and social and communal action are all essential as we struggle to define ourselves as Jews and as North Americans in the context of contemporary multiculturalism.

Notes

1.   The equation of "diversity" with "visible minority" has meant, among other things, the negation of the diversity of people (like Jews) who belong to "invisible minorities." According to this way of thinking, Jews cannot be included in discussions of diversity because, in a white world, we can "pass," and therefore we are really "just like everybody else." This argument—which obviously reflects an appalling ignorance of Jewish history and also conveniently ignores the existence of non-white Jews (e.g., those from Ethiopia, Yemen, and various other Middle Eastern and North African countries)—claims that Jews are too much a part of the dominant culture and not sufficiently oppressed to be defined as a "diverse" ethnic, cultural, or racial group.

2.   In this joke, a woman runs up to a dead man who has been hit by a car and starts spooning chicken soup into his mouth. A doctor comes over and says, "Madam, it won't help." "Maybe it won't help," she answers, "but it can't hurt!"

3.   For an argument to use in these kinds of situations, see Gold (1996).

References

Alexander, Edward. "Multiculturalism's Jewish Problem." *Academic Questions* (Fall 1992).

Beck, Evelyn. "Judaism, Feminism and Psychology: Making the Links Visible." Paper presented at the First International Conference on Judaism, Feminism and Psychology, Seattle, Wash., 1992.

B'nai Brith Canada League for Human Rights. 1994 Audit of Anti-Semitic Incidents. Downsview: Author, 1995.

Gold, Nora. "On Diversity, Jewish Women, and Social Work." *Canadian Social Work Review* 10, no. 2 (1993):240–55.

————. 1996. "Putting Anti-Semitism on the Anti-Racism Agenda in Schools of Social Work in North America." *Journal of Social Work Education* 32, no. 1 (1996):77–89.

hooks, bell. "Keeping a Legacy of Shared Struggle." *Z Magazine* (September 1992):3–25.

Pogrebin, Lettin Cottin. *Deborah, Golda, and Me: Being Female and Jewish in America.* Toronto: Doubleday, 1991.

Saunders, Marlene, Nora Gold, George Johnson, and Ralph Garber. "Exploring the Implications of Black-Jewish Relations for Teaching Empowerment and Diversity." Paper presented at the annual program meeting, Council on Social Work Education, San Diego, March 2–5, 1995.

Soifer, Steven. "Infusing Content about Jews and About anti-Semitism into the Curricula." *Journal of Social Work Education* 27, no. 2 (1991):156–167.

West, Cornel. "How to End the Impasse." *New York Times*, April 14, 1993.

Facilitating Multicultural Progress
Community Economic Development
and the American Jewish Community

JEFFREY DEKRO

Multiculturalism, often understood as an amalgam of social, cultural, and political elements, also requires the development of an economic base. Ultimately, every community's most serious concerns relate to social dignity *and* to economic equity: (1) Are we accorded genuine cultural and political rights, participation, and expression? (2) Do we also have genuine financial opportunity with sufficient resources to fulfill all our potential? The second question is critical because without sufficient economic wherewithal, cultural development will be slowed or even undermined. Between communities with unequal opportunities and financial resources, both these questions are often at the root of highly exacerbated and competitive, even antagonistic, power relationships. Intergroup tensions and hatreds may result.

Although discussion about multiculturalism *per se* has stimulated an often hostile debate, most American Jews share the goals of obliterating explicit legal and other social discrimination or prejudice. American Jews have prized the sharing of traditional values in intergroup dialogue to help eliminate bias and create the possibility for genuine respect. Such discussions are welcome trust-building processes that can sustain and expand our nation's civic and religious liberties and freedom.

But what specifically can the relatively well-off Jewish community offer low-income communities and, thereby, help expand America's potential? The American Jewish community's socioeconomic structure is itself a model blend of cultural mores and customs that facilitates greater economic security. One historical strength of the American Jewish community is that its organizational structure (a network of religious and secular institutions), its mores and customs (a mixture of respect for family and community and support for social justice), and its economic development capacity (well-developed financial and entrepreneurial skills) have been in harmony. As a result, both individuals and the larger American Jewish community have benefited: numerous individuals and families became wealthy at the same time that communal bonds and values were strengthened.

Further, it can be said that the interpenetration of cultural and economic factors is a weave of mutually supportive elements that gives texture to the conventional Jewish community. These synergistic factors advance both cultural expression and economic interests. For example: (1) Membership in Jewish country clubs across the country depends on the capacity to show evidence of contributions to the local federation and/or United Way. (2) Access to increased business contacts is provided through the respective business and professional divisions of every local Jewish community federation.

In addition to financial assets, American Jews have acquired tremendous organizational and technical expertise as a result of more than a century of institution building. For example, as part of the community's economic development in the late nineteenth and early twentieth centuries, American Jews created Hebrew Free Loan Societies and Landsmanschaften Societies, the former for local residents, and the latter for local residents from a particular town in Europe. Up until the early 1930s, Hebrew Free Loan Societies financed Jewish business activity in New England because commercial banks there would not lend to Jews. Given that background, the Jewish community would do well to assist low-income economic development today with financing and credit. Direct economic assistance can be combined with technical advice from experienced developers, bankers, and managers. To whatever degree possible, both financial and technical assistance should be funneled through institutions located in and controlled by residents of low-income communities, helping poor communities replicate American Jewish community development. Thus, by helping strengthen the capacity for both economic and cultural development, American Jews can assist others in proceeding on their own long march from society's margins to its center.

American Jewish relations with minority and low-income communities also have a shadow side. Due to the disproportionate numbers of Jewish teachers, social workers, attorneys, shopkeepers, and property owners, the encounter between the poor and the Jewish middle class has been intimate and conflicted. Sometimes the simple facts of the American Jewish community's enviable status and history inspire resentment by other groups. Further, vocal opposition to affirmative action by the Anti-Defamation League and tensions between Orthodox and/or Hasidic communities and their non-white neighbors have fostered an impression of Black-Jewish friction, in particular. All this has tended to eclipse the reality of mutual cooperation—and indifference. Just as active Jewish support for, and participation in, the Civil Rights Movement strengthened relations between Jews and African Americans, so now a strong and active Jewish commitment to low-income community economic development could play a healing role in the attenuated connections that exist. In the face of declining Jewish population and political clout, such alliances may also be important for the sake of Jewish self-interest.

Community Needs and Initiatives: Capital for a "Culture of Achievement"

Poor people need financial resources and the skills to use them effectively to develop viable community-based institutions without a downward spiral of society-wide exploitation, despair, and violence. Speaking at the Jewish Funders Network national conference in November 1991, Michael Freedland, director of community lending at Citibank–California, pointed to the three most essential components of successful community development: capacity and leadership development, capital availability, and ongoing review and evaluation. Since the mid-1970s, many successful institutions have been created to provide these ingredients to help poor people effectively transform their lives and communities. The most prominent of these economic development institutions include community development corporations (CDCs), which coordinate planning, development, and implementation of projects to assure that jobs, housing, and essential goods and services will be available in low-income areas.

To realize the low-income community development goals that CDCs promote, financing must be secured. In poor communities, however, conventional credit sources such as banks and savings and loans often do not provide needed funds. As a result, community development financial institutions (CDFIs) have been established to provide loan capital to poor neighborhoods by capturing and recycling money already in the community and by seeking additional investment money elsewhere.

As a group, CDFIs have become highly effective community-based institutions that provide a full range of financial services to individuals and small businesses. In particular, as community development lenders, CDFIs assure that loans will be properly made, managed, used, repaid, and recirculated to create additional economic opportunities for residents. They also collaborate with CDCs to make loans for better housing, new businesses, and expansion of existing community services. There are four types of CDFIs: community development credit unions (CDCUs), community development banks (CDBs), and community development loan funds (CDLFs) and microenterprise loan funds provide financial services to individuals and small businesses. They also collaborate with CDCs to make loans for better housing, new businesses, and expansion of existing community services. (See Appendix.)

The hallmark of both CDCs and CDFIs is that they are run by and for the community members, who carefully attend to the community's needs and to the quality of life for its residents. These institutions have a mission to instill dignity, develop skills and capacities, nurture leadership, and establish power and autonomy for whole communities; they rely on participation, leadership, and control by residents in the areas where they are located. The integral connection between the neighborhoods, and the CDCs and CDFIs is an essential premise of overall community development. The community organizations constitute the infrastructure by which people in poor neighborhoods, tribal reservations, and economically depressed regions gain skills and leadership training, legal assistance, managerial expertise, and investment and equity capital to initiate and sustain development efforts.

These are the reasons why community development organizations are so essential. This is especially true about CDFIs, which make it possible for people who know each other to handle sensible banking and credit matters directly on a more personal basis. CDFIs not only promote economic development; they also create institutions with the capacity to add directly to the well-being of low-income communities instead of relying on outside, indirect, and trickle-down approaches to poverty, marginalization, and disempowerment. CDFIs (and CDCs) are platforms for the development of community-wide and solid personal identity, family life, and cultural expression in place of empty platitudes, unfulfilled dreams, and demoralizing despair.

According to the 1991 National Congress for Community Economic Development study, *Changing the Odds,* 2,000 CDCs nationwide have developed nearly 320,000 affordable housing units and created almost 90,000 permanent jobs. CDFIs have been stalwart lending partners to the CDCs, providing much of the necessary financial capital for these initiatives. CDCs and CDFI have been remarkably successful despite overwhelming public disinvestment that began during the Reagan/Bush years. These budget cuts followed longstanding bank and insurance company redlining that worked to exclude poor people and low-income communities from participating in viable economic development planning and programs.

In the summer of 1994 the Clinton administration pushed the Community Development Financial Institutions Act through Congress. Passed unanimously by the Senate and with only twelve dissenting House votes, the CDFI Act was originally designed to provide CDFIs with a total of $382 million of federal money, depending on a dollar-for-dollar match from private investors, including the business, foundation, and religious communities. (Ultimately, $52 million was authorized.)

(What is interesting from a Jewish perspective is that the CDFI Act established a process that is very similar to classic Jewish *tzedakah*: "pooled" resources were to be drawn from both the community's representative [i.e., government] as well as from other individual sources [i.e., private philanthropic and religious sector] for "socially responsible" purposes.)

The CDFI Act was drafted to stimulate faster and responsible growth by CDFIs through the use of both *equity* and *debt* financing. In the past, foundations and religious institutions often gave money (equity financing) to low-income community development projects. But grant money was always limited and CDFIs themselves required more credit than was available to promote economic development at a level that would really make a difference. In addition, since management, accountability, and evaluation procedures were often inadequate, community residents, boards and staff, and funders were frequently left dissatisfied. For these reasons, recent and current efforts to capitalize CDCs and CDFIs have increasingly turned to making loans that must be repaid (debt financing). Despite the extensive Republican budget cuts, the CDFI Act has made both equity and debt financing available through a process whereby private investment or grants will release matching federal dollars.

Limited American Jewish Support
for Community Economic Development

Unfortunately, to date, American Jewish institutional support for low-income community economic development has been very limited. In many poor and non-Jewish minority areas, that absence, perceived in context with other tensions with the Jewish community, can easily be interpreted as a reflection of how little commitment American Jews have to the flowering of other groups' lives and cultures. It is not surprising, then, that among the tensions arising between the American Jewish and, for example, African American communities, the absence of institutional Jewish support for low-income community economic development is acutely felt and resented. Hence, we can begin to appreciate Louis Farrakhan's success in making one of his basic charges that Jews are hypocrites who do not "walk the talk." For many, Farrakhan's demagoguery has the ring of truth because the Jewish community is a powerful and legitimate political and economic force in American society despite being a small population group. According to Gerald Bubis, the Jewish community, constituting about 2.5 percent of the population, either owns or directly controls between 8–10 percent of the U.S. Gross Domestic Product. This is an astounding figure, about which Jews are both proud and simultaneously anxious regarding the conclusions that others might illegitimately draw.

In the context of community relations with other minority groups, the material wealth of American Jews as a whole could be an extraordinary resource to help promote justice and equity for our nation's urban, rural, and tribal poor. Although Protestant and Catholic religious institutions and organizations have been prominent supporters of community economic development, the Jewish community has lagged far behind in supporting such efforts. Only a few anecdotes are needed to give tone to the limited context of Jewish efforts in support of low-income community development and CDFIs.

1. In 1987 a six-month concerted organizing effort failed to persuade a liberal Philadelphia-area Jewish organization to invest as little

as $1,000 of its endowment in the Delaware Valley Community Reinvestment Fund. DVCRF was a young and uninsured community loan fund, taking investments at below-market rates and making collateralized loans in poor neighborhoods for housing and economic development. The group finally decided to continue investing in a local savings and loan's certificates of deposit. Today the S&L is gone. After years of problem loans, the institution was purchased by an out-of-town bank. Meantime, DVCRF has grown to more than $10 million in assets and still has a perfect lending record.

2. In 1993, in a midsize East Coast city, a Jewish investor/businessman offered a challenge from his synagogue to the local federation. Members of the congregation promised to raise $20,000 or more if the federation or its endowment would match that investment in the local community reinvestment fund. Federation staff and leaders rejected the deal, saying that their endowment managers had achieved a consistent 17 percent rate of return and would not make any investment that could not at least equal that performance.

3. Overall, virtually no Jewish institutional investment, deposits, or supporting grants have been made to CDFIs. When Community Capital Bank of Brooklyn was being established, extensive efforts were undertaken to solicit Jewish community investment from New York and elsewhere. These attempts, including letters as well as group and personal meetings, succeeded in obtaining only five Jewishly identified investments over fifteen months. By fall 1993 Community Capital Bank had $13.6 million in total deposits, but only $160,000 from Jewish institutions. This figure compares with $3 million in deposits from other religious institutions.

4. Limited as the above example suggests, visible Jewish participation in forming Community Capital Bank actually exceeds Jewish involvement to date in the more than forty community development loan funds nationwide. The National Association of Community Loan Funds reported in 1993 that of the approximately $23 million investment capital from religious institutions (23 percent of the total $100 million), less than one-tenth of one percent comes from Jewish institutions—something less than $25,000.

This record is all the more unfortunate since CDFIs are reminiscent of and function similarly to Hebrew Free Loan and Landsmanschaften Societies, which American Jews organized to build a communal economic base in the late nineteenth and early twentieth centuries. Those institutions made it possible for American Jews to obtain credit that they could not otherwise get due to the anti-Semitic policies of local commercial banks. Historical awareness and communal memory should lead American Jews to recognize how important CDFIs are to low-income communities today.

CDFIs are an essential arena of activity for low-income community development. American Jewish institutional support for CDFIs could be an important sign of commitment to broader multicultural work, where our experience and strengths are greatly needed and can be effectively put to use for social justice. Ultimately, only by establishing direct institutional contacts between the Jewish community and comparable programs that operate under direct control of low-income communities, such as CDFIs, can greater understanding and trust be generated and sustained.

American Jewish Community Tzedakah Efforts

Despite the American Jewish community's reluctance to support these forms of low-income community economic development, there are many historical precedents for Jewish involvement in other forms of social and economic justice work. Jews have always provided money to rescue captives, support immigrants, and underwrite economic revitalization. In Rabbinic times, institutions were developed to meet intracommunity needs. In premodern Jewish life, the *kuppah* ("community fund") was organized and administered by communal leaders. In 1892 the Hebrew Free Loan Society was formed in New York as a communal tool to help East European Jews seek financial autonomy. Operationally, Jews have always given *tzedakah* to help other Jews attain economic self-reliance. Jews have also often given *tzedakah* to non-Jews, basing such actions on the defensive principle *mipnei darkhai shalom* ("in order to pursue the paths of peace [with non-Jews]").

In the United States, Jewish support for poor non-Jews has developed in three stages, of which the first two essentially preserve the classic view toward *tzedakah* (fundamentally serving the Jewish community's needs). In the first stage, direct, small-scale, local intervention was provided for poor people in areas where Jews lived with non-

Jews, so *tzedakah* was available generally without regard to religion (race was historically not an issue). Later, in the second stage, Jews allocated *tzedakah* to federation agencies, which also received government contracts that supported infrastructure and projects primarily benefiting many minority poor as well as impoverished (mostly elderly) Jews and immigrants from the former Soviet Union. (Today, government grants for federation programs and services serving the general poor provide substantially more capital for the Jewish community's own needs than would otherwise be available from federation campaigns.)

In the third stage, many Jews began giving as individuals and as members of private family foundations to support projects that mostly benefited poor non-Jews and also explicitly promoted social change rather than social services. This model of philanthropy was given full communal expression in the 1980s through the formation of several national public foundations that promote visibly identified Jewish support of economic justice for people who are overwhelmingly not Jewish. For example, Mazon: A Jewish Response to Hunger, is the largest funder of hunger relief and advocacy projects in the United States. The Jewish Fund for Justice makes grants nationwide for grassroots advocacy and organizing activities that deal with poverty and economic inequity. Lastly, The Shefa ("Abundance") Fund provides a vehicle for individual Jewish funders to make funder-directed grants for social and economic justice. (Outside the United States, the American Jewish World Service promotes economic development and empowerment in the third world.) While each of these foundations is committed explicitly to social change by enabling minority poor people to lift themselves and alter the nature of their own conditions, it is, nevertheless, worth noting that, still related to a traditional *tzedakah* model, they all have developed some components of their programs to serve the Jewish community internally.

There are also many independent Jewish family foundations and thousands of individual Jews who personally contribute time, energy, and money to relief efforts for poor people in the United States, including emergency food, clothing, shelter, drug treatment, housing, advocacy, and community organization. Although they do not operate in a Jewish context, a Jewish sense of prophetic mission and responsibility frequently motivates their activity.

Jewish Institutional Uses of Debt Financing
for Community Development and Economic Justice

Among the array of Jewish institutional responses to poverty, only a few *tzedakah* initiatives specifically embody economic self-help principles and facilitate community-based development. Some of these programs benefit the Jewish community exclusively, but they often also affect wider constituencies. The following list is not exhaustive and it is growing, but it does describe some of the country's existing projects. All of them reflect a sophisticated awareness of the need to meet both vital Jewish and general community housing and capital maintenance needs by maximizing available personnel and financial resources.

1. In the 1990s S. H. and Helen R. Scheuer Family Foundation made a $1.3 million matching grant for an interest-free loan fund so Jewish families from the former Soviet Union can occupy vacant apartments in New York's Co-op City. Co-op City is currently a mostly African American development whose residents want increased housing integration. The program is managed by the Metropolitan New York Coordinating Council on Jewish Poverty, which represents the city's Jewish poor and their neighborhoods, the Hebrew Free Loan Society, and the Co-op City's board.

2. The Chicago Jewish Council on Urban Affairs organized its Community Ventures Program, which has procured several million dollars of foundation and individual investments for low-income and minority housing projects. Community Ventures has leveraged more than $60 million for single-room occupancy housing in Chicago.

3. YACHAD, the Jewish Community Housing Development Corporation of Greater Washington, D.C., was organized as a result of a Jewish community study aimed at mobilizing communal resources to help provide more affordable housing in the nation's capital. It has a $100,000 revolving loan fund.

4. In the wake of the LA riots, federation leaders have begun a coordinated effort by Jewish businesspeople to make business investment and community revitalization loans in South Central

and other low-income neighborhoods. No investment pool yet exists.

5. In Milwaukee, a small group of wealthy Jews has each contributed $10,000 to produce a loan fund of nearly $200,000 that they administer to provide start-up and expansion for local African American entrepreneurs.

6. Led by the Straus Foundation in Baltimore, local Jewish foundations have made nearly $1 million in grants and loans to the Nehemiah Project, a highly successful, nationally known community-based development project.

7. The Boston Jewish Community Relations Council is beginning to cooperate with the Boston Community Development Loan Fund to organize local Jewish investment.

8. At the national level, The Shefa Fund, located in Philadelphia, has launched the Tzedek (Justice) Economic Development Campaign (TzEDeC) to stimulate increased visible American Jewish institutional investment in low-income community economic development nationwide. TzEDeC's first breakthrough came when the Reform Movement's Rabbinic Pension Fund voted to buy $50,000 certificates of deposition in four community development banks across the country.

All these programs and initiatives depend on successfully pairing local community needs for capital with Jewish institutional resources. They constitute an important first step toward Jewish involvement in community economic development. However, the amount of resources that have been provided are extremely limited, especially when considered in relation to the total amount of the American Jewish community's institutional wealth, which exceeds $8 billion in assets.

Obstacles to Jewish Involvement in Community Development

So what is the problem? American Jews and Jewish institutions have consistently participated in and contributed to social service, relief, educational, and even advocacy and community organizations' programs for the nation's poor and minorities. Nevertheless, there has been almost no national Jewish institutional backing for low-income, community-based economic development initiatives. Thus, although minority groups have acted on their own behalf to create structures that emulate historic Jewish patterns of mutual support through community organization, Jewish institutional investment has been lacking. To alter this pattern, we must recognize what structural obstacles inhibit Jewish communal support for low-income community economic development.

1. The Jewish community is highly decentralized. Unlike the Protestant and Catholic communities, American Jewish life is not predominately organized along religious lines. Rather, the largest, most prominent, and financially secure Jewish institutions are secular and Israel-oriented. From one local Jewish community to the next, diverse configurations and interests compete for the allegiance and resources of individual Jews. Although the Jewish community is well coordinated, few mechanisms and perhaps even fewer opportunities exist to explore and shape economic development policy on issues other than those of exclusive Jewish communal concern.

2. Jewish community institutions have historically operated on the basis of available cash rather than with the benefit of endowment capital. As a result, little reserve money was available for long-term investment. (Israel bonds are the one obvious exception, providing an interesting precedent and suggesting a persuasive rationale for attracting Jewish institutional capital for social investment programs.) Only in the past two decades have substantial assets been accumulated for Jewish federation endowments and family foundations. Beginning now, American Jewish philanthropic capital could become a tremendous source for financing start-up and established community economic development projects.

3. Conventional fiduciary concerns associated with "risk" and "return" are exacerbated for Jews by deep-seated security fears. Historically, many Jewish fortunes have been made partially in response to anti-Semitism, especially the Holocaust. As a result, both private foundation and community endowment capital is often regarded as a resource pool for exclusively Jewish needs. Fund management may also be very conservative in order to preserve capital for crises like Middle East war or emergency assistance for endangered Jewish communities in such places as Ethiopia or the former Soviet Union. When Israel ob-

tains a secure peace, many of the American Jewish community's anxieties about money could be reduced.

4. Jewish communities in North America and worldwide continue to face many pressing problems. These include meeting immigration and social welfare needs in Israel and the United States; protecting Jews worldwide from anti-Semitism and its attendant, potentially lethal, threats; promoting Jewish education and culture; and maintaining necessary Jewish institutions.

5. American Jewry has been in an angry, defensive stance about the attitudes of other minority communities toward Israel for years. Relations between American Jews and other minority groups, especially African Americans, have been very difficult for years. Contributing factors have included the longstanding Arab boycott of Israel, adoption of the United Nations resolution that "Zionism is racism," and news reports about collaborations between Israel and South Africa in nuclear bomb technology as well as Israeli arms shipments to Central America. Recent events in the United Nations and in the Mideast, including, of course, the Middle East peace process, can be expected to reduce tensions tremendously in this area. Much work must still be done, however, to effect a real reconciliation that will assuage the hurt feelings of many American Jews.

6. The persistent reality of Black anti-Semitism in particular remains a troublesome obstacle to cultivating Jewish empathy and support for economic development in African American neighborhoods. Despite a productive history of mutual support, cooperation, and achievement in many Civil Rights struggles, Jews and African Americans have had pointed disagreements arising from strikingly different views of their respective interests. Vocal disputes over quotas and preferential treatment in education and employment, Jesse Jackson's presidential campaigns, the popular success of Louis Farrakhan, and the emergence of cultural diversity and autonomy as public issues have heightened the tensions between the Jewish and African American communities. Over the past two generations, the gap has widened as Jews as a community have grown more affluent and moved from the cities to the suburbs. Worst of all, violence between Jews and Blacks in Crown Heights has further antagonized negative feelings and undermined efforts at reconciliation and cooperation. All this has substantially decreased the sense of commonality and affinity that Jews and African Americans previously felt toward one another.

7. Finally, the emergence of community-based development enterprise and financing is relatively new. As a result, there are not enough accessible, quality materials about CDCs and CDFIs for foundation decision makers. Relatively few people can competently discuss these issues with foundation trustees and endowment managers who make grants and investment decisions. Like their counterparts in the wider philanthropic universe, American Jewish funders generally know little about community economic development issues and strategies. Moreover, professional advisors are often reluctant to start complicated discussions about the needs, opportunities, limitations, regulations, and accountability pertaining to investment in low-income development projects. As a result, funder deliberations usually focus on traditional grant making rather than on more innovative philanthropic options for support of community development.

The American Jewish Community's Capital: Where Is It?

By taking note of CDFI successes, the American Jewish community could design and implement coordinated initiatives to assist low-income community economic development nationwide. The extent of Jewish organizational and financial resources should embolden us to undertake model programs that will empower people in poor communities and permit us to fulfill the tenets of our historical values and experience. We can utilize our communal material wealth to show respect for the social and economic development of other minority groups by providing support to community-based organizations that fulfill the interests of people in those communities.

Excluding personal and business assets, the American Jewish community's wealth is in three primary places: synagogues and organizations, federation community foundations, and private family foundations. According to conservative estimates of the Shefa Fund, the total money in our community coffers is $8 billion, and growing. By conducting a comprehensive education and outreach program, a relatively huge amount of capital could be organized for investment in community economic development institutions, like CDFIs, while simultaneously maintaining the level of grant funds for other important programs.

1. Synagogue and organization bank accounts for long-term projects and endowments nationwide contain well over $1 billion. Much of this money is operating capital for ongoing activities; however, the largest portion is in general endowments and special funds for prayer-books, flowers, libraries, and other prestigious programs. Another substantial sum is in accounts with extended time horizons, stretching from receipt to expenditure of monies. For example, membership dues often come in at the beginning of the activity year and are spent throughout the fiscal cycle. Building funds often contain large sums of money that are expended during lengthy building or rehabilitation processes. Finally, rabbinic and communal worker pension funds are another rapidly growing source of investment capital.

2. Across the country, 101 federation-related community foundations now have endowments amounting to more than $3 billion. These endowments have been built up over the past twenty years and are still growing at a fantastic rate. Within the federation movement, these funds are regarded as critical resources because, although the annual campaign revenues continue at very high rates, demographics suggest that middle-age and younger Jews do not have the same giving patterns as their parents and grandparents. The endowments provide a means for federations to "capture and recycle" the community's capital—precisely the same strategy adopted by CDFIs. The assets and their returns, including interest, dividends, and capital gains, produce income for federation campaigns, new projects, and charitable causes that donors can designate on an "advisory" basis. The federation endowments are in a special Internal Revenue Service category called "public" foundations, whose trustees are charged to act in the community's best interests. CDFI representatives and their allies in the Jewish community can initiate a campaign to involve federation endowments in community development projects.

3. There are as many as six thousand private Jewish foundations with at least $4 billion or more in assets. Consistent with the Jewish community's traditionally cohesive nature (a factor in significant flux today!), these foundations are important funding sources both for, and also from, the Jewish community. In many cases, they function as parallels to the endowments that churches have developed historically. For example, some private philanthropies are formally linked to their local federations as "supporting" foundations. Due to the close operational ties that these foundations have to other Jewish institutions and

charitable beneficiaries, they should be considered a significant part of the Jewish community's public institutional wealth.

The American Jewish Community's Capital: How Can It Promote Community Development?

Any strategy to use Jewish institutional wealth to assist low-income community economic development must involve plans for both liquid and capital assets. First, all Jewish institutions should carefully examine where they do their normal banking and how they handle their cash management. By choosing to deposit Jewish institutional funds in local banks that make loans for home mortgages and small businesses in low-income areas, Jewish institutions can help strengthen the economic and social bases of their own inner cities.

Jewish organizations, endowments, and private foundations can also use funds that do not need to be readily available to buy insured certificates of deposits (CDs) in development credit unions and banks. Most CDFIs also offer "development" deposits and CDs for investors outside their service areas.

Federation endowments and private foundations can also make program related investments (PRIs) with limited amounts of their endowment capital to grow the assets of community-based housing and economic development projects as well as to CDFIs. PRIs are a special IRS-approved method to increase the leverage of endowment capital by using it as debt financing, in the form of loans and loan guarantees, for projects that advance an organization's core mission. PRIs may also be equity investments that give the investor institution an ownership share in the project or organization. Public and private foundation PRIs to CDFIs and other community development projects are direct and socially responsible investments that have been widely used across the country. For example, the S. H. and Helen R. Scheuer Family Foundation made a $3 million PRI to create an interest-free revolving loan fund for New York UJA-Federation approved capital improvements to Jewish YMHAs and community centers.

Another strategy is to invest Jewish community employee pension funds in CDFIs and other low-income economic development projects. Institutions can organize their pension plans so that the money is invested in socially responsible mutual funds that place a portion of their assets in community development projects. To increase the amount of pension monies handled this way, thorough research must be done about how Jewish communal pension funds are now invested. It will take concerted organizing to develop new patterns of pension investment by the Jewish community's largest organizations.

Conclusion

We can view economic development and multiculturalism as twin goals of the Leviticus injunction, "Justice! You shall pursue justice!" Following the exodus from Egypt, the ancient Israelites established a framework that combined cultural-religious and economic elements to define themselves fully. Over many subsequent centuries, that paradigm has also guided a multitude of religious, ethnic, and national groups in their efforts to shape viable societies.

As progenitors of and heirs to this model, American Jews would do well to note how we became recent successful practitioners of our own traditional wisdom. We have long recognized the relationship among economic self sufficiency, security, and cultural richness. In addition to providing direct and emergency aid to our own poor and needy, Jewish communities historically have developed highly sophisticated networks of long-term economic self-help and development. Although we have often extended aid to non-Jews in need, in the context of multiculturalism's emphasis on community empowerment, our history of important social services is not enough. If we want to encourage minority community development in a multicultural environment, we must combine our verbal support with institutional financial resources so that other groups can also firmly establish their own social, cultural, and economic foundations. This will require expanding the relatively few existing local Jewish efforts that support community economic development and also undertaking national initiatives. If American Jews do these things, our nation's distinct communities can create a single society that is genuinely richer because we share our resources in a common quest for social and cultural dignity as well as economic equity.

Appendix

There are four types of community development financial institutions (CDFIs):

1. Community development credit unions (CDCUs) are non-profit financial institutions owned and controlled by their members to benefit both low-income residents and their communities. CDCUs have more than $500 million in deposits and provide basic banking services in areas where few or even no commercial banks are located. They offer savings and checking accounts, check cashing, and other cash services. CDCU boards of directors set the rate and frequency of interest to be paid on regular savings accounts and certificates of deposit. Rates are generally competitive with those of regular commercial banks, savings and loans, and other credit unions.

2. Community development loan funds (CDLFs) have special structures and a focus that enable them to obtain investment capital from private sources including institutions and individuals who want to make social investments in low-income areas. CDLFs act as brokers for investors by making loans for housing and small business projects that directly benefit the wider community rather than individual owners and entrepreneurs. They provide start-up and expansion capital for projects of CDCs, workers' cooperatives, and other nonprofits. Sometimes CDLFs make "bridge loans" to nonprofits awaiting promised grant or contract funds. CDLFs sometimes make loans to developers and businesspeople for housing and other projects that clearly benefit low-income people. CDLFs also involve conventional lenders, such as banks, savings and loans, and insurance companies, in community lending. CDLFs are chartered as nonprofit organizations whose boards of directors come from three groups: social investors, community borrowers, and community developers and advocates. The investment solicitation processes of CDLFs are regulated by state and federal rules. CDLFs operate according to established lending and financial management principles that are explicitly defined in emerging industry standards.

With more than $100 million in assets, CDLFs provide below-market interest rates to investors who accept social benefits as a complement to the financial returns they receive. The low interest rates are subsidies for the lending rates that CDLFs offer to borrowers. Altogether, CDLFs have made $100 million in loans that have leveraged another $750 million more from other private and public sources.

Investments in CDLFs are neither insured nor guaranteed so the principal is at risk. However, even though CDLFs do not employ traditional risk management techniques, they have very successful lending records. At the end of 1990, reported loan default losses for all CDLFs amounted to only 1.3 percent of all loans made.

3. Community development banks (CDBs) are full-service, federally insured depository institutions with a dual mission to operate safely and profitably and to provide credit for grassroots economic activity, including housing and small business development and neighborhood rehabilitation. CDBs are distinguished from other banks by their commitment to realize profit by advancing the interests of the community as a whole, including both residents and the locale itself. As pioneered by the South Shore Bank in Chicago, CDBs have shown a nimble willingness to promote urban and rural community economic development by creating various nonprofit and for-profit subsidiaries. In combination with the CDB, these related corporate entities form an effective infrastructure to provide training assistance for new developers and entrepreneurs, to offer loans for investments that are riskier than those usually made by commercial banks, and to assist other community groups with strategic planning and solicitation of seed funding and venture capital. The CDBs use bank profits to help finance the subsidiaries' community development activities.

To obtain additional lending capital, CDBs offer "development deposits" to attract social investments from individuals and institutions outside the bank's service area. CDB development deposits are significant because they represent an influx of investment capital, reversing the tendency by which money flows out of low-income communities. There are only three community development banks in the country that are exclusively focused on community revitalization: South Shore Bank in Chicago, Elkhorn Bank in Arkadelphia, Arkansas, and Community Capital Bank in Brooklyn. South Shore Bank is regionalizing activities by assisting bank and lending programs in Kansas City, Kansas, and in the Upper Peninsula of Michigan. Community Capital helped form a new CBD in the San Francisco Bay Area that is expected to open in the spring of 1996. Community development activists in several of the cities are also trying to launch development banks.

4. Microenterprise loan funds lend small sums of money for very small, often start-up businesses. Microenterprise loan funds are based on models first developed outside the United States, especially in Bangladesh. They often function as borrowing–lending circles of peers, whereby initial sums of money are loaned and must be fully re-paid by everyone before additional capital is made available for further loans. As such, microenterprise loans often operate as part of a dual strategy for both human and economic development. Individuals par-ticipate in these programs to gain life skills, enhance personal esteem, acquire business skills, and promote economic development.

Loans are frequently made for labor-intensive activities for which the borrower already has the requisite skills (e.g., sewing and haircut-ting). Women, especially of color and on welfare, are most often the participants in microenterprise loan funds. Microenterprise loans do not usually exceed $5,000 and may be as small as $250. These funds are often administered by free-standing, community-based nonprofit organizations, and occasionally by either public agencies or other CDFIs, such as a loan fund. In their scale and in the mix of both human and capital development, microenterprise loan funds, among all the types of CDFIs, most closely resemble Hebrew Free Loan Societies.

What Does It Mean to Be an "American"?

MICHAEL WALZER

There is no country called America. We live in the United States *of America,* and we have appropriated the adjective "American" even though we can claim no exclusive title to it. Canadians and Mexicans are also Americans, but they have adjectives more obviously their own, and we have none. Words like "unitarian" and "unionist" won't do; our sense of ourselves is not captured by the mere fact of our union, however important that is. Nor will "statist," even "united statist," serve our purposes; a good many of the citizens of the United States are antistatist. Other countries, wrote the "American" political theorist Horace Kallen, get their names from the people, or from one of the peoples, who inhabit them. "The United States, on the other hand, has a peculiar anonymity."[1] It is a name that doesn't even pretend to tell us who lives here. Anybody can live here, and just about everybody does—men and women from all the world's peoples. (The *Harvard Encyclopedia of American Ethnic Groups* begins with Acadians and Afghans and ends with Zoroastrians.[2]) It is peculiarly easy to become an American. The adjective provides no reliable information about the origins, histories, connections, or cultures of those whom it designates. What does it say, then, about their political allegiance?

Patriotism and Pluralism

American politicians engage periodically in a fierce competition to demonstrate their patriotism. This is an odd competition, surely, for in most countries the patriotism of politicians is not an issue. There are

Michael Walzer, "What Does It Mean to Be an 'American'?" from *Social Research* (Volume 57, No.3, Fall 1990), reprinted by permission of the author.

other issues, and this question of political identification and commitment rarely comes up; loyalty to the *patrie,* the fatherland (or motherland), is simply assumed. Perhaps it isn't assumed here because the United States isn't a *patrie.* Americans have never spoken of their country as a fatherland (or a motherland). The kind of natural or organic loyalty that we (rightly or wrongly) recognize in families doesn't seem to be a feature of our politics. When American politicians invoke the metaphor of family they are usually making an argument about our mutual responsibilities and welfarist obligations, and among Americans, that is a controversial argument.[3] One can be an American patriot without believing in the mutual responsibilities of American citizens—indeed, for some Americans disbelief is a measure of one's patriotism.

Similarly, the United States isn't a "homeland" (where a national family might dwell), not, at least, as other countries are, in casual conversation and unreflective feeling. It is a country of immigrants who, however grateful they are for this new place, still remember the old places. And their children know, if only intermittently, that they have roots elsewhere. They, no doubt, are native grown, but some awkward sense of newness here, or of distant oldness, keeps the tongue from calling this land "home." The older political uses of the word "home," common in Great Britain, have never taken root here: home countries, home station, Home Office, home rule. To be "at home" in America is a personal matter: Americans have homesteads and homefolks and hometowns, and each of these is an endlessly interesting topic of conversation. But they don't have much to say about a common or communal home.

Nor is there a common *patrie,* but rather many different ones—a multitude of fatherlands (and motherlands). For the children, even the grandchildren, of the immigrant generation, one's *patrie,* the "native land of one's ancestors," is somewhere else. The term "Native Americans" designates the very first immigrants, who got here centuries before any of the others. At what point do the rest of us, native grown, become natives? The question has not been decided; for the moment, however, the language of nativism is mostly missing (it has never been dominant in American public life), even when the political reality is plain to see. Alternatively, nativist language can be used against the politics of nativism, as in these lines of Horace Kallen, the theorist of an anonymous America: "Behind [the individual] in time and tremendously in him in quality are his ancestors; around him in space are his relatives and kin, carrying in common with him the inherited organic set from a remoter common ancestry. In all these he lives and moves and has his being. They constitute his, literally, *natio,* the inwardness of his nativity."[4] But since there are so many "organic sets" (language is deceptive here: Kallen's antinativist nativism is cultural, not biological), none of them can rightly be called "American." Americans have no inwardness of their own; they look inward only by looking backward.

According to Kallen, the United States is less importantly a union of states than it is a union of ethnic, racial, and religious groups—a union of otherwise unrelated "natives." What is the nature of this union? The Great Seal of the United States carries the motto *E pluribus unum,* "From many, one," which seems to suggest that manyness must be left behind for the sake of oneness. Once there were many, now the many have merged or, in Israel Zangwell's classic image, been melted down into one. But the Great Seal presents a different image: the "American" eagle holds a sheaf of arrows. Here there is no merger or fusion but only a fastening, a putting together: many-in-one. Perhaps the adjective "American" describes this kind of oneness. We might say, tentatively, that it points to the citizenship, not the nativity or nationality, of the men and women it designates. It is a political adjective, and its politics is liberal in the strict sense: generous, tolerant, ample, accommodating—it allows for the survival, even the enhancement and flourishing, of manyness.

On this view, appropriately called "pluralist," the word "from" on the Great Seal is a false preposition. There is no movement from many to one, but rather a simultaneity, a coexistence—once again, many-in-one. But I don't mean to suggest a mystery here, as in the Christian conception of a God who is three-in-one. The language of pluralism is sometimes a bit mysterious—thus Kallen's description of America as a "nation of nationalities" or John Rawls's account of the liberal state as a "social union of social unions"—but it lends itself to a rational unpacking.[5] A sheaf of arrows is not, after all, a mysterious entity. We can find analogues in the earliest forms of social organization: tribes composed of many clans, clans composed of many families. The conflicts of loyalty and obligation, inevitable products of pluralism, must arise in these cases too. And yet, they are not exact analogues of the American case, for tribes and clans lack Kallen's "anonymity." American pluralism is, as we shall see, a peculiarly modern phenomenon—not mysterious but highly complex.

In fact, the United States is not a "nation of nationalities" or a "social union of social unions." At least, the singular nation or union is not constituted by, it is not a combination or fastening together of, the plural nationalities or unions. In some sense, it includes them; it provides a framework for their coexistence; but they are not its parts. Nor are the individual states, in any significant sense, the parts that make up the United States. The parts are individual men and women. The United States is an association of citizens. Its "anonymity" consists in the fact that these citizens don't transfer their collective name to the association. It never happened that a group of people called Americans came together to form a political society called America. The people are Americans only by virtue of having come together. And whatever identity they had before becoming Americans, they retain (or, better, they are free to retain) afterward. There is, to be sure, another view of Americanization, which holds that the process requires for its success the mental erasure of all previous identities—forgetfulness or even, as one enthusiast wrote in 1918, "absolute forgetfulness."[6] But on the pluralist view, Americans are allowed to remember who they were and to insist, also, on *what else they are.*

They are not, however, bound to the remembrance or to the insistence. Just as their ancestors escaped the old country, so they can if they choose escape their old identities, the "inwardness" of their nativity. Kallen writes of the individual that "whatever else he changes, he cannot change his grandfather."[7] Perhaps not; but he can call his grandfather a "greenhorn," reject his customs and convictions, give up the family name, move to a new neighborhood, adopt a new "lifestyle."

He doesn't become a better American by doing these things (though that is sometimes his purpose), but he may become an American simply, an American and nothing else, freeing himself from the hyphenation that pluralists regard as universal on this side, though not on the other side, of the Atlantic Ocean. But, free from hyphenation, he seems also free from ethnicity: "American" is not one of the ethnic groups recognized in the United States census. Someone who is only an American is, so far as our bureaucrats are concerned, ethnically anonymous. He has a right, however, to his anonymity; that is part of what it means to be an American.

For a long time, British-Americans thought of themselves as Americans simply—and not anonymously: they constituted, so they would have said, a new ethnicity and a new nationality, into which all later immigrants would slowly assimilate. "Americanization" was a political program designed to make sure that assimilation would not be too slow a process, at a time, indeed, when it seemed not to be a recognizable *process* at all. But though there were individuals who did their best to assimilate, that is, to adopt, at least outwardly, the mores of British-Americans, that soon ceased to be a plausible path to an "American" future. The sheer number of non-British immigrants was too great. If there was to be a new nationality, it would have to come out of the melting pot, where the heat was applied equally to all groups, the earlier immigrants as well as the most recent ones. The anonymous American was, at the turn of the century, say, a placeholder for some unknown future person who would give cultural content to the name. Meanwhile, most Americans were hyphenated Americans, more or less friendly to their grandfathers, more or less committed to their manyness. And pluralism was an alternative political program designed to legitimate this manyness and to make it permanent—which would leave those individuals who were Americans and nothing else permanently anonymous, assimilated to a cultural nonidentity.

Citizens

But though these anonymous Americans were not better Americans for being or for having become anonymous, it is conceivable that they were, and are, better American *citizens*. If the manyness of America is cultural, its oneness is political, and it may be the case that men and women who are free from non-American cultures will commit themselves more fully to the American political system. Maybe cultural anonymity is the best possible grounding for American politics. From the beginning, of course, it has been the standard claim of British-Americans that their own culture is the best grounding. And there is obviously much to be said for that view. Despite the efforts of hyphenated Americans to describe liberal and democratic politics as a kind of United Way to which they have all made contributions, the genealogy of the American political system bears a close resemblance to the genealogy of the Sons and Daughters of the American Revolution—ethnic organizations if there ever were any![8] But this genealogy must also account for the flight across the Atlantic and the Revolutionary War. The parliamentary oligarchy of eighteenth-century Great Britain wasn't, after all, all that useful a model for America. When the ancestors of the Sons and Daughters described their political achievement as a "new order for the ages," they were celebrating a break with their own ethnic past almost as profound as that which later Americans were called upon to make. British-Americans who refused the break called themselves "Loyalists," but they were called disloyal by their opponents and treated even more harshly than hyphenated Americans from Germany, Russia, and Japan in later episodes of war and revolution.

Citizenship in the "new order" was not universally available, since Blacks and women and Indians (Native Americans) were excluded, but it was never linked to a single nationality. "To be or to become an American," writes Philip Gleason, "a person did not have to be of any particular national, linguistic, religious, or ethnic background. All he had to do was to commit himself to the political ideology centered on the abstract ideals of liberty, equality, and republicanism,"[9] These abstract ideals made for a politics separated not only from religion but from culture itself or, better, from all the particular forms in which religious and national culture was, and is, expressed—hence a politics "anonymous" in Kallen's sense. Anonymity suggests autonomy too, though I don't want to claim that American politics was not qualified in important ways by British Protestantism, later by Irish Catholicism, later still by German, Italian, Polish, Jewish, African, and Hispanic religious commitments and political experience. But these qualifications never took what might be called a strong adjectival form, never became permanent or exclusive qualities of America's abstract politics and citizenship. The adjective "American" named, and still names, a politics that is relatively unqualified by religion or nationality or, alternatively, that is qualified by so many religions and nationalities as to be free from any one of them.

It is this freedom that makes it possible for America's oneness to encompass and protect its manyness. Nevertheless, the conflict between the one and the many is a pervasive feature of American life. Those Americans who attach great value to the oneness of citizenship and the centrality of political allegiance must seek to constrain the influence of cultural manyness; those who value the many must disparage the one. The conflict is evident from the earliest days of the republic, but I will begin my own account of it with the campaign to restrict immigration and naturalization in the 1850s. Commonly called "nativist" by historians, the campaign was probably closer in its politics to a Rousseauian republicanism.[10] Anti-Irish and anti-Catholic bigotry played a large part in mobilizing support for the American (or American Republican) party, popularly called the Know-Nothings; and the political style of the party, like that of contemporary abolitionists and free-soilers, displayed many of the characteristics of Protestant moralism. But in its self-presentation, it was above all republican, more concerned about the civic virtue of the new immigrants than about their ethnic lineages, its religious critique focused on the ostensible connection between Catholicism and tyranny. The legislative program of the Know-Nothings had to do largely with questions of citizenship at the national level and of public education at the local level. In Congress, where the party had 75 representatives (and perhaps another 45 sympathizers, out of a total of 234) at the peak of its strength in 1855, it seemed more committed to restricting the suffrage than to cutting off immigration. Some of its members would have barred "paupers" from entering the United States, and others would have required an oath of allegiance from all immigrants immediately upon landing. But their energy was directed mostly toward revising the naturalization laws.[11] It was not the elimination of manyness but its disenfranchisement that the Know-Nothings championed.

Something like this was probably the position of most American "nativists" until the last years of the nineteenth century. In 1845, when immigration rates were still fairly low, a group of "native Americans" meeting in Philadelphia declared that they would "kindly receive [all] persons who came to America, and give them every privilege except office and suffrage."[12] I would guess that the nativist view of American Blacks was roughly similar. Most of the northern Know-Nothings (the party's greatest strength was in New England) were strongly opposed to slavery, but it did not follow from that opposition that they were prepared to welcome former slaves as fellow citizens. The logic of events led to citizenship, after a bloody war, and the Know-Nothings, by then loyal Republicans, presumably supported that outcome. But the logic of republican principle, as they understood it, would have suggested some delay. Thus a resolution of the Massachusetts legislature in 1856 argued that "republican institutions were especially adapted to an educated and intelligent people, capable of *and accustomed to* self-government. Free institutions could be confined safely only to free men."[13] The legislators went on to urge a twenty-one-year residence requirement for naturalization. Since it was intended that disenfranchised residents should nonetheless be full members of civil society, another piece of Know-Nothing legislation would have provided that any alien free white person (this came from a Mississippi senator) should be entitled after twelve months' residence "to all the protection of the government, and [should] be allowed to inherit, and hold, and transmit real estate . . . in the same manner as though he were a citizen."[14]

Civil society, then, would include a great variety of ethnic and religious and perhaps even racial groups, but the members of these groups would acquire the "inestimable" good of citizenship only after a long period of practical education (but does one learn just by watching?) in democratic virtue. Meanwhile, their children would get a formal education. Despite their name, the Know-Nothings thought that citizenship was a subject about which a great deal had to be known. Some of them wanted to make attendance in public schools compulsory, but, faced with constitutional objections, they insisted only that no public funding should go to the support of parochial schools. It is worth emphasizing that the crucial principle here was not the separation of church and state. The Know-Nothing party did not oppose sabbatarian laws.[15] Its members believed that tax money should not be used to underwrite social manyness—not in the case of religion, obviously, but also not in the case of language and culture. Political identity, singular in form, would be publicly inculcated and defended; the plurality of social identities would have to be sustained in private.

I don't doubt that most nativists hoped that plurality would not, in fact, be sustained. They had ideas, if not sociological theories, about the connection of politics and culture—specifically, as I have said, republican politics and British Protestant culture. I don't mean to underestimate the centrality of these ideas: this was presumably the knowledge that the Know-Nothings were concealing when they claimed to know nothing. Nonetheless, the logic of their position, as of any "American" republican position, pressed toward the creation of a politics independent of all the ethnicities and religions of civil society. Otherwise too many people would be excluded; the political world would look too much like Old England and not at all like the "new order of the ages," not at all like "America." Nor could American nativists challenge ethnic and religious pluralism directly, for both were protected (as the parochial schools were protected) by the constitution to which they claimed a passionate attachment. They could only insist that passionate attachment should be the mark of all citizens—and set forth the usual arguments against the seriousness of love at first sight and in favor of long engagements. They wanted what Rousseau wanted: that citizens should find the greater share of their happiness in public (political) rather than in private (social) activities.[16] And they were prepared to deny citizenship to men and women who seemed to them especially unlikely to do that.

No doubt, again, public happiness came easily to the nativists because they felt so entirely at home in American public life. But we should not be too quick to attribute this feeling to the carry-over of ethnic consciousness into the political sphere. For American politics in the 1850s was already so open, egalitarian, and democratic (relative to European politics) that almost anyone could feel at home in it. Precisely because the United States was no one's *national* home, its politics was universally accessible. All that was necessary in principle was ideological commitment, in practice, a good line of talk. The Irish did very well and demonstrated as conclusively as one could wish that "British" and "Protestant" were not necessary adjectives for American politics. They attached to the many, not to the one.

For this reason, the symbols and ceremonies of American citizenship could not be drawn from the political culture or history of British-Americans. Our Congress is not a Commons; Guy Fawkes Day is not an American holiday; the Magna Carta has never been one of our sacred texts. American symbols and ceremonies are culturally anonymous, invented rather than inherited, voluntaristic in style, narrowly political in content: the flag, the Pledge, the Fourth, the Constitution. It is entirely appropriate that the Know-Nothing party had its origin in the Secret Society of the Star-Spangled Banner. And it is entirely understandable that the flag and the Pledge continue, even today, to figure largely in political debate. With what reverence should the flag be treated? On what occasions must it be saluted? Should we require school children to recite the Pledge, teachers to lead the recitation? Questions like these are the tests of a political commitment that can't be assumed, because it isn't undergirded by the cultural and religious commonalities that make for mutual trust. The flag and the Pledge are, as it were, all we have. One could suggest, of course, alternative and more practical tests of loyalty—responsible participation in political life, for example. But the real historical alternative is the test proposed by the cultural pluralists: one proves one's Americanism, in their view, by living in peace with all the other "Americans," that is, by agreeing to respect social manyness rather than by pledging allegiance to the "one and indivisible" republic. And pluralists are led on by the logic of this argument to suggest that citizenship is something less than an "inestimable" good.

Hyphenated Americans

Good it certainly was to be an American citizen. Horace Kallen was prepared to call citizenship a "great vocation," but he clearly did not believe (in the 1910s and '20s, when he wrote his classic essays on cultural pluralism) that one could make a life there. Politics was a necessary, but not a spiritually sustaining activity. It was best understood in instrumental terms; it had to do with the arrangements that made it possible for groups of citizens to "realize and protect" their diverse cultures and "attain the excellence appropriate to their kind."[17] These arrangements, Kallen thought, had to be democratic, and democracy required citizens of a certain sort—autonomous, self-disciplined, capable of cooperation and compromise. "Americanization" was entirely legitimate insofar as it aimed to develop these qualities; they made up Kallen's version of civic virtue, and he was willing to say that they should be common to all Americans. But, curiously perhaps, they did not touch the deeper self. "The common city-life, which depends upon like-mindedness, is not inward, corporate, and inevitable, but external, inarticulate, and incidental . . . not the expression of a homogeneity of heritage, mentality, and interest."[18]

Hence Kallen's program: assimilation "in matters economic and political," dissimilation "in cultural consciousness."[19] The hyphen joined these two processes in one person, so that a Jewish-American (like Kallen) was similar to other Americans in his economic and political activity, but similar only to other Jews at the deeper level of culture.[20] It is clear that Kallen's "hyphenates," whose spiritual life is located so emphatically to the left of the hyphen, cannot derive the greater part of their happiness from their citizenship. Nor, in a sense, should they, since culture, for the cultural pluralists, is far more important than politics and promises a more complete satisfaction. Pluralists, it seems, do not make good republicans—for the same reason that republicans, Rousseau the classic example, do not make good pluralists. The two attend to different sorts of goods.

Kallen's hyphenated Americans can be attentive and conscientious citizens, but on a liberal, not a republican model. This means two things. First, the various ethnic and religious groups can intervene in political life only in order to defend themselves and advance their common interests—as in the case of the NAACP or the Anti-Defamation League—but not in order to impose their culture or their values. They have to recognize that the state is anonymous (or, in the language of contemporary political theorists, neutral) at least in this sense: that it can't take on the character or the name of any of the groups that it includes. It isn't a nation-state of a particular kind and it isn't a Christian republic. Second, the primary political commitment of individual citizens is to protect their protection, to uphold the democratic framework within which they pursue their more substantive activities. This commitment is consistent with feelings of gratitude, loyalty, even patriotism of a certain sort, but it doesn't make for fellowship. There is indeed *union* in politics (and economics) but union of a sort that precludes intimacy. "The political and economic life of the commonwealth," writes Kallen, "is a single unit and serves as the foundation and background for the realization of the distinctive individuality of each *natio*."[21] Here pluralism is straightforwardly opposed to republicanism: politics offers neither self-realization nor communion. All intensity lies, or should lie, elsewhere.

Kallen believes, of course, that this "elsewhere" actually exists; his is not a utopian vision; it's not a case of "elsewhere, perhaps." The "organic groups" that make up Kallen's America appear in public life as interest groups only, organized for the pursuit of material and social goods that are universally desired but sometimes in short supply and often unfairly distributed. That is the only appearance countenanced by a liberal and democratic political system. But behind it, concealed from public view, lies the true significance of ethnicity or religion: "It is the center at which [the individual] stands, the point of his most intimate social relations, therefore of his intensest emotional life."[22] I am inclined to say that this is too radical a view of ethnic and religious identification, since it seems to rule out moral conflicts in which the individual's emotions are enlisted, as it were, on both sides. But Kallen's more important point is simply that there is space and opportunity *elsewhere* for the emotional satisfactions that politics can't (or shouldn't) provide. And because individuals really do find this satisfaction, the groups within which it is found are permanently sustainable: they won't melt down, not, at least, in any ordinary (noncoercive) social process. Perhaps they can be repressed, if the repression is sufficiently savage; even then, they will win out in the end.

Kallen wasn't entirely unaware of the powerful forces making for cultural meltdown, even without repression. He has some strong lines on the effectiveness of the mass media—though he knew these only in their infancy and at a time when newspapers were still a highly localized medium and the foreign-language press flourished. In his analysis and critique of the pressure to conform, he anticipated what became by the 1950s a distinctively American genre of social criticism. It isn't always clear whether he sees pluralism as a safeguard against or an antidote for the conformity of ethnic-Americans to that spiritless "Americanism" he so much disliked, a dull protective coloring that destroys all inner brightness. In any case, he is sure that inner brightness will survive, "for Nature is naturally pluralistic; her unities are eventual, not primary."[23] Eventually, he means, the American union will prove to be a matter of "mutual accommodation," leaving intact the primacy of ethnic and religious identity. In the years since Kallen wrote, this view has gathered a great deal of ideological, but much less of empirical, support. "Pluralist principles . . . have been on the ascendancy," writes a contemporary critic of pluralism, "precisely at a time when ethnic differences have been on the wane."[24] What if the "excellence" appropriate to our "kind" is, simply, an American excellence? Not necessarily civic virtue of the sort favored by nativists, republicans, and contemporary communitarians, but nonetheless some local color, a brightness of our own?

Peripheral Distance

This local color is most visible, I suppose, in popular culture—which is entirely appropriate in the case of the world's first mass democracy. Consider, for example, the movie *American in Paris,* where the hero is an American simply and not at all an Irish- or German- or Jewish-American. Do we drop our hyphens when we travel abroad? But what are we, then, without them? We carry with us cultural artifacts of a quite specific sort: *"une danse americaine,"* Gene Kelly tells the French children as he begins to tap dance. What else could he call it, this melted-down combination of Northern English clog dancing, the Irish jig and reel, and African rhythmic foot stamping, to which had been added, by Kelly's time, the influence of the French and Russian ballet? Creativity of this sort is both explained and celebrated by those writers and thinkers, heroes of the higher culture, that we are likely to recognize as distinctively American: thus Emerson's defense of the experimental life (I am not sure, though, that he would have admired tap dancing), or Whitman's democratic inclusiveness, or the pragmatism of Peirce and James.

"An American nationality," writes Gleason, "does in fact exist."[25] Not just a political status, backed up by a set of political symbols and ceremonies, but a full-blooded nationality, reflecting a history and a culture—exactly like all the other nationalities from which Americans have been, and continue to be, recruited. The ongoing immigration makes it difficult to see the real success of Americanization in creating distinctive types, characters, styles, artifacts of all sorts which, were Gene Kelly to display them to his Parisian neighbors, they would rightly recognize as "American." More important, Americans recognize one another, take pride in the things that fellow Americans have made and done, identify with the national community. So, while there no doubt are people plausibly called Italian-Americans or Swedish-Americans, spiritual (as well as political) life—this is Gleason's view—is lived largely to the right of the hyphen: contrasted with real Italians and real Swedes, these are real Americans.

This view seems to me both right and wrong. It is right in its denial of Kallen's account of America as an anonymous nation of named nationalities. It is wrong in its insistence that America is a nation like all the others. But the truth does not lie, where we might naturally be led to look for it, somewhere between this rightness and this wrongness—as if we could locate America at some precise point along the continuum that stretches from the many to the one. I want to take the advice of that American song, another product of the popular culture, which tells us: "Don't mess with mister in-between."[26] If there are cultural artifacts, songs and dances, styles of life and even philosophies, that are distinctively American, there is also an idea of America that is itself distinct, incorporating oneness and manyness in a "new order" that may or may not be "for the ages" but that is certainly for us, here and now.

The cultural pluralists come closer to getting the new order right than do the nativists and the nationalists and the American communitarians. Nonetheless, there is a nation and a national community and, by now, a very large number of native Americans. Even first- and second-generation Americans, as Gleason points out, have graves to visit and homes and neighborhoods to remember *in this country,* on this side of whatever waters their ancestors crossed to get here.[27] What is distinctive about the nationality of these Americans is not its insubstantial character—substance is quickly acquired—but its nonexclusive character. Remembering the God of the Hebrew Bible, I want to argue that America is not a jealous nation. In this sense, at least, it is different from most of the others.

Consider, for example, a classic moment in the ethnic history of France: the debate over the emancipation of the Jews in 1790 and '91. It is not, by any means, a critical moment; there were fewer than 35,000 Jews in revolutionary France, only 500 in Paris. The Jews were not economically powerful or politically significant or even intellectually engaged in French life (all that could come only after emancipation). But the debate nonetheless was long and serious, for it dealt with the meaning of citizenship and nationality. When the Constituent Assembly voted for full emancipation in September 1791, its position was summed up by Clermont-Tonnerre, a deputy of the Center, in a famous sentence: "One must refuse everything to the Jews as a nation, and give everything to the Jews as individuals. . . . It would be repugnant to have . . . a nation within a nation."[28] The Assembly's vote led to the disestablishment of Jewish corporate existence in France, which had been sanctioned and protected by the monarchy. "Refusing everything to the Jews as a nation" meant withdrawing the sanction, denying the protection. Henceforth Jewish communities would be voluntary associations, and individual Jews would have rights against the community as well as against the state: Clermont-Tonnerre was a good liberal.

But the Assembly debate also suggests that most of the deputies favoring emancipation would not have looked with favor even on the voluntary associations of the Jews, insofar as these reflected national sensibility or cultural difference. The future Girondin leader Brissot, defending emancipation, predicted that Jews who became French citizens would "lose their particular characteristics." I suspect that he could hardly imagine a greater triumph of French *civisme* than this— as if the secular Second Coming, like the religious version, awaited only the conversion of the Jews. Brissot thought the day was near: "Their eligibility [for citizenship] will regenerate them."[29] Jews could be good citizens only insofar as they were regenerated, which meant, in effect, that they could be good citizens only insofar as they became French. (They must, after all, have some "particular characteristics," and if not their own, then whose?) Their emancipators had, no doubt, a generous view of their capacity to do that but would not have been generous in the face of resistance (from the Jews or from any other of the corporate groups of the old regime). The price of emancipation was assimilation.

This has been the French view of citizenship ever since. Though they have often been generous in granting the exalted status of citizen to foreigners, the successive republics have been suspicious of any form of ethnic pluralism. Each republic really has been "one and indivisible," and it has been established, as Rousseau thought it should be, on a strong national oneness. Oneness all the way down is, on this view, the only guarantee that the general will and the common good will triumph in French politics.

America is very different, and not only because of the eclipse of republicanism in the early nineteenth century. Indeed, republicanism has had a kind of afterlife as one of the legitimating ideologies of American politics. The Minute Man is a republican image of embodied citizenship. Reverence for the flag is a form of republican piety. The Pledge of Allegiance is a republican oath. But emphasis on this sort of thing reflects social disunity rather than unity; it is a straining after oneness where oneness doesn't exist. In fact, America has been, with severe but episodic exceptions, remarkably tolerant of ethnic pluralism (far less so of racial pluralism).[30] I don't want to underestimate the human difficulties of adapting even to a hyphenated Americanism, nor to deny the bigotry and discrimination that particular groups have encountered. But tolerance has been the cultural norm.

Perhaps an immigrant society has no choice; tolerance is a way of muddling through when any alternative policy would be violent and dangerous. But I would argue that we have, mostly, made the best of this necessity, so that the virtues of toleration, in principle though by no means always in practice, have supplanted the singlemindedness of republican citizenship. We have made our peace with the "particular characteristics" of all the immigrant groups (though not, again, of all the racial groups) and have come to regard American nationality as an addition to rather than a replacement for ethnic consciousness. The hyphen works, when it is working, more like a plus sign. "American," then, is a name indeed, but unlike "French" or "German" or "Italian" or "Korean" or "Japanese" or "Cambodian," it can serve as a second name. And as in those modern marriages where two patronymics are joined, neither the first nor the second name is dominant: here the hyphen works more like a sign of equality.

We might go farther than this: in the case of hyphenated Americans, it doesn't matter whether the first or the second name is dominant. We insist, most of the time, that the "particular characteristics" associated with the first name be sustained, as the Know-Nothings urged, without state help—and perhaps they will prove unsustainable on those terms. Still, an ethnic American is someone who can, in principle, live his spiritual life as he chooses, *on either side of the hyphen*. In this sense, American citizenship is indeed anonymous, for it doesn't require a full commitment to American (or to any other) nationality. The distinctive national culture that Americans have created doesn't underpin, it exists alongside of, American politics. It follows, then, that the people I earlier called Americans simply, Americans and nothing else, have in fact a more complicated existence than those terms suggest. They are American-Americans, one more group of hyphenates (not quite the same as all the others), and one can imagine them attending to the cultural aspects of their Americanism and refusing the political commitment that republican ideology demands. They might still be good or bad citizens. And similarly, Orthodox Jews as well as secular (regenerate) Jews, Protestant fundamentalists as well as liberal Protestants, Irish republicans as well as Irish Democrats, black nationalists as well as black integrationists—all these can be good or bad citizens, given the American (liberal rather than republican) understanding of citizenship.

One step more is required before we have fully understood this strange America: it is not the case that Irish-Americans, say, are culturally Irish and politically American, as the pluralists claim (and as I have been assuming thus far for the sake of the argument). Rather, they are culturally Irish-American and politically Irish-American. Their culture has been significantly influenced by American culture; their politics is still, both in style and substance, significantly ethnic. With them, and with every ethnic and religious group except the American-Americans, hyphenation is doubled. It remains true, however, that what all the groups have in common is most importantly their citizenship and what most differentiates them, insofar as they are still differentiated, is their culture. Hence the alternation in American life of patriotic fevers and ethnic revivals, the first expressing a desire to heighten the commonality, the second a desire to reaffirm the difference.

At both ends of this peculiarly American alternation, the good that is defended is also exaggerated and distorted, so that pluralism itself is threatened by the sentiments it generates. The patriotic fevers are the symptoms of a republican pathology. At issue here is the all-important ideological commitment that, as Gleason says, is the sole prerequisite of American citizenship. Since citizenship isn't guaranteed by oneness all the way down, patriots or superpatriots seek to guarantee it by loyalty oaths and campaigns against "un-American" activities. The Know-Nothing party having failed to restrict naturalization, they resort instead to political purges and deportations. Ethnic revivals are less militant and less cruel, though not without their own pathology. What is at issue here is communal pride and power—a demand for political recognition without assimilation, an assertion of interest-group politics against republican ideology, an effort to distinguish this group (one's own) from all the others. American patriotism is always strained and nervous because hyphenation makes indeed for dual loyalty but seems, at the same time, entirely American. Ethnic revivalism is also strained and nervous, because the hyphenates are already Americans, on both sides of the hyphen.

In these circumstances, republicanism is a mirage, and American nationalism or communitarianism is not a plausible option; it doesn't reach to our complexity. A certain sort of communitarianism is available to each of the hyphenate groups—except, it would seem, the American-Americans, whose community, if it existed, would deny the Americanism of all the others. So Horace Kallen is best described as a Jewish (-American) communitarian and a (Jewish-) American liberal, and this kind of coexistence, more widely realized, would constitute the pattern he called cultural pluralism. But the different ethnic and religious communities are all of them far more precarious than he thought, for they have, in a liberal political system, no corporate form or legal structure or coercive power. And, without these supports, the "inherited organic set" seems to dissipate—the population lacks cohesion, cultural life lacks coherence. The resulting "groups" are best conceived, John Higham suggests, as a core of activists and believers and an expanding periphery of passive members or followers, lost, as it were, in a wider America.[31] At the core, the left side of the (double) hyphen is stronger; along the periphery, the right side is stronger, though never fully dominant. Americans choose, as it were, their own location; and it appears that a growing number of them are choosing to fade into the peripheral distances. They become American-Americans, though without much passion invested in the becoming. But if the core doesn't hold, it also doesn't disappear; it is still capable of periodic revival.

At the same time, continued large-scale immigration reproduces a Kallenesque pluralism, creating new groups of hyphenate Americans and encouraging revivalism among activists and believers in the old groups. America is still a radically unfinished society, and for now, at least, it makes sense to say that this unfinishedness is one of its distinctive features. The country has a political center, but it remains in every other sense decentered. More than this, the political center, despite occasional patriotic fevers, doesn't work against decentering elsewhere. It neither requires nor demands the kind of commitment that would put the legitimacy of ethnic or religious identification in doubt. It doesn't aim at a finished or fully coherent Americanism. Indeed, American politics, itself pluralist in character, *needs* a certain sort of incoherence. A radical program of Americanization would *really* be un-American. It isn't inconceivable that America will one day become an American nation-state, the many giving way to the one, but that is not what it is now; nor is that its destiny. America has no singular national destiny—and to be an "American" is, finally, to know that and to be more or less content with it.

Notes

1.   Horace M. Kallen, *Culture and Democracy in the United States* (New York: Boni and Liveright, 1924), p. 51.

2.   *Harvard Encyclopedia of American Ethnic Groups,* ed. Stephan Thernstrom (Cambridge, Mass.: Harvard University Press, 1980).

3. Mario Cuomo's speech at the 1984 Democratic Party Convention provides a nice example of this sort of argument.

4. Kallen, *Culture and Democracy,* p. 94.

5. Ibid., p. 122 (cf. p. 116); John Rawls, *A Theory of Justice* (Cambridge, Mass.: Harvard University Press, 1971), p. 527.

6. Quoted in Kallen, *Culture and Democracy,* p. 138; the writer was superintendent of New York's public schools.

7. Kallen, *Culture and Democracy,* p. 94.

8. See Kallen's account of how British-Americans were forced into ethnicity: *Culture and Democracy,* pp. 99f.

9. P. Gleason, "American Identity and Americanization," in *Harvard Encyclopedia,* p. 32.

10. On the complexities of "nativism," see John Higham, *Send These to Me: Jews and Other Immigrants in Urban America* (New York: Atheneum, 1975), pp. 102–15. For an account of the Know-Nothings different from mine, to which I am nonetheless indebted, see S. M. Lipset and Earl Raab, *The Politics of Unreason: Right-wing Extremism in America,* 1790–1970, (New York: Harper and Row, 1970), chap. 2.

11. Frank George Franklin, *The Legislative History of Naturalization in the United States* (New York: Arno, 1969), chaps. 11–14.

12. Ibid., p. 247.

13. Ibid., p. 293 (emphasis added).

14. Ibid.

15. Lipset and Raab, *Politics of Unreason,* p. 46.

16. Jean-Jacques Rousseau, *The Social Contract,* trans. G. D. H. Cole (New York: Dutton, 1950), bk. III, chap. 15, p. 93.

17. Kallen, *Culture and Democracy,* p. 61.

18. Ibid., p. 78.

19. Ibid., pp. 114–15.

20. It is interesting that both nativists and pluralists wanted to keep the market free of ethnic and religious considerations. The Know-Nothings, since they thought that democratic politics was best served by British ethnicity and Protestant religion, set the market firmly within civil society, allowing full market rights even to new and Catholic immigrants. Kallen, by contrast, since he understands civil society as a world of ethnic and religious groups, assimilates the market to the universality of the political sphere, the "common city-life."

21. Kallen, *Culture and Democracy,* p. 124.

22. Ibid., p. 200.

23. Ibid., p. 179.

24. Stephen Steinberg, *The Ethnic Myth: Race, Ethnicity, and Class in America* (Boston: Beacon, 1981), p. 254.

25. Gleason, "American Identity," p. 56.

26. The song is "Accentuate the Positive," which is probably what I am doing here.

27. Gleason, "American Identity," p. 56.

28. Quoted in Gary Kates, "Jews into Frenchmen: Nationality and Representation in Revolutionary France," *Social Research* 56 (Spring 1989): 229. See also the discussion in Arthur Hertzberg, *The French Enlightenment and the Jews: The Origins of Modern Anti-Semitism* (New York: Schocken, 1970), pp. 360–62.

29.   Kates, "Jews into Frenchmen," p. 229.

30.   The current demand of (some) Black Americans that they be called African-Americans represents an attempt to adapt themselves to the ethnic paradigm—imitating, perhaps, the relative success of various Asian American groups in a similar adaptation. But names are no guarantees; nor does antinativist pluralism provide sufficient protection against what is all too often an *ethnic*-American racism. It has been argued that this racism is the necessary precondition of hyphenated ethnicity: the inclusion of successive waves of ethnic immigrants is possible only because of the permanent exclusion of Black Americans. But I don't know what evidence would demonstrate *necessity* here: I am inclined to reject the metaphysical belief that all inclusion entails exclusion. A historical and empirical account of the place of Blacks in the "system" of American pluralism would require another essay.

31.   Higham, *Send These to Me*, p. 242.

Contributors

MARTHA ACKELSBERG is professor of government and Women's Studies at Smith College, where she is also a member of the Advisory Committee on Jewish Studies. Her writings include *Free Women of Spain: Anarchism and the Struggle for the Emancipation of Women* and a variety of articles on women's activism, reconceptualizing families and family life in the modern period, Spanish anarchism, and Jewish feminism. Ackelsberg was a founding member of Ezrat Nashim (the first women's organization in recent years to argue for equality for women in Judaism) and of B'not Esh (a Jewish feminist spirituality collective).

REENA BERNARDS is the co-coordinator of The Dialogue Project Between American Jewish and Palestinian Women. She lives in Washington, D.C., and works as a trainer and consultant to nonprofit organizations in strategic planning, leadership development, and multicultural diversity. Her clients include the League of Women Voters, the National Wildlife Federation, and the New Israel Fund. She holds a master's degree in public administration from Harvard University John F. Kennedy School of Government and a bachelor's degree in sociology from Brandies University.

JONATHAN BOYARIN's involvement in the dynamics of Jewish community life was nurtured in the Jewish chicken farming community of Farmingdale, N.J. He has pursued this interest in studies of memoirs of twentieth-century Polish Jews; in fieldwork with Jewish communities in Paris, Jerusalem, and New York City; and in essays articulating the new field of Jewish Cultural Studies. The books resulting from his research include *Polish Jews in Paris: The Ethnography of Memory, Storm from Paradise: The Politics of Jewish Memory,* and *A Storyteller's World: The Education of Shlomo Noble in Europe and America.*

MARLA BRETTSCHNEIDER is a professor of political science and Women's Studies at the University of New Hampshire. She has written numerous articles and is the author of *Cornerstones of Peace: Jewish Identity Politics and Democratic Theory.*

JEFFREY DEKRO is president and founder of The Shefa Fund, a public foundation established in 1988 to promote Jewish social responsibility and to assist individuals in exploring their identities as progressive Jews with wealth. He is also a co-initiator of the Jewish Funders Network, which facilitates communication and cooperation among North American Jewish funders and foundations. Author of numerous articles, Dekro is co-author of *Jews, Money and Social Responsibility: Developing a "Torah of Money" for Contemporary Life,* and *Building Community, Creating Justice: A Guide for Organizing Tzedakah Collectives.*

NORA GOLD is a Ph.D. and active Jewish feminist. She currently holds the position of assistant professor at the School of Social Work, McMaster University, Ontario, Canada. She has studied and published on the relationship between anti-Semitism and racism and issues of concern for Jewish women.

BOB GOLDFARB studied government at Harvard College and earned a Master's in business administration at the Harvard Business School. He is a member of Jewish Activist Gays and Lesbians (JAGL), as well as the Gay and Lesbian Committee of Congregation B'Nai Jeshurun of New York, and serves on the board of directors of the World Congress of Gay and Lesbian Jewish Organizations.

GERALD HORNE, who teaches at the University of California–Santa Barbara, is the author of *Black Liberation/Red Scare: Ben Davis and the Communist Party,* and most recently *Fire This Time: The Watts Uprising and the 1960s.* He is now writing *Class Struggle in Hollywood: Trade Unionists, Mobsters, Moguls, Stars, Politicians and Reds, 1945–6.*

EPHRAIM ISAAC is the director of the Institute of Semitic Studies in Princeton, N.J. He was born in Ethiopia, where he got his early education, and speaks seventeen languages. He is author of numerous books and articles, including *The Book of Enoch* and *An Ethiopic History of Joseph,* and is currently working on a new edition of the "Dead Sea Scrolls Fragments of the Book of Enoch."

MELANIE KAYE/KANTROWITZ is an activist, writer, and teacher, currently working as the executive director of Jews for Racial and Economic Justice. She graduated from City College, earned a Ph.D. in comparative literature from the University of California–Berkeley, and has taught and worked in movements for social change all over the country. She returned to New York in 1990 specifically to do antiracist work in a Jewish context. In addition to her many articles, Kaye/Kantrowitz is the author of *The Issue Is Power: Essays on Women, Jews, Violence and Resistance* and *My Jewish Face and Other Stories,* co-editor of *The Tribe of Dina: A Jewish Women's Anthology,* and former editor and publisher of *Sinister Wisdom,* a lesbian-feminist journal.

CLARE KINBERG lives in Eugene, Oregon, and is managing editor of *Bridges,* a journal for Jewish feminists and our friends. (Subscriptions $15/one year/two issues: All correspondence to *Bridges,* PO Box 24839, Eugene, OR 97402, (503) 935-5720).

NAOMI NIM holds a doctorate in multicultural education from the University of San Francisco. She is an educator, activist, and researcher whose work has focused on the transformation of public education, community conflict resolution, and Middle East peace.

ELLEN OSTERHAUS is a multicultural curriculum specialist, K–5, in the Madison Metropolitan School District (MMSD) in Wisconsin. Osterhaus has been working in multicultural education for the past fifteen years, providing staff inservice, curriculum development for MMSD, and consulting with school districts and other educational institutions on the national, state, and local levels.

REBECCA POSNER is from Montreal. She recently completed a master's degree in the history of Spanish feminism. She has worked on multicultural issues for many years in various forums and is currently working as a freelance writer and film editor in New York City.

LEORA SAPOSNIK is the Holocaust consultant and multicultural resource assistant for the Madison Metropolitan School District in Wisconsin. She is also currently pursuing a doctorate in modern European Jewish history with an emphasis on the Holocaust. Saposnik teaches an annual staff enrichment course entitled "Teaching about the Holocaust," and often lectures to students and teachers in the Madison schools. She is the recipient of a grant to collect oral histories of Madison survivors.

TOBA SPITZER is a student at the Reconstructionist Rabbinical College in Philadelphia. She has been involved in the movement for Israeli-Palestinian peace as well as working as a Jewish educator and organizer promoting youth involvement in grassroots community groups. She is currently working on Jewish approaches to liberation theology.

EVELYN TORTON BECK is professor of Women's Studies and Jewish Studies at the University of Maryland–College Park, where she served as director of the Women's Studies Program from 1984 to 1993. Among her writings are *Kafka and the Yiddish Theatre: Its Impact on His Work*, *The Prism of Sex: Essays in the Sociology of Knowledge*, *Nice Jewish Girls: A Lesbian Anthology*, and translations from the Yiddish of I. B. Singer. She lectures widely across the United States, Europe, Japan, and Canada on issues related to "difference," especially at the intersection of anti-Semitism and misogyny with other hate crimes. Beck is a pioneer in the fields of Women's Studies, Jewish Studies, and Lesbian Studies. Her analysis of the baiting of young Jewish women as "Jewish American Princesses" was heard on National Public Radio.

MICHAEL WALZER is the UPS Foundation Professor of Social Science at the Institute for Advanced Study in Princeton, N.J., and the author of many books, including *Exodus and Revolution*, *Spheres of Justice*, and *What It Means to Be an American*.

CORNEL WEST is author of the best-selling *Race Matters* and nine other books. He is a professor of Afro-American studies and the philosophy of religion at Harvard University.

FELICE YESKEL is a white, Jewish (Ashkenazi), lesbian who grew up working class in New York City. She has been an activist for over twenty years in many social change movements: feminism, lesbian and gay liberation, anti-intervention, peace, and disarmament. She is currently the co-coordinator of the Share the Wealth Project, organizing to revitalize America through redistributing wealth. She has a Ph.D. in organizational development and is an adjunct faculty member in the Social Justice Education Program at the University of Massachusetts–Amherst, teaching graduate courses on oppression theory, training design and methodology, classism, racism, sexism, heterosexism, anti-Semitism, and ableism. Yeskel is also co-director of Diversity Works, Inc., an organization of social justice educators working with groups and organizations across the United States on multiculturalism. Other articles have appeared in *Twice Blessed: On Being Lesbian, Gay and Jewish, Out of the Class Closet: Lesbians Speak, Bridges, Sojourner,* the *Journal of Holistic Education, The Women's Review of Books,* and the forthcoming *Teaching for Social Diversity and Social Justice: A Sourcebook for Teachers and Trainers.*